IDW

Facebook: **facebook.com/idwpublishing**
Twitter: **@idwpublishing**
YouTube: **youtube.com/idwpublishing**
Tumblr: **tumblr.idwpublishing.com**
Instagram: **instagram.com/idwpublishing**

COVER ART BY
JAMES BIGGIE

COLLECTION EDITS BY
JUSTIN EISINGER
AND ALONZO SIMON

COLLECTION DESIGN BY
JEFF POWELL

PUBLISHER
TED ADAMS

ISBN: 978-1-63140-875-5   20 19 18 17   2 3 4 5

Originally published as ARCHANGEL issues #1–5.

Ted Adams, CEO & Publisher
Greg Goldstein, President & COO
Robbie Robbins, EVP/Sr. Graphic Artist
Chris Ryall, Chief Creative Officer
David Hedgecock, Editor-in-Chief
Laurie Windrow, Senior VP of Sales & Marketing
Matthew Ruzicka, CPA, Chief Financial Officer
Lorelei Bunjes, VP of Digital Services
Jerry Bennington, VP of New Product Development

WILLIAM GIBSON'S
ARCHANGEL

Script by **WILLIAM GIBSON**
with **MICHAEL ST. JOHN SMITH**

Created by **WILLIAM GIBSON**
and **MICHAEL ST. JOHN SMITH**

Art by **BUTCH GUICE,**
ALEJANDRO BARRIONUEVO,
and **WAGNER REIS**

Inks by **TOM PALMER**
with **BUTCH GUICE**

Colors by **DIEGO RODRIGUEZ**
and **WES DZIOBA**

Letters by **SHAWN LEE**
and **GILBERTO LAZCANO**

Editing and **MICHAEL BENEDETTO**
Story Breakdown by

Series Edits by **DAVID HEDGECOCK**

Special thanks to Jeff Webber for his invaluable assistance
and participation in production of this series.

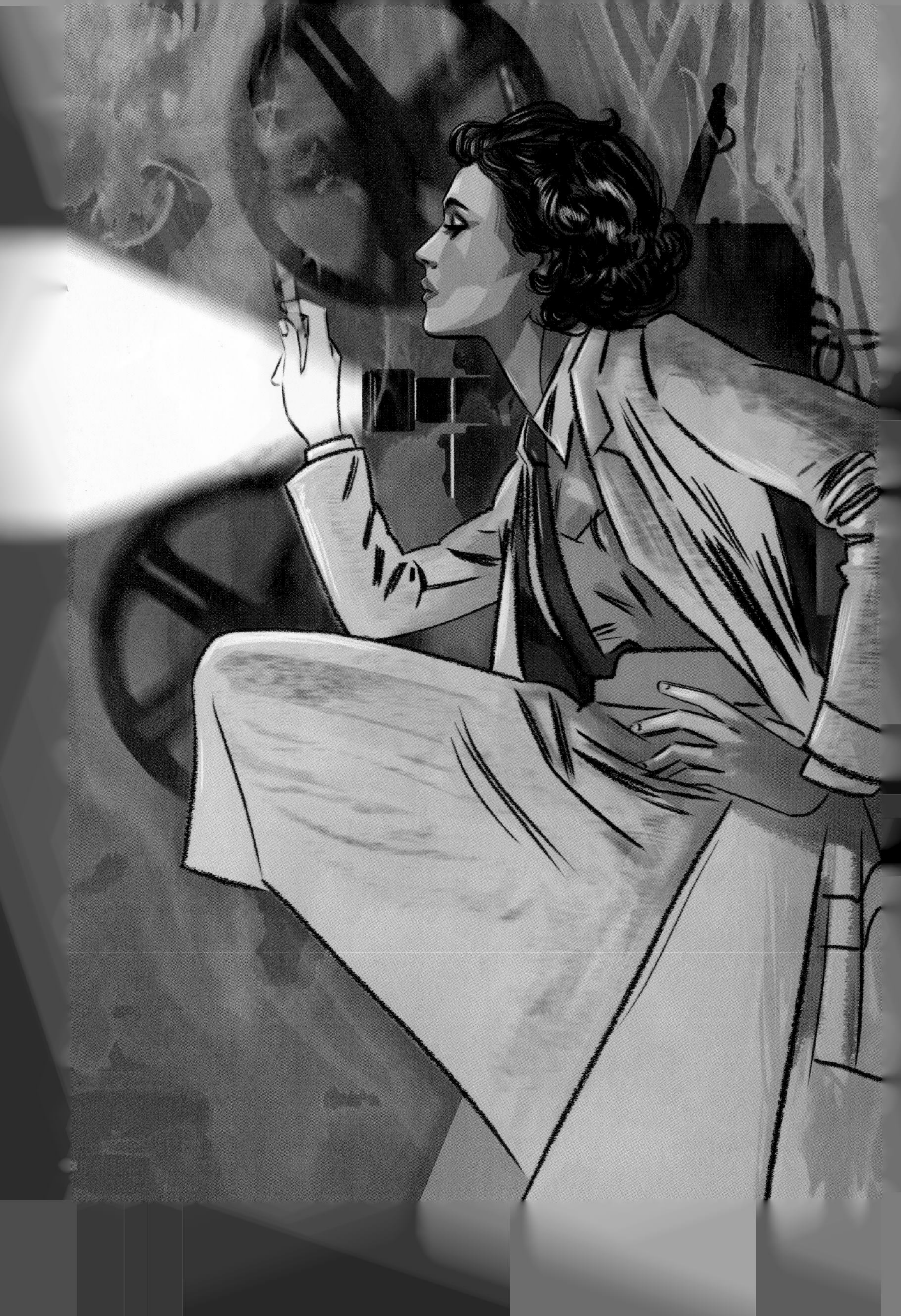

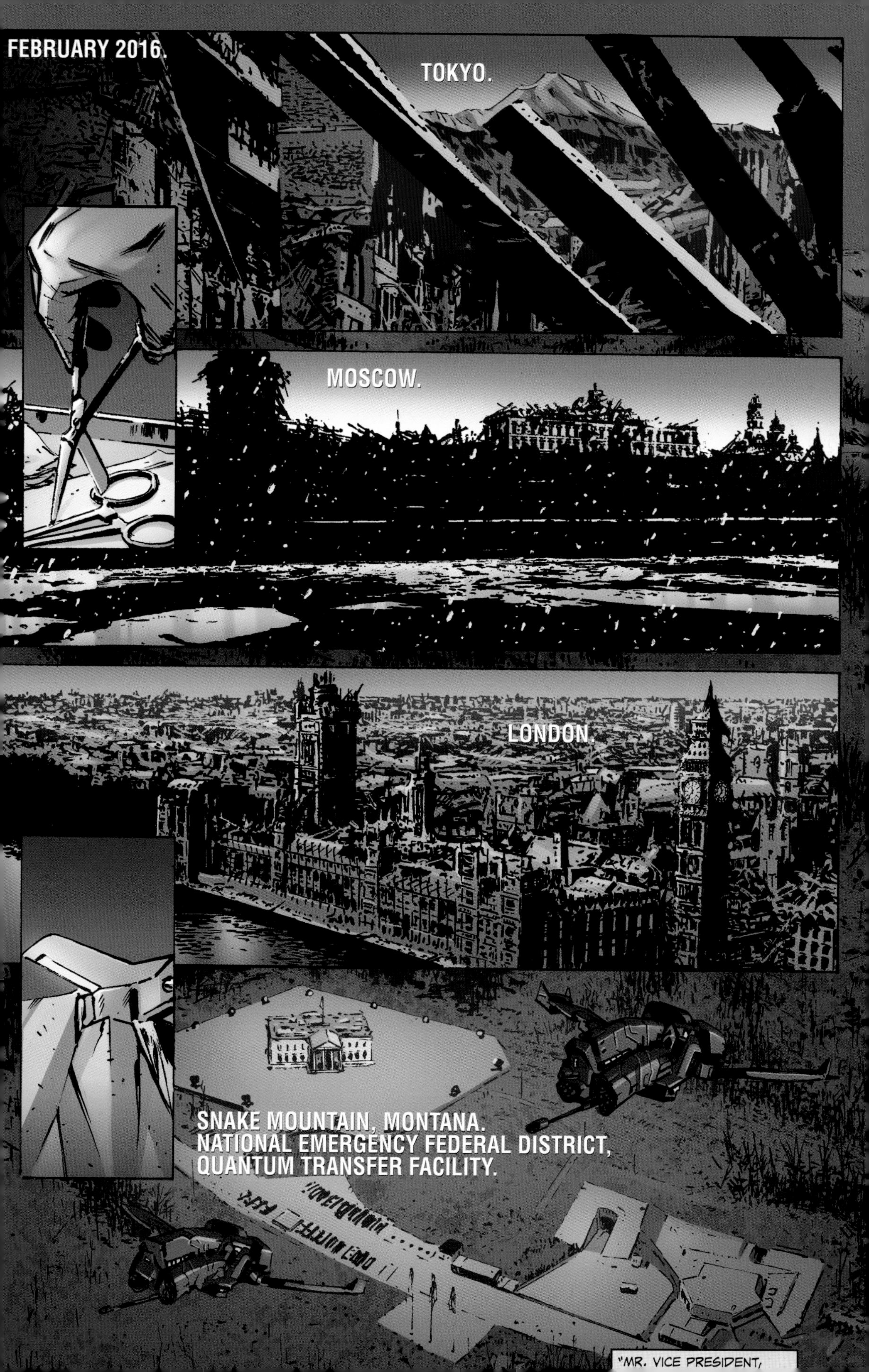

FEBRUARY 2016.
TOKYO.
MOSCOW.
LONDON.
SNAKE MOUNTAIN, MONTANA.
NATIONAL EMERGENCY FEDERAL DISTRICT,
QUANTUM TRANSFER FACILITY.
"MR. VICE PRESIDENT,

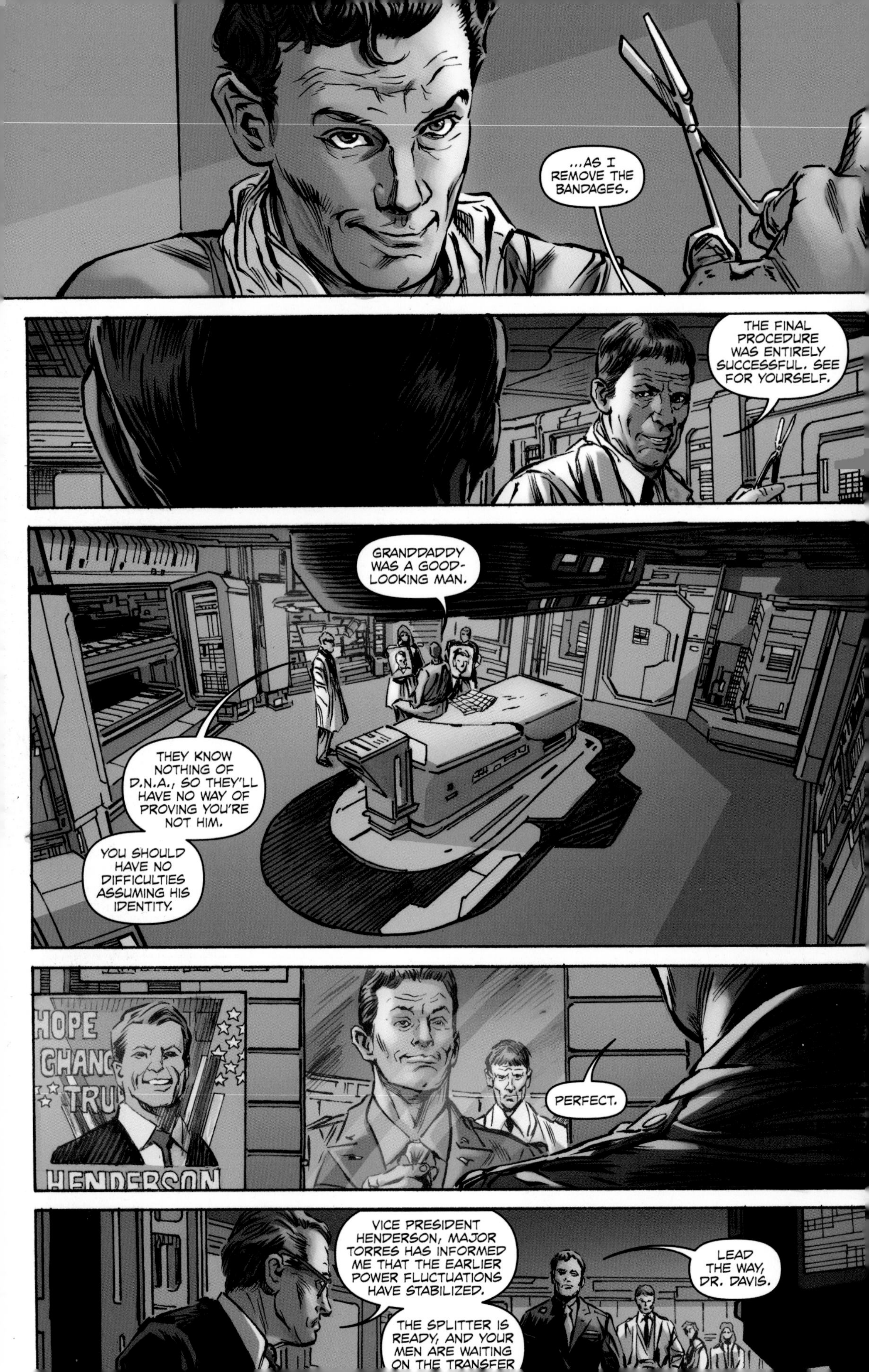
...AS I REMOVE THE BANDAGES.
THE FINAL PROCEDURE WAS ENTIRELY SUCCESSFUL. SEE FOR YOURSELF.
GRANDDADDY WAS A GOOD-LOOKING MAN.
THEY KNOW NOTHING OF D.N.A., SO THEY'LL HAVE NO WAY OF PROVING YOU'RE NOT HIM.
YOU SHOULD HAVE NO DIFFICULTIES ASSUMING HIS IDENTITY.
HOPE
CHANG
TRU
HENDERSON
PERFECT.
VICE PRESIDENT HENDERSON, MAJOR TORRES HAS INFORMED ME THAT THE EARLIER POWER FLUCTUATIONS HAVE STABILIZED.
THE SPLITTER IS READY, AND YOUR MEN ARE WAITING ON THE TRANSFER
LEAD THE WAY, DR. DAVIS.

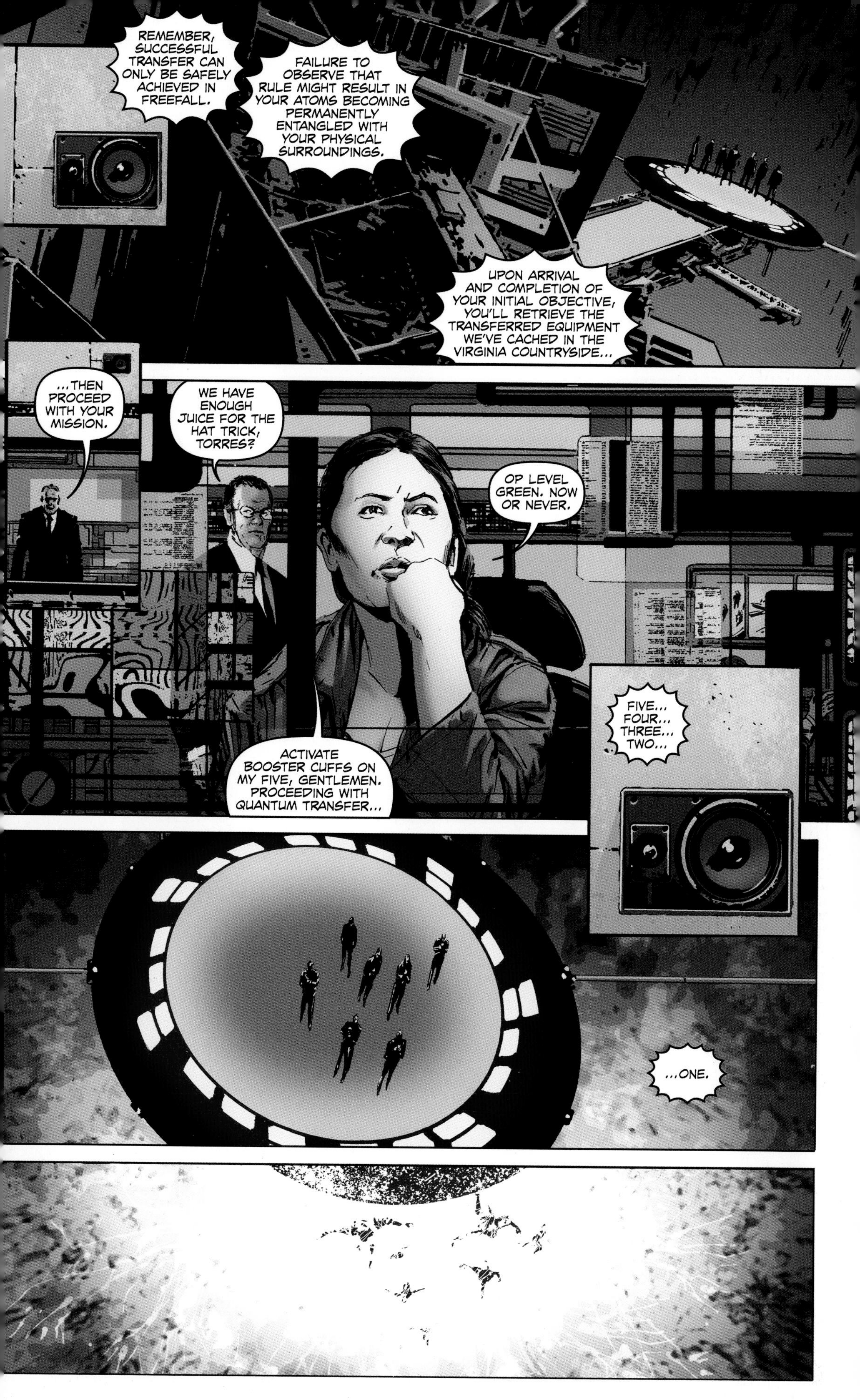

REMEMBER, SUCCESSFUL TRANSFER CAN ONLY BE SAFELY ACHIEVED IN FREEFALL.
FAILURE TO OBSERVE THAT RULE MIGHT RESULT IN YOUR ATOMS BECOMING PERMANENTLY ENTANGLED WITH YOUR PHYSICAL SURROUNDINGS.
UPON ARRIVAL AND COMPLETION OF YOUR INITIAL OBJECTIVE, YOU'LL RETRIEVE THE TRANSFERRED EQUIPMENT WE'VE CACHED IN THE VIRGINIA COUNTRYSIDE...
...THEN PROCEED WITH YOUR MISSION.
WE HAVE ENOUGH JUICE FOR THE HAT TRICK, TORRES?
OP LEVEL GREEN. NOW OR NEVER.
ACTIVATE BOOSTER CUFFS ON MY FIVE, GENTLEMEN. PROCEEDING WITH QUANTUM TRANSFER...
FIVE... FOUR... THREE... TWO...
...ONE.

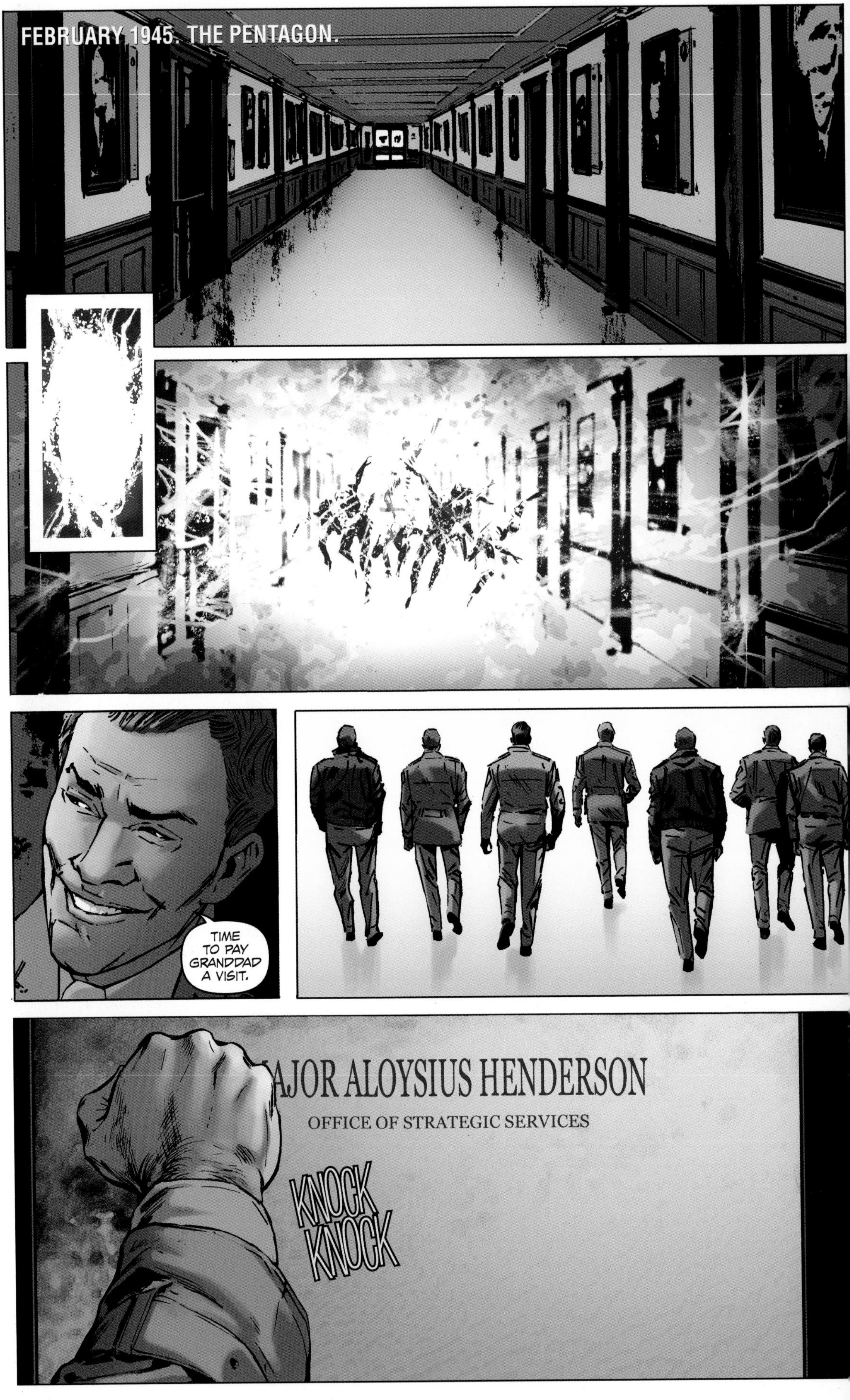
FEBRUARY 1945. THE PENTAGON.
TIME TO PAY GRANDDAD A VISIT.
MAJOR ALOYSIUS HENDERSON
OFFICE OF STRATEGIC SERVICES
KNOCK KNOCK

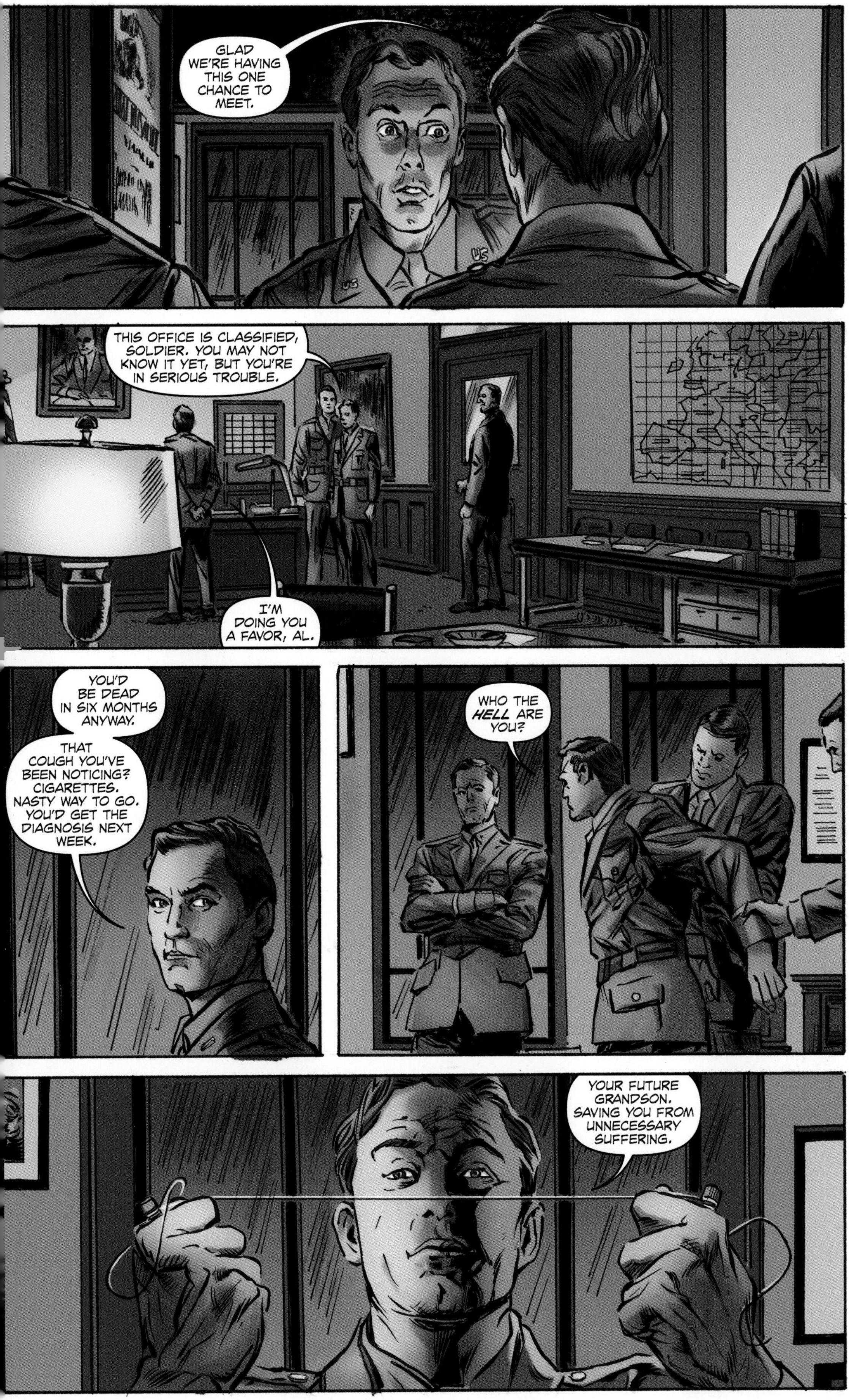
GLAD WE'RE HAVING THIS ONE CHANCE TO MEET.
THIS OFFICE IS CLASSIFIED, SOLDIER. YOU MAY NOT KNOW IT YET, BUT YOU'RE IN SERIOUS TROUBLE.
I'M DOING YOU A FAVOR, AL.
YOU'D BE DEAD IN SIX MONTHS ANYWAY.
THAT COUGH YOU'VE BEEN NOTICING? CIGARETTES. NASTY WAY TO GO. YOU'D GET THE DIAGNOSIS NEXT WEEK.
WHO THE HELL ARE YOU?
YOUR FUTURE GRANDSON. SAVING YOU FROM UNNECESSARY SUFFERING.

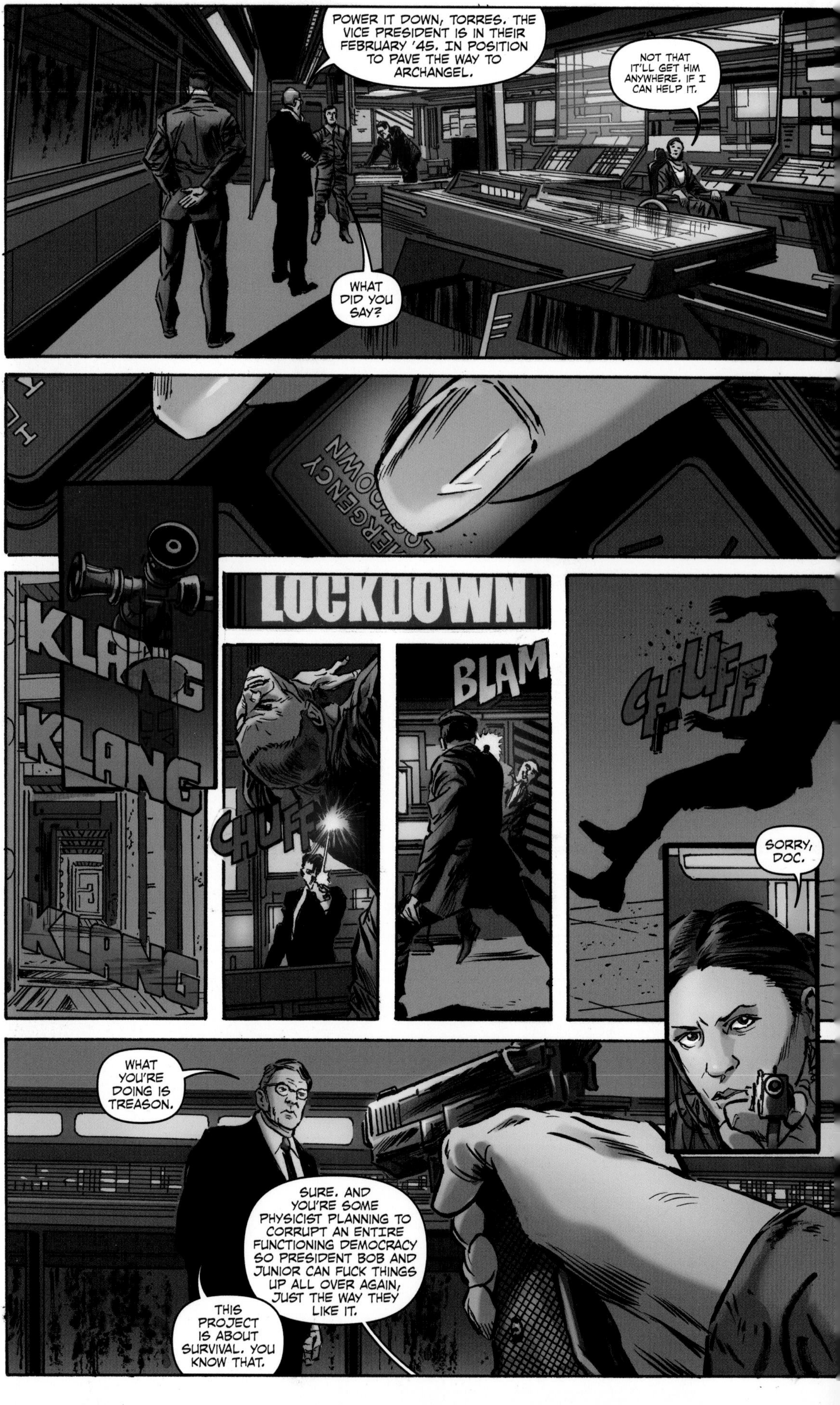

POWER IT DOWN, TORRES. THE VICE PRESIDENT IS IN THEIR FEBRUARY '45. IN POSITION TO PAVE THE WAY TO ARCHANGEL.
NOT THAT IT'LL GET HIM ANYWHERE, IF I CAN HELP IT.
WHAT DID YOU SAY?
EMERGENCY LOCKDOWN
KLANG
KLANG
KLANG
LOCKDOWN
CHUFF
BLAM
CHUFF
SORRY, DOC.
WHAT YOU'RE DOING IS TREASON.
SURE. AND YOU'RE SOME PHYSICIST PLANNING TO CORRUPT AN ENTIRE FUNCTIONING DEMOCRACY SO PRESIDENT BOB AND JUNIOR CAN FUCK THINGS UP ALL OVER AGAIN, JUST THE WAY THEY LIKE IT.
THIS PROJECT IS ABOUT SURVIVAL. YOU KNOW THAT.

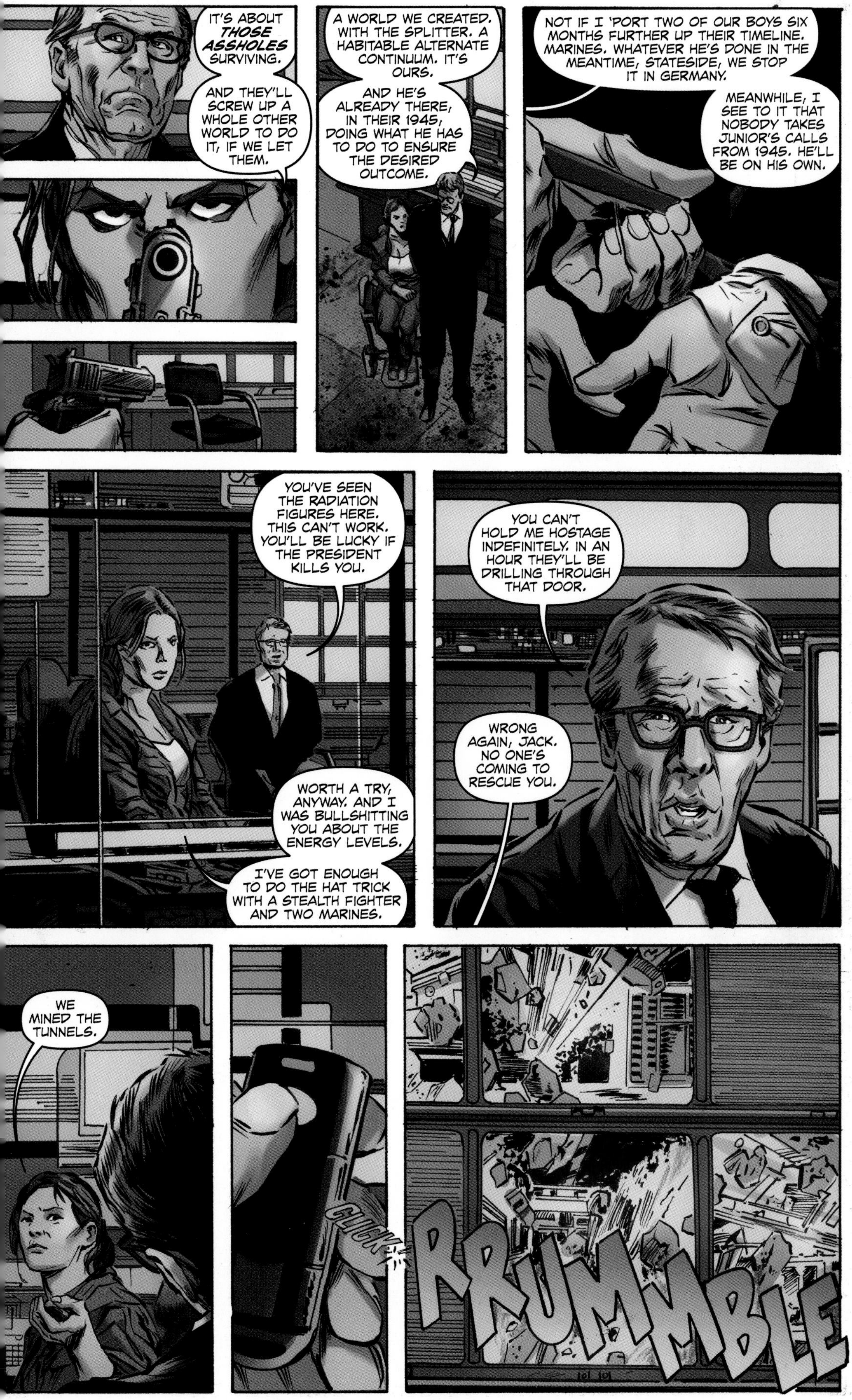
IT'S ABOUT *THOSE ASSHOLES* SURVIVING.
AND THEY'LL SCREW UP A WHOLE OTHER WORLD TO DO IT, IF WE LET THEM.
A WORLD WE CREATED. WITH THE SPLITTER. A HABITABLE ALTERNATE CONTINUUM. IT'S OURS.
AND HE'S ALREADY THERE, IN THEIR 1945, DOING WHAT HE HAS TO DO TO ENSURE THE DESIRED OUTCOME.
NOT IF I 'PORT TWO OF OUR BOYS SIX MONTHS FURTHER UP THEIR TIMELINE. MARINES. WHATEVER HE'S DONE IN THE MEANTIME, STATESIDE, WE STOP IT IN GERMANY.
MEANWHILE, I SEE TO IT THAT NOBODY TAKES JUNIOR'S CALLS FROM 1945. HE'LL BE ON HIS OWN.
YOU'VE SEEN THE RADIATION FIGURES HERE. THIS CAN'T WORK. YOU'LL BE LUCKY IF THE PRESIDENT KILLS YOU.
WORTH A TRY, ANYWAY. AND I WAS BULLSHITTING YOU ABOUT THE ENERGY LEVELS.
I'VE GOT ENOUGH TO DO THE HAT TRICK WITH A STEALTH FIGHTER AND TWO MARINES.
YOU CAN'T HOLD ME HOSTAGE INDEFINITELY. IN AN HOUR THEY'LL BE DRILLING THROUGH THAT DOOR.
WRONG AGAIN, JACK. NO ONE'S COMING TO RESCUE YOU.
WE MINED THE TUNNELS.
CLICK
RRUMMBLE

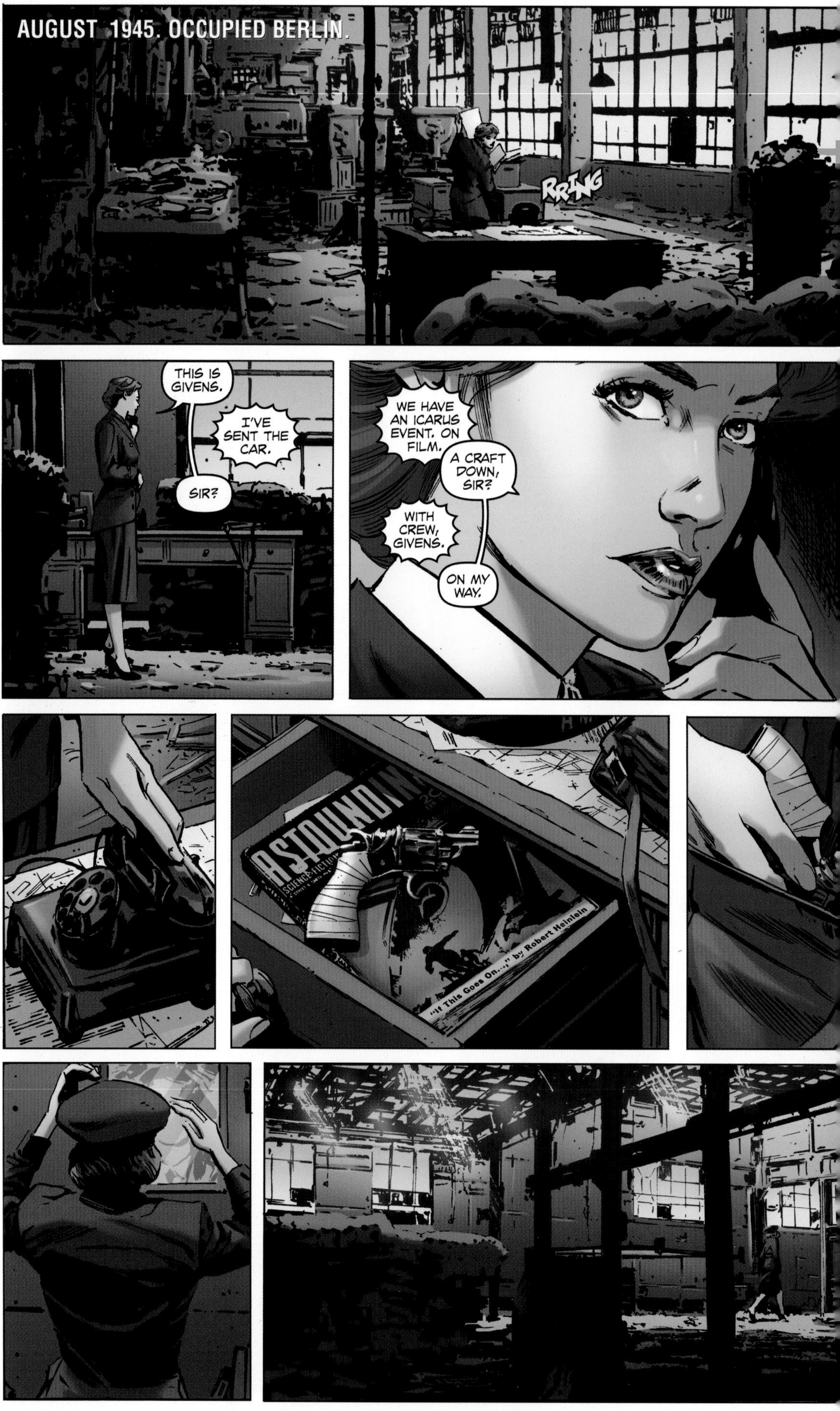
AUGUST 1945. OCCUPIED BERLIN.
RRING
THIS IS GIVENS.
I'VE SENT THE CAR.
SIR?
WE HAVE AN ICARUS EVENT. ON FILM.
A CRAFT DOWN, SIR?
WITH CREW, GIVENS.
ON MY WAY.
ASTOUND
SCIENCE-FICTION
"If This Goes On...," by Robert Heinlein

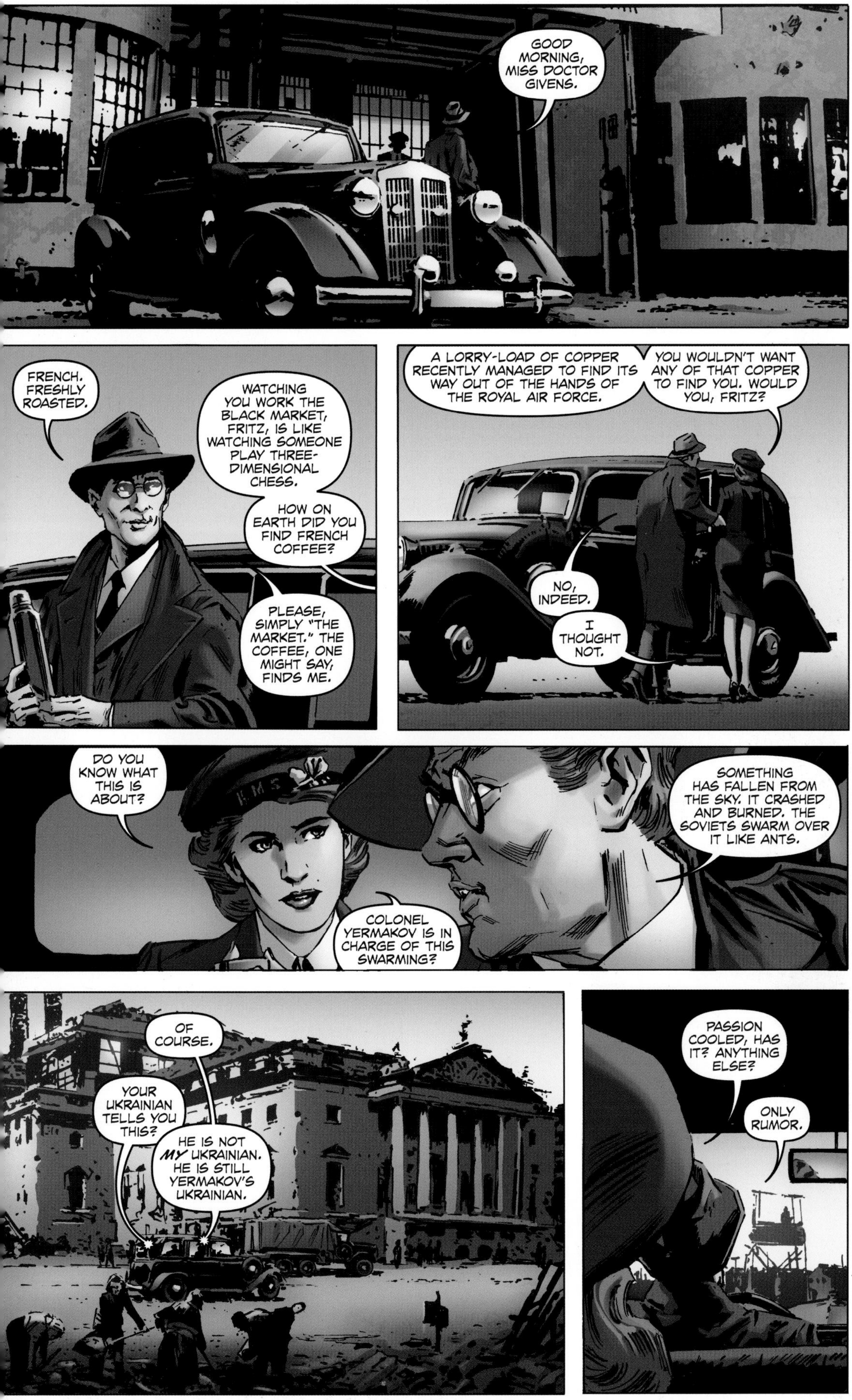
GOOD MORNING, MISS DOCTOR GIVENS.
FRENCH. FRESHLY ROASTED.
WATCHING YOU WORK THE BLACK MARKET, FRITZ, IS LIKE WATCHING SOMEONE PLAY THREE-DIMENSIONAL CHESS.
HOW ON EARTH DID YOU FIND FRENCH COFFEE?
PLEASE, SIMPLY "THE MARKET." THE COFFEE, ONE MIGHT SAY, FINDS ME.
A LORRY-LOAD OF COPPER RECENTLY MANAGED TO FIND ITS WAY OUT OF THE HANDS OF THE ROYAL AIR FORCE.
YOU WOULDN'T WANT ANY OF THAT COPPER TO FIND YOU. WOULD YOU, FRITZ?
NO, INDEED.
I THOUGHT NOT.
DO YOU KNOW WHAT THIS IS ABOUT?
SOMETHING HAS FALLEN FROM THE SKY. IT CRASHED AND BURNED. THE SOVIETS SWARM OVER IT LIKE ANTS.
COLONEL YERMAKOV IS IN CHARGE OF THIS SWARMING?
OF COURSE.
YOUR UKRAINIAN TELLS YOU THIS?
HE IS NOT *MY* UKRAINIAN. HE IS STILL YERMAKOV'S UKRAINIAN.
PASSION COOLED, HAS IT? ANYTHING ELSE?
ONLY RUMOR.

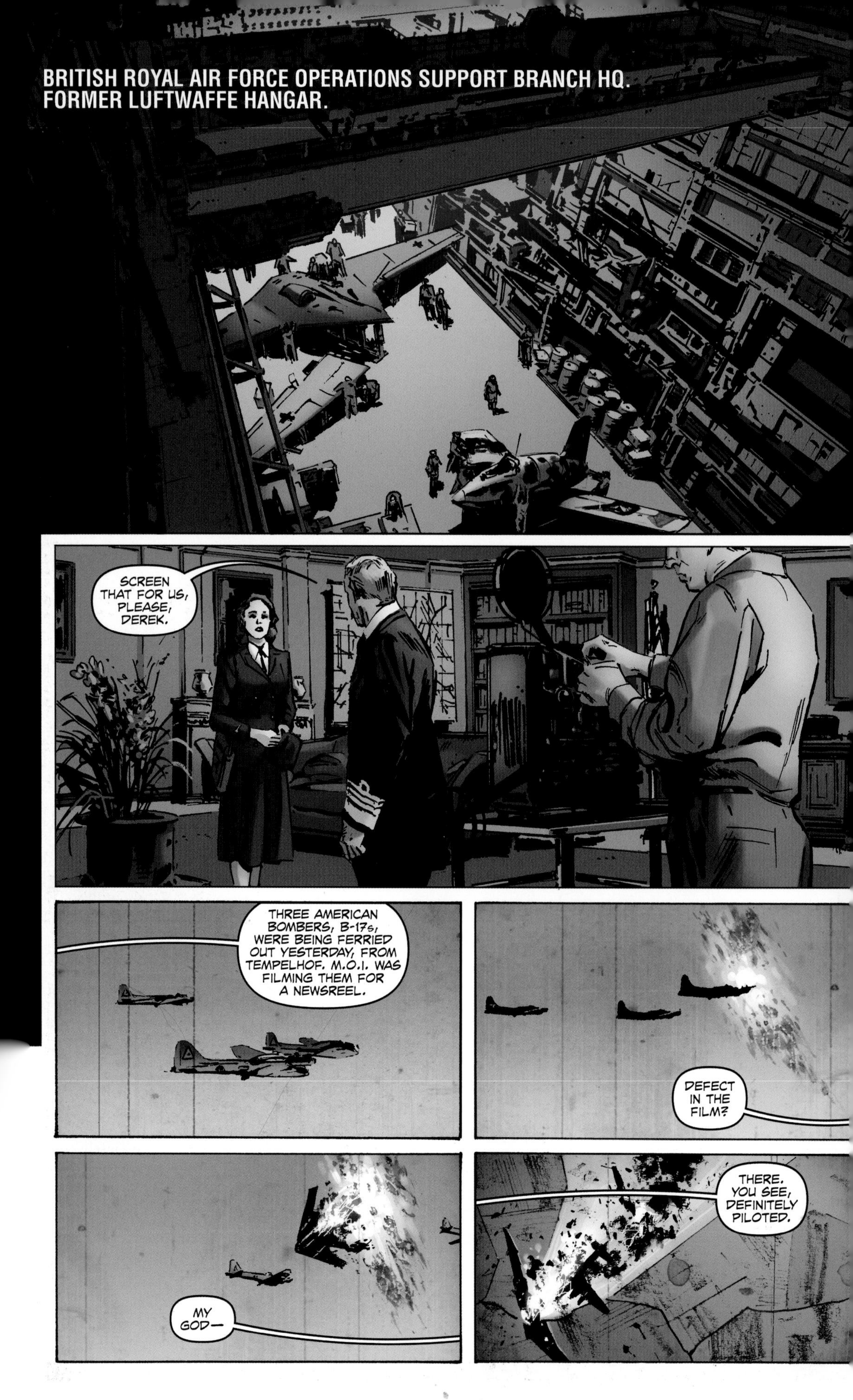
BRITISH ROYAL AIR FORCE OPERATIONS SUPPORT BRANCH HQ. FORMER LUFTWAFFE HANGAR.
SCREEN THAT FOR US, PLEASE, DEREK.
THREE AMERICAN BOMBERS, B-17s, WERE BEING FERRIED OUT YESTERDAY, FROM TEMPELHOF. M.O.I. WAS FILMING THEM FOR A NEWSREEL.
DEFECT IN THE FILM?
MY GOD—
THERE. YOU SEE, DEFINITELY PILOTED.

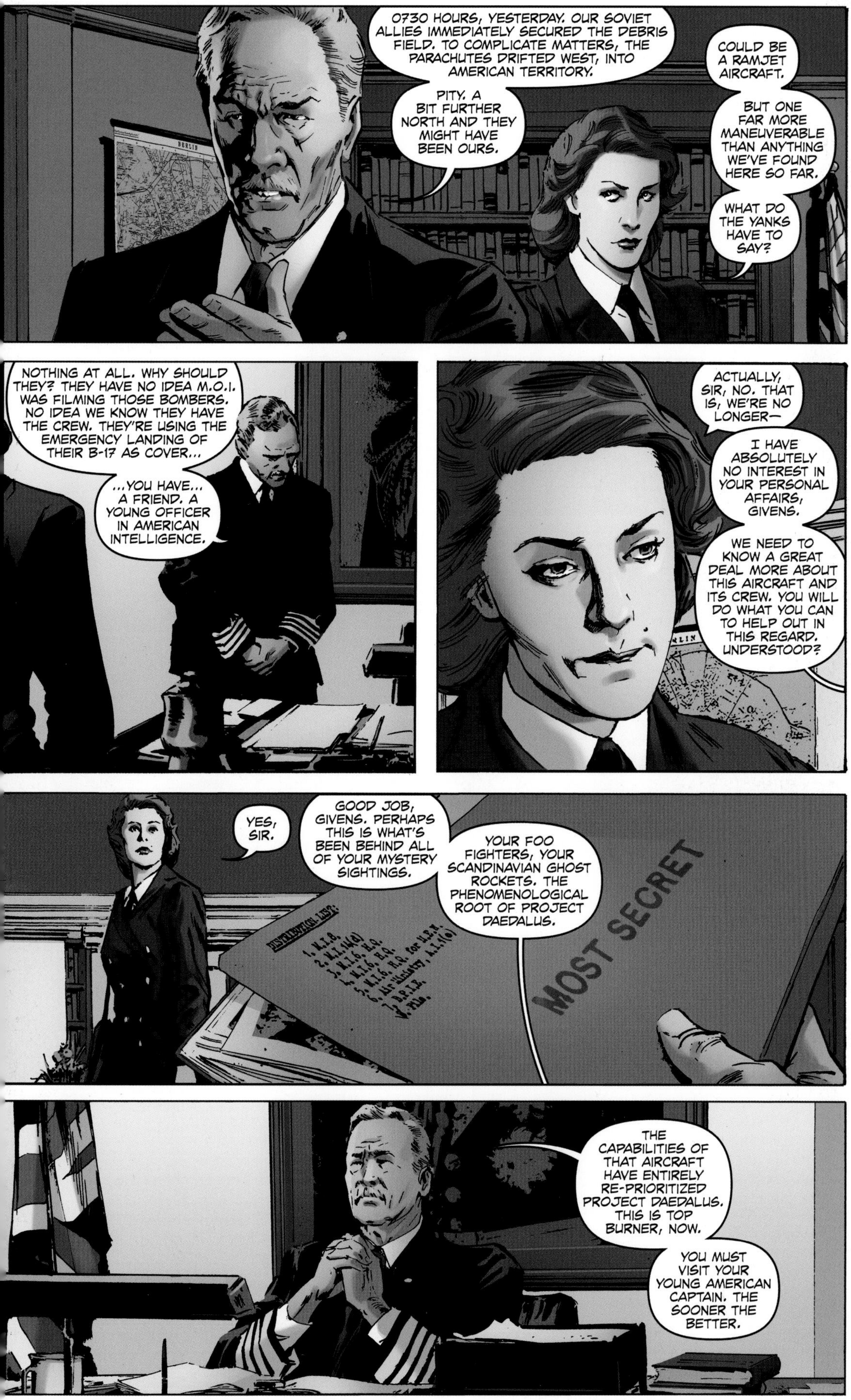
0730 HOURS, YESTERDAY. OUR SOVIET ALLIES IMMEDIATELY SECURED THE DEBRIS FIELD. TO COMPLICATE MATTERS, THE PARACHUTES DRIFTED WEST, INTO AMERICAN TERRITORY.
PITY. A BIT FURTHER NORTH AND THEY MIGHT HAVE BEEN OURS.
COULD BE A RAMJET AIRCRAFT.
BUT ONE FAR MORE MANEUVERABLE THAN ANYTHING WE'VE FOUND HERE SO FAR.
WHAT DO THE YANKS HAVE TO SAY?
NOTHING AT ALL. WHY SHOULD THEY? THEY HAVE NO IDEA M.O.I. WAS FILMING THOSE BOMBERS. NO IDEA WE KNOW THEY HAVE THE CREW. THEY'RE USING THE EMERGENCY LANDING OF THEIR B-17 AS COVER...
...YOU HAVE... A FRIEND. A YOUNG OFFICER IN AMERICAN INTELLIGENCE.
ACTUALLY, SIR, NO. THAT IS, WE'RE NO LONGER—
I HAVE ABSOLUTELY NO INTEREST IN YOUR PERSONAL AFFAIRS, GIVENS.
WE NEED TO KNOW A GREAT DEAL MORE ABOUT THIS AIRCRAFT AND ITS CREW. YOU WILL DO WHAT YOU CAN TO HELP OUT IN THIS REGARD. UNDERSTOOD?
YES, SIR.
GOOD JOB, GIVENS. PERHAPS THIS IS WHAT'S BEEN BEHIND ALL OF YOUR MYSTERY SIGHTINGS.
YOUR FOO FIGHTERS, YOUR SCANDINAVIAN GHOST ROCKETS. THE PHENOMENOLOGICAL ROOT OF PROJECT DAEDALUS.
MOST SECRET
THE CAPABILITIES OF THAT AIRCRAFT HAVE ENTIRELY RE-PRIORITIZED PROJECT DAEDALUS. THIS IS TOP BURNER, NOW.
YOU MUST VISIT YOUR YOUNG AMERICAN CAPTAIN. THE SOONER THE BETTER.

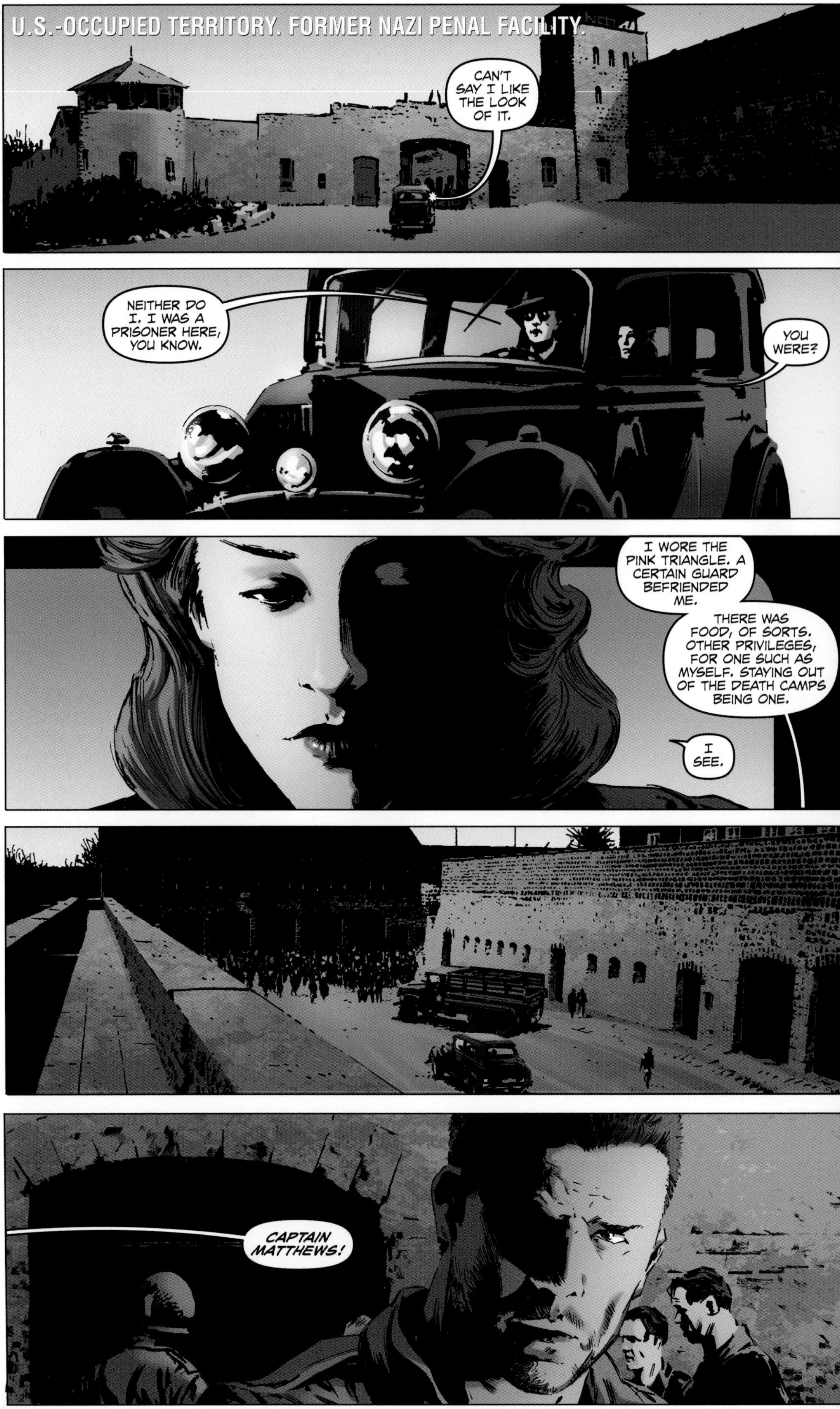
U.S.-OCCUPIED TERRITORY. FORMER NAZI PENAL FACILITY.
CAN'T SAY I LIKE THE LOOK OF IT.
NEITHER DO I. I WAS A PRISONER HERE, YOU KNOW.
YOU WERE?
I WORE THE PINK TRIANGLE. A CERTAIN GUARD BEFRIENDED ME.
THERE WAS FOOD, OF SORTS. OTHER PRIVILEGES, FOR ONE SUCH AS MYSELF. STAYING OUT OF THE DEATH CAMPS BEING ONE.
I SEE.
CAPTAIN MATTHEWS!

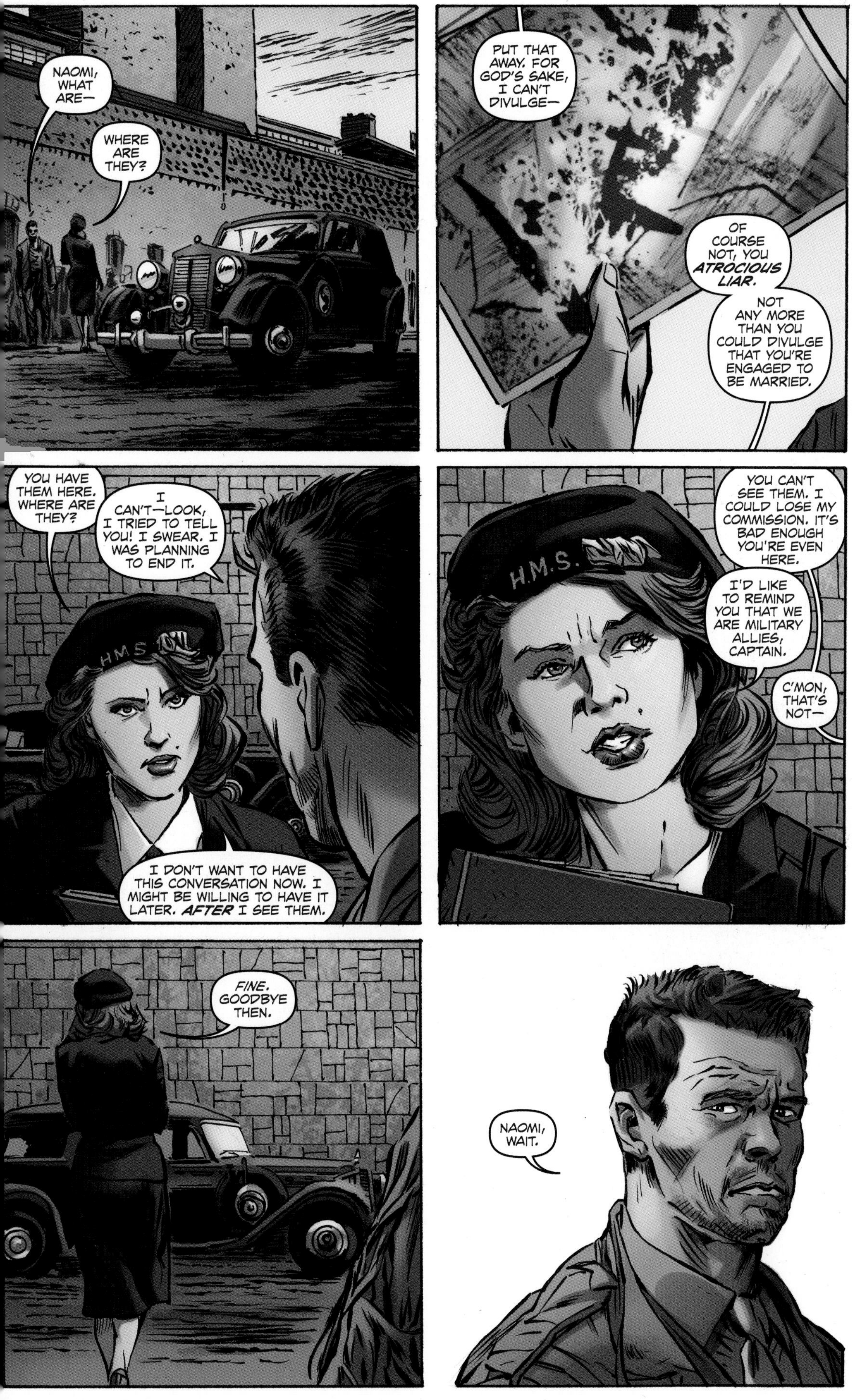
NAOMI, WHAT ARE—
WHERE ARE THEY?
PUT THAT AWAY. FOR GOD'S SAKE, I CAN'T DIVULGE—
OF COURSE NOT, YOU *ATROCIOUS LIAR.*
NOT ANY MORE THAN YOU COULD DIVULGE THAT YOU'RE ENGAGED TO BE MARRIED.
YOU HAVE THEM HERE. WHERE ARE THEY?
I CAN'T—LOOK, I TRIED TO TELL YOU! I SWEAR. I WAS PLANNING TO END IT.
I DON'T WANT TO HAVE THIS CONVERSATION NOW. I MIGHT BE WILLING TO HAVE IT LATER. *AFTER* I SEE THEM.
H.M.S.
YOU CAN'T SEE THEM. I COULD LOSE MY COMMISSION. IT'S BAD ENOUGH YOU'RE EVEN HERE.
I'D LIKE TO REMIND YOU THAT WE ARE MILITARY ALLIES, CAPTAIN.
C'MON, THAT'S NOT—
FINE. GOODBYE THEN.
NAOMI, WAIT.

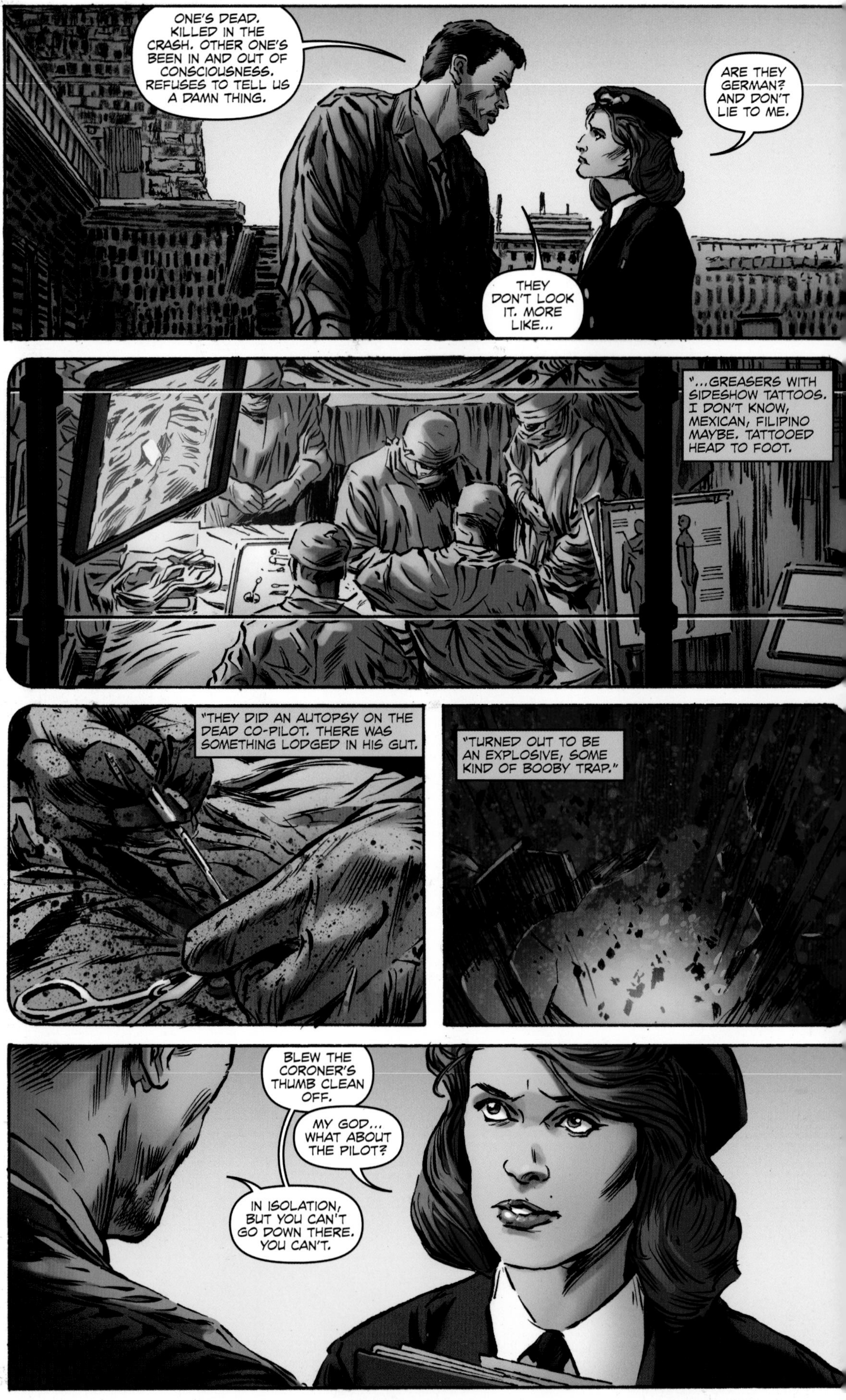
ONE'S DEAD. KILLED IN THE CRASH. OTHER ONE'S BEEN IN AND OUT OF CONSCIOUSNESS. REFUSES TO TELL US A DAMN THING.
ARE THEY GERMAN? AND DON'T LIE TO ME.
THEY DON'T LOOK IT. MORE LIKE...
"...GREASERS WITH SIDESHOW TATTOOS. I DON'T KNOW, MEXICAN, FILIPINO MAYBE. TATTOOED HEAD TO FOOT.
"THEY DID AN AUTOPSY ON THE DEAD CO-PILOT. THERE WAS SOMETHING LODGED IN HIS GUT.
"TURNED OUT TO BE AN EXPLOSIVE, SOME KIND OF BOOBY TRAP."
BLEW THE CORONER'S THUMB CLEAN OFF.
MY GOD... WHAT ABOUT THE PILOT?
IN ISOLATION, BUT YOU CAN'T GO DOWN THERE. YOU CAN'T.

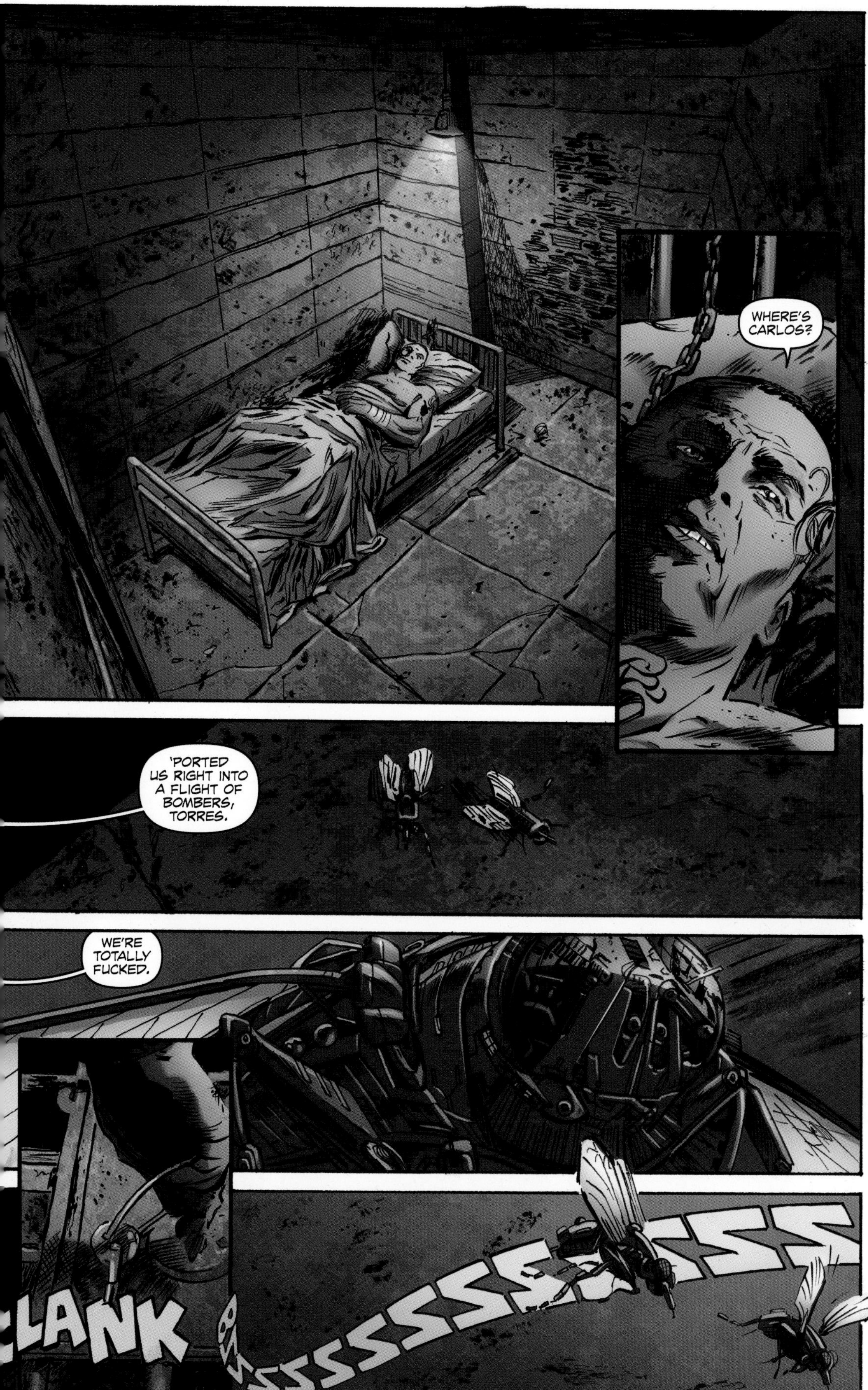
WHERE'S CARLOS?
'PORTED US RIGHT INTO A FLIGHT OF BOMBERS, TORRES.
WE'RE TOTALLY FUCKED.
LANK
BSSSSSSSSSSSSS

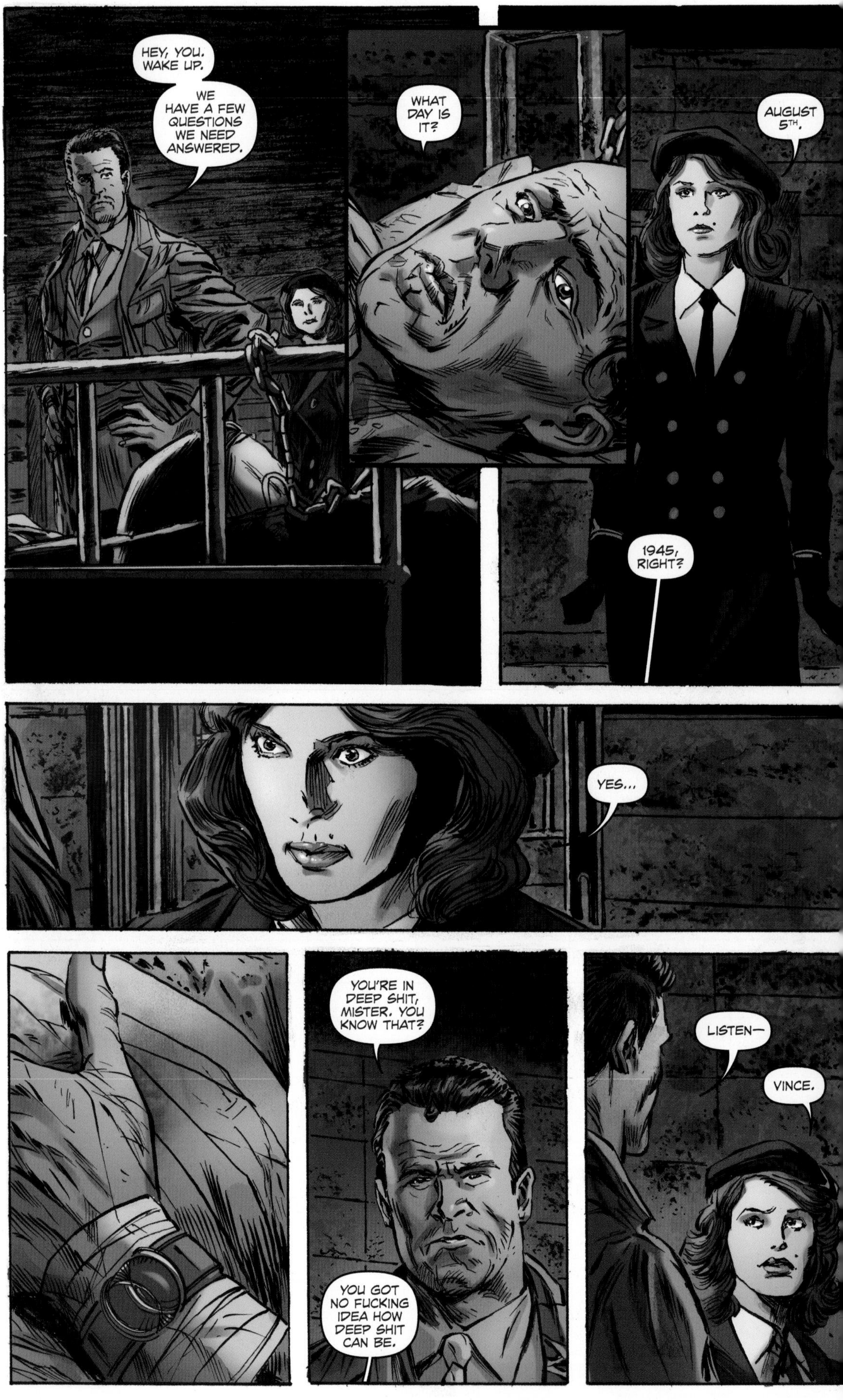
HEY, YOU. WAKE UP.
WE HAVE A FEW QUESTIONS WE NEED ANSWERED.
WHAT DAY IS IT?
AUGUST 5TH.
1945, RIGHT?
YES...
YOU'RE IN DEEP SHIT, MISTER. YOU KNOW THAT?
YOU GOT NO FUCKING IDEA HOW DEEP SHIT CAN BE.
LISTEN—
VINCE.

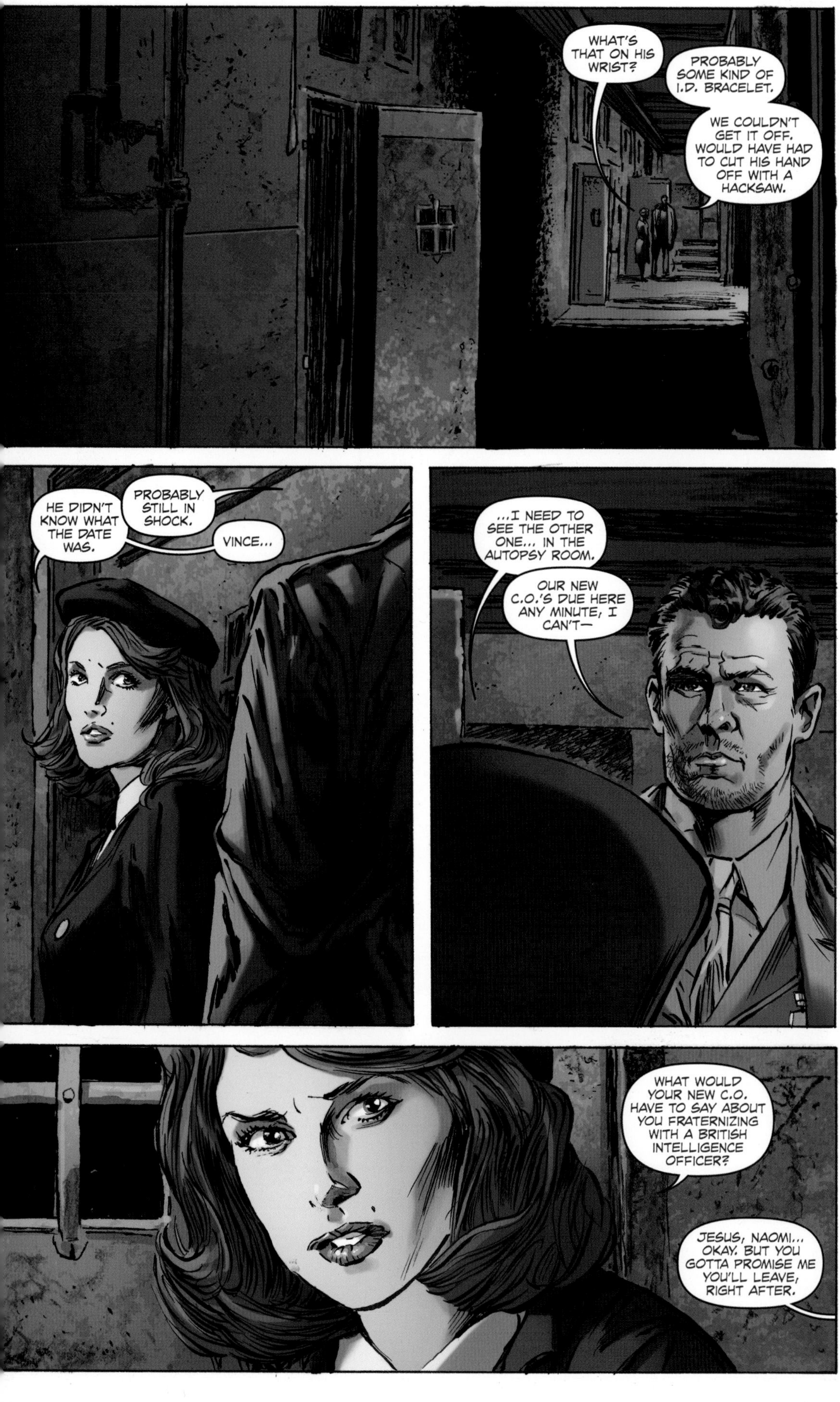
WHAT'S THAT ON HIS WRIST?
PROBABLY SOME KIND OF I.D. BRACELET.
WE COULDN'T GET IT OFF. WOULD HAVE HAD TO CUT HIS HAND OFF WITH A HACKSAW.
HE DIDN'T KNOW WHAT THE DATE WAS.
PROBABLY STILL IN SHOCK.
VINCE...
...I NEED TO SEE THE OTHER ONE... IN THE AUTOPSY ROOM.
OUR NEW C.O.'S DUE HERE ANY MINUTE, I CAN'T—
WHAT WOULD YOUR NEW C.O. HAVE TO SAY ABOUT YOU FRATERNIZING WITH A BRITISH INTELLIGENCE OFFICER?
JESUS, NAOMI... OKAY. BUT YOU GOTTA PROMISE ME YOU'LL LEAVE, RIGHT AFTER.

CAUSE OF DEATH?

LOOKS AS THOUGH HE SWALLOWED AN AMERICAN CIGARETTE LIGHTER.

MISSING THE BACK OF HIS HEAD. PROBABLY WHEN THEY CLIPPED THE B-17.

WHATEVER HE SWALLOWED, THE DOC'S SHORT A THUMB.

HE'S WEARING ONE OF THOSE I.D. BRACELETS, TOO. AND THESE MARKINGS.

THEY'RE BOTH COVERED WITH THAT STUFF.

AND WHATEVER THEY WERE FLYING, IT DEFINITELY WASN'T OURS.

HOW DO YOU KNOW? EVEN IF YOU AREN'T LYING TO ME, WHY WOULD YOU BE AWARE OF EVERY SECRET U.S. WEAPONS PROJECT?

WHAT IF THIS WERE ONE OF YOUR OWN EXPERIMENTAL AIRCRAFT?

FLOWN BY TATTOOED *SIDESHOW FREAKS?* I DON'T THINK SO.

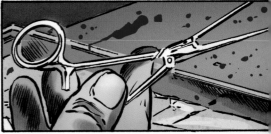

PLASTIC?

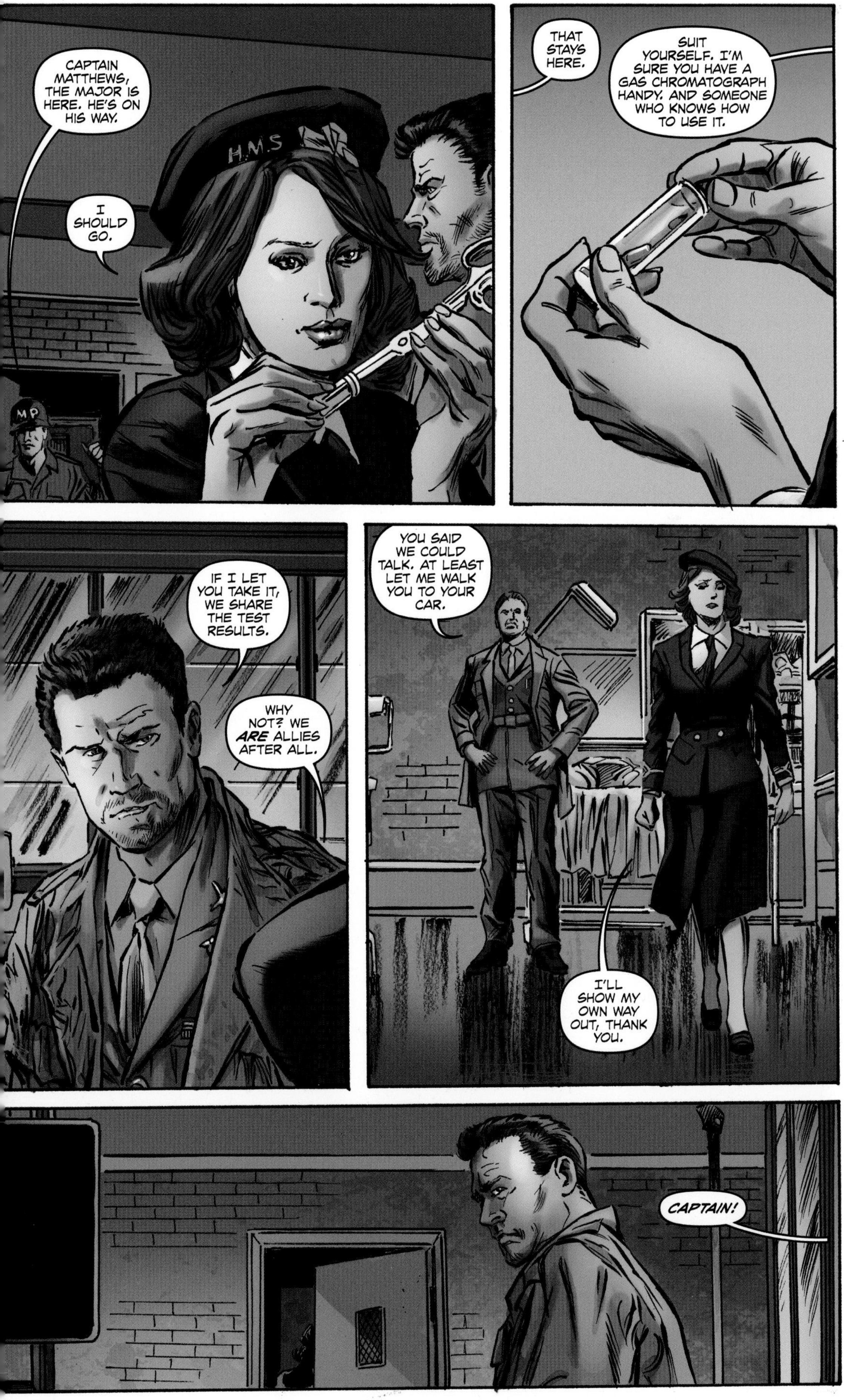
CAPTAIN MATTHEWS, THE MAJOR IS HERE. HE'S ON HIS WAY.
I SHOULD GO.
THAT STAYS HERE.
SUIT YOURSELF. I'M SURE YOU HAVE A GAS CHROMATOGRAPH HANDY. AND SOMEONE WHO KNOWS HOW TO USE IT.
H.M.S
MP
IF I LET YOU TAKE IT, WE SHARE THE TEST RESULTS.
WHY NOT? WE ARE ALLIES AFTER ALL.
YOU SAID WE COULD TALK. AT LEAST LET ME WALK YOU TO YOUR CAR.
I'LL SHOW MY OWN WAY OUT, THANK YOU.
CAPTAIN!

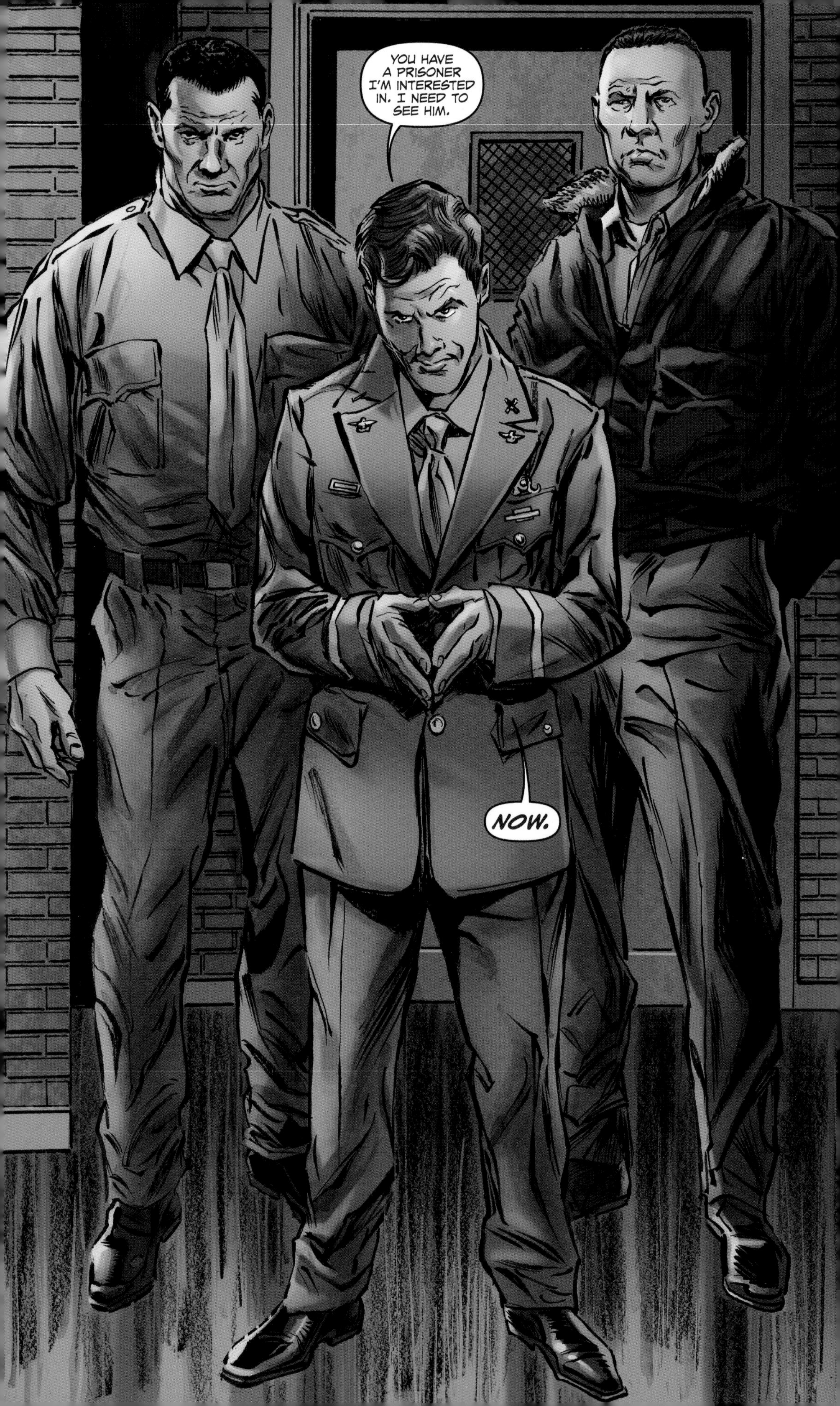
YOU HAVE A PRISONER I'M INTERESTED IN. I NEED TO SEE HIM.
NOW.

TWO

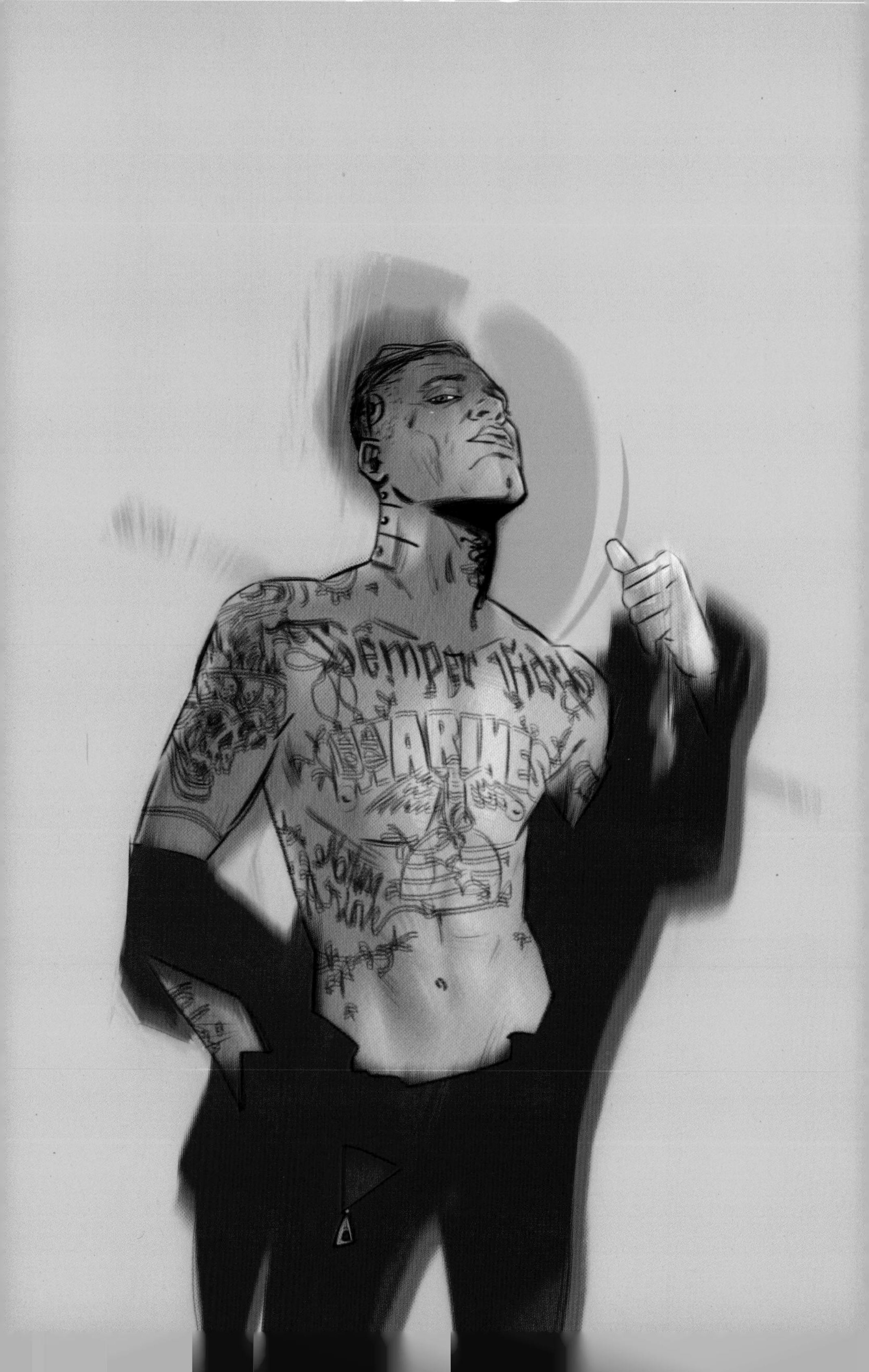

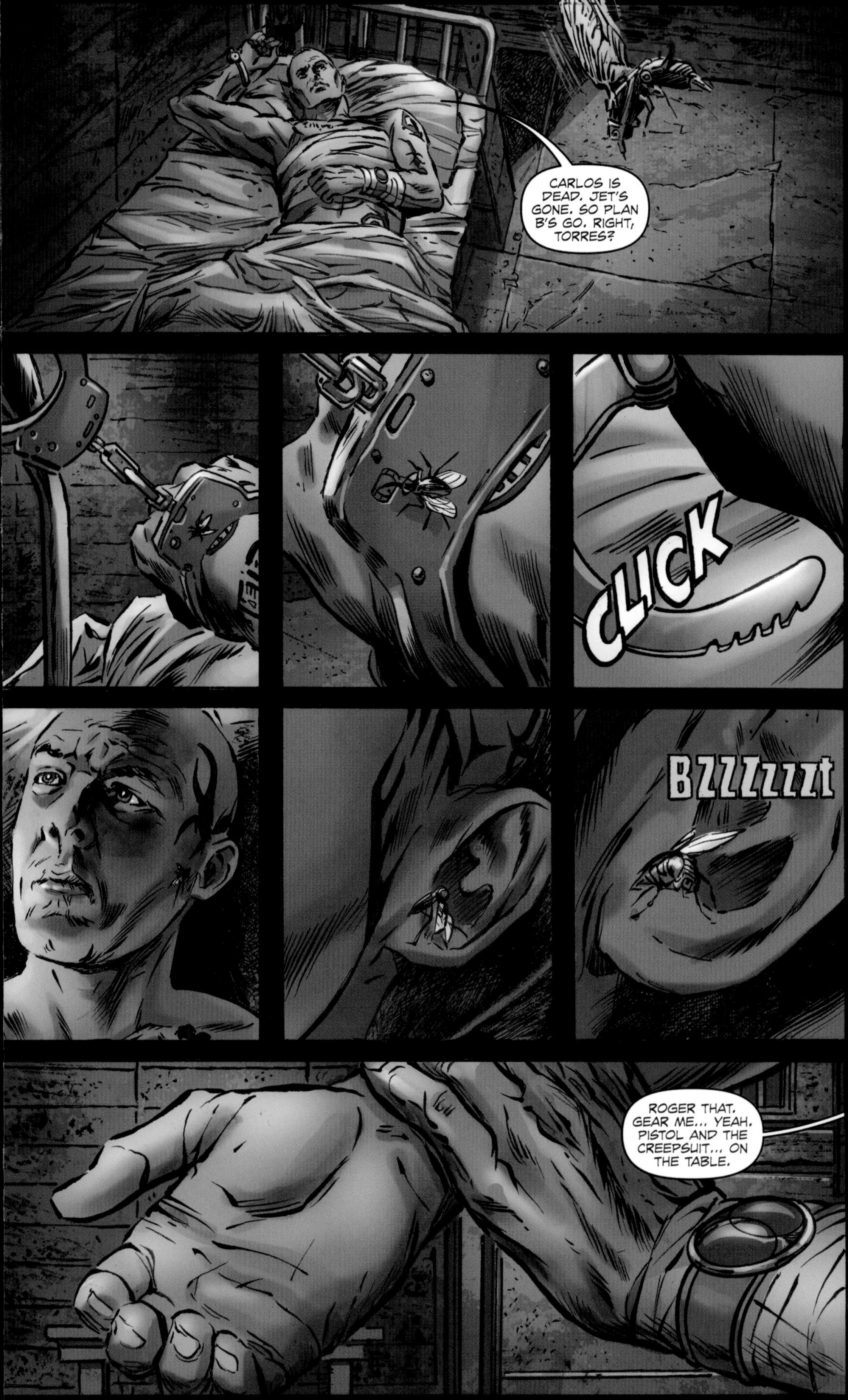
CARLOS IS DEAD. JET'S GONE. SO PLAN B'S GO. RIGHT, TORRES?
CLICK
BZZZzzzt
ROGER THAT. GEAR ME... YEAH. PISTOL AND THE CREEPSUIT... ON THE TABLE.

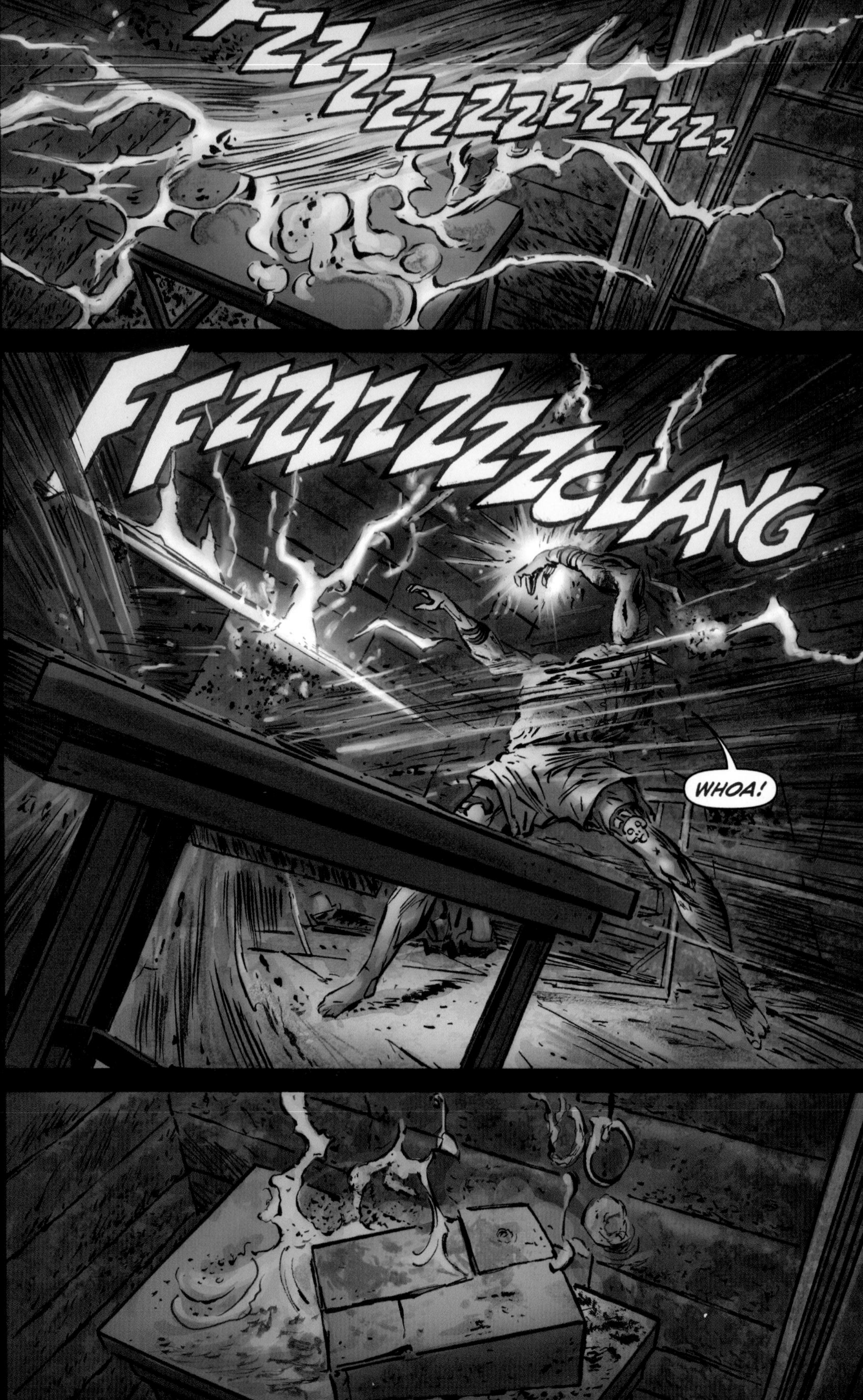
FZZZZZZZZZZZZZZz
FFZZZZZZZZCLANG
WHOA!

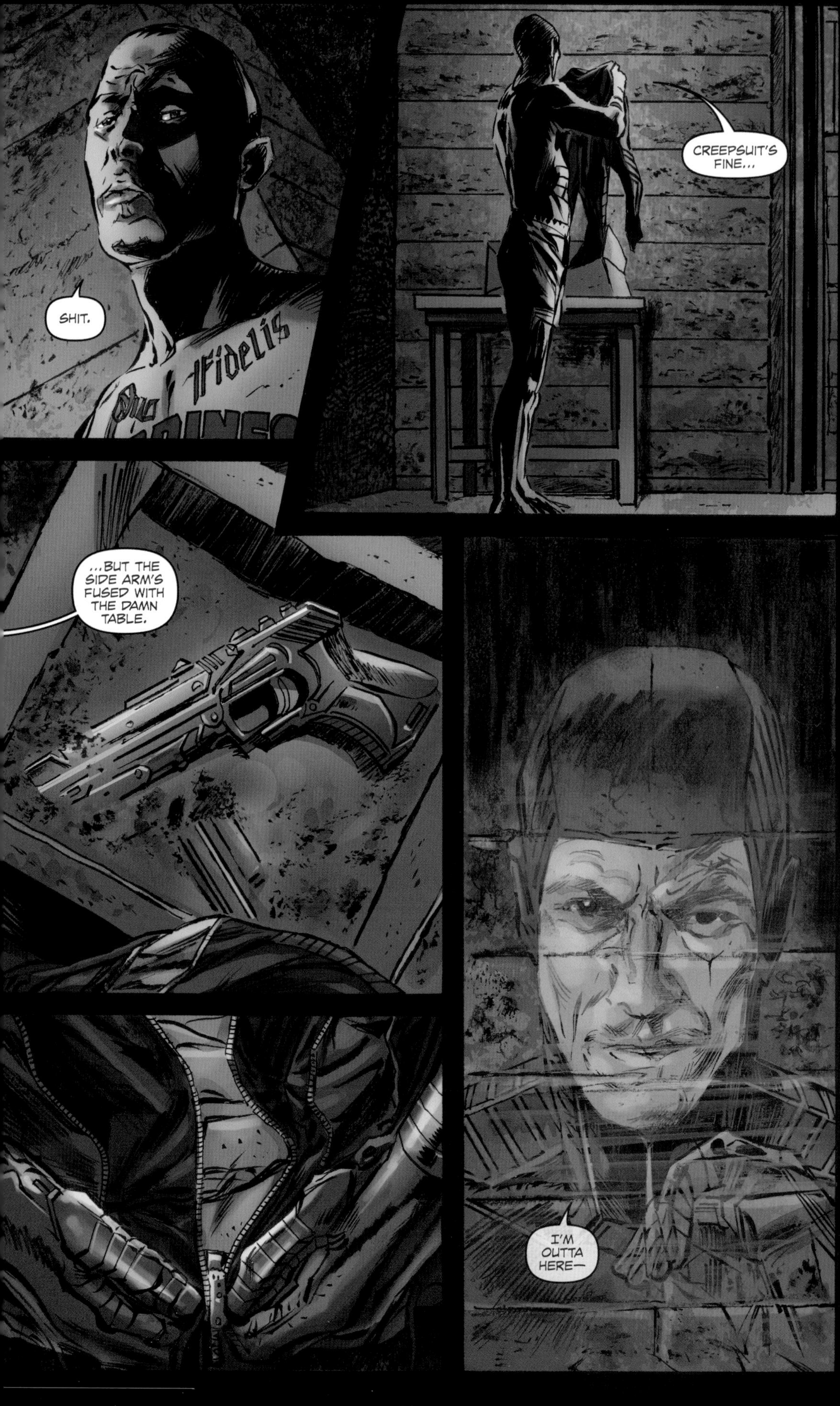
SHIT.
CREEPSUIT'S FINE...
...BUT THE SIDE ARM'S FUSED WITH THE DAMN TABLE.
I'M OUTTA HERE—

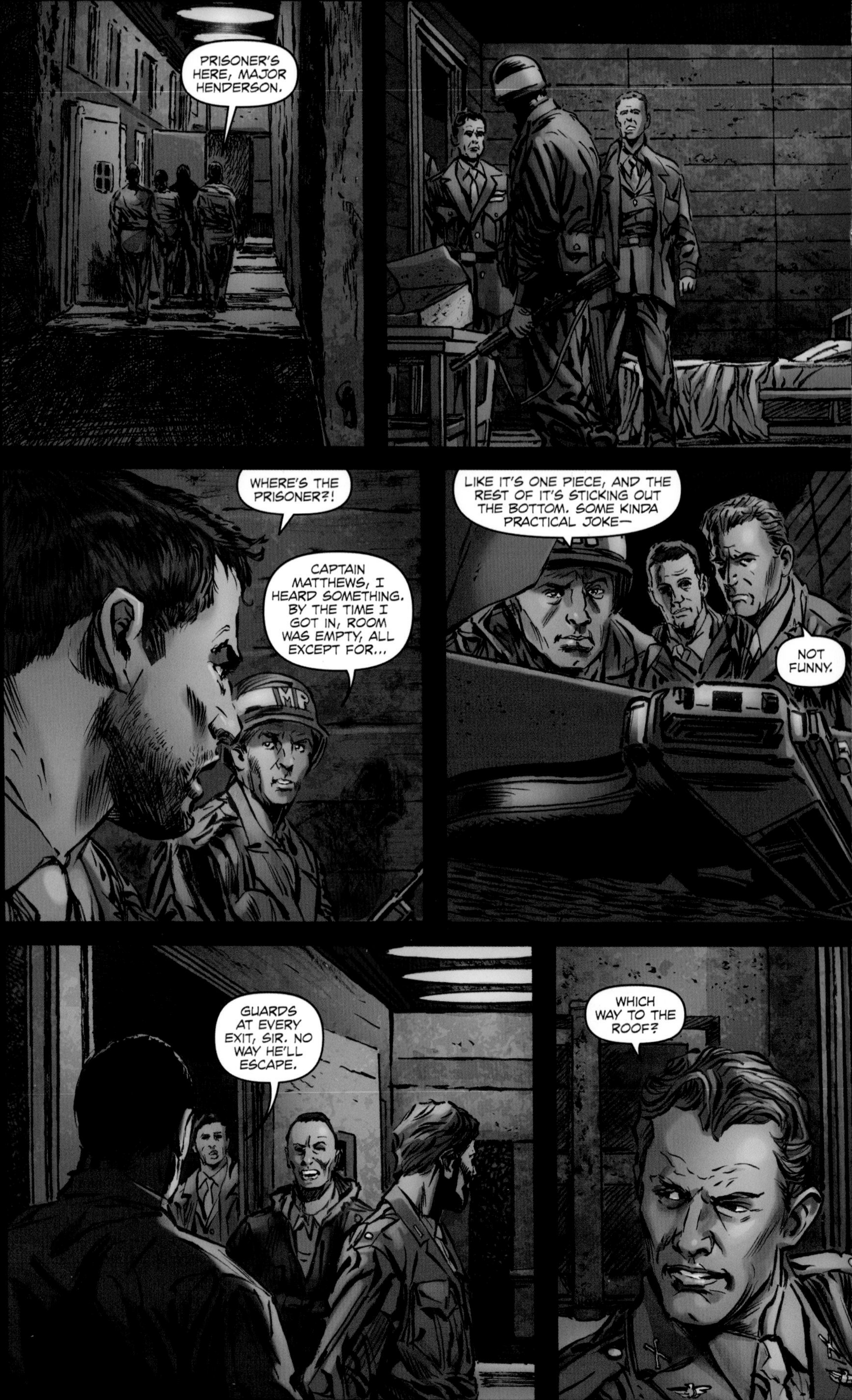
PRISONER'S HERE, MAJOR HENDERSON.
WHERE'S THE PRISONER?!
CAPTAIN MATTHEWS, I HEARD SOMETHING. BY THE TIME I GOT IN, ROOM WAS EMPTY, ALL EXCEPT FOR...
MP
LIKE IT'S ONE PIECE, AND THE REST OF IT'S STICKING OUT THE BOTTOM. SOME KINDA PRACTICAL JOKE—
NOT FUNNY.
GUARDS AT EVERY EXIT, SIR. NO WAY HE'LL ESCAPE.
WHICH WAY TO THE ROOF?

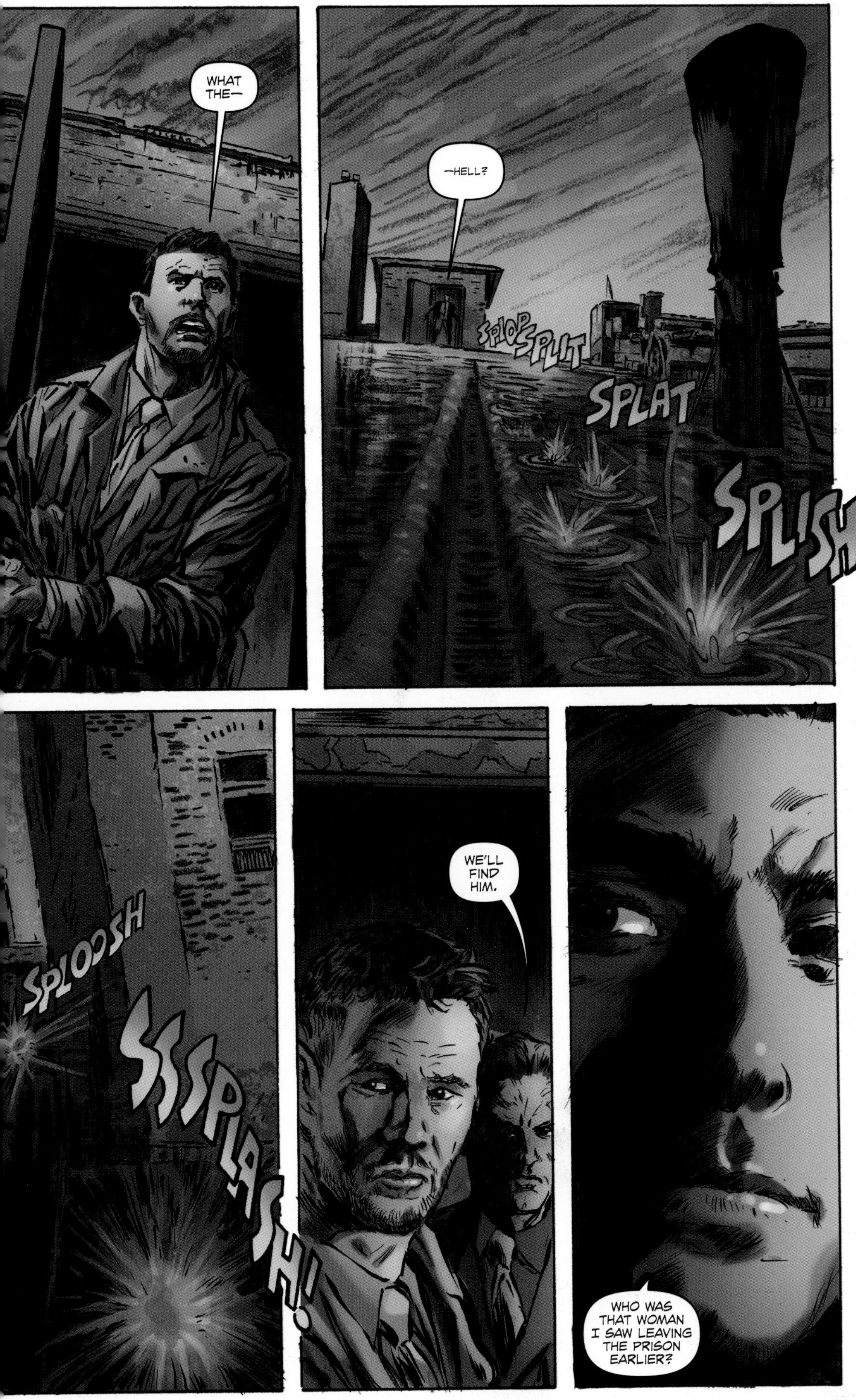
WHAT THE—
—HELL?
SPLOP
SPLIT
SPLAT
SPLISH
SPLOOSH
SSSPLASH!
WE'LL FIND HIM.
WHO WAS THAT WOMAN I SAW LEAVING THE PRISON EARLIER?

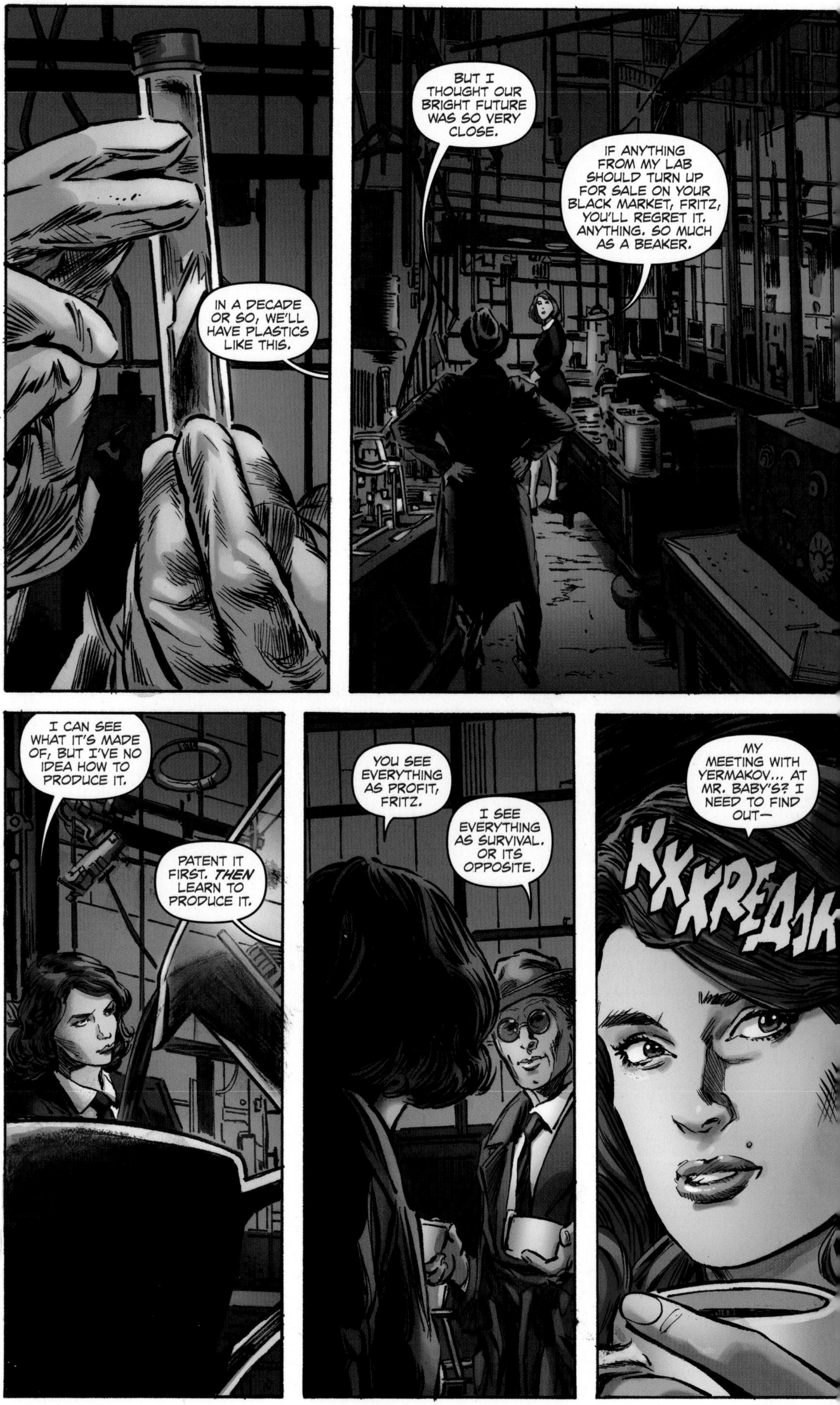
IN A DECADE OR SO, WE'LL HAVE PLASTICS LIKE THIS.
BUT I THOUGHT OUR BRIGHT FUTURE WAS SO VERY CLOSE.
IF ANYTHING FROM MY LAB SHOULD TURN UP FOR SALE ON YOUR BLACK MARKET, FRITZ, YOU'LL REGRET IT. ANYTHING. SO MUCH AS A BEAKER.
I CAN SEE WHAT IT'S MADE OF, BUT I'VE NO IDEA HOW TO PRODUCE IT.
PATENT IT FIRST. *THEN* LEARN TO PRODUCE IT.
YOU SEE EVERYTHING AS PROFIT, FRITZ.
I SEE EVERYTHING AS SURVIVAL. OR ITS OPPOSITE.
MY MEETING WITH YERMAKOV... AT MR. BABY'S? I NEED TO FIND OUT—
KKXREAAK

GO.

WHATEVER DETONATED IN THE DEAD MAN'S STOMACH WAS MADE OF A PLASTIC THAT DOESN'T EXIST TODAY.

H. G. LS WROTE OOK, *THE VISIBLE MAN.*

I'M GIVENS. *NAOMI GIVENS.* AND YOU ARE...?

I'M THE PILOT.

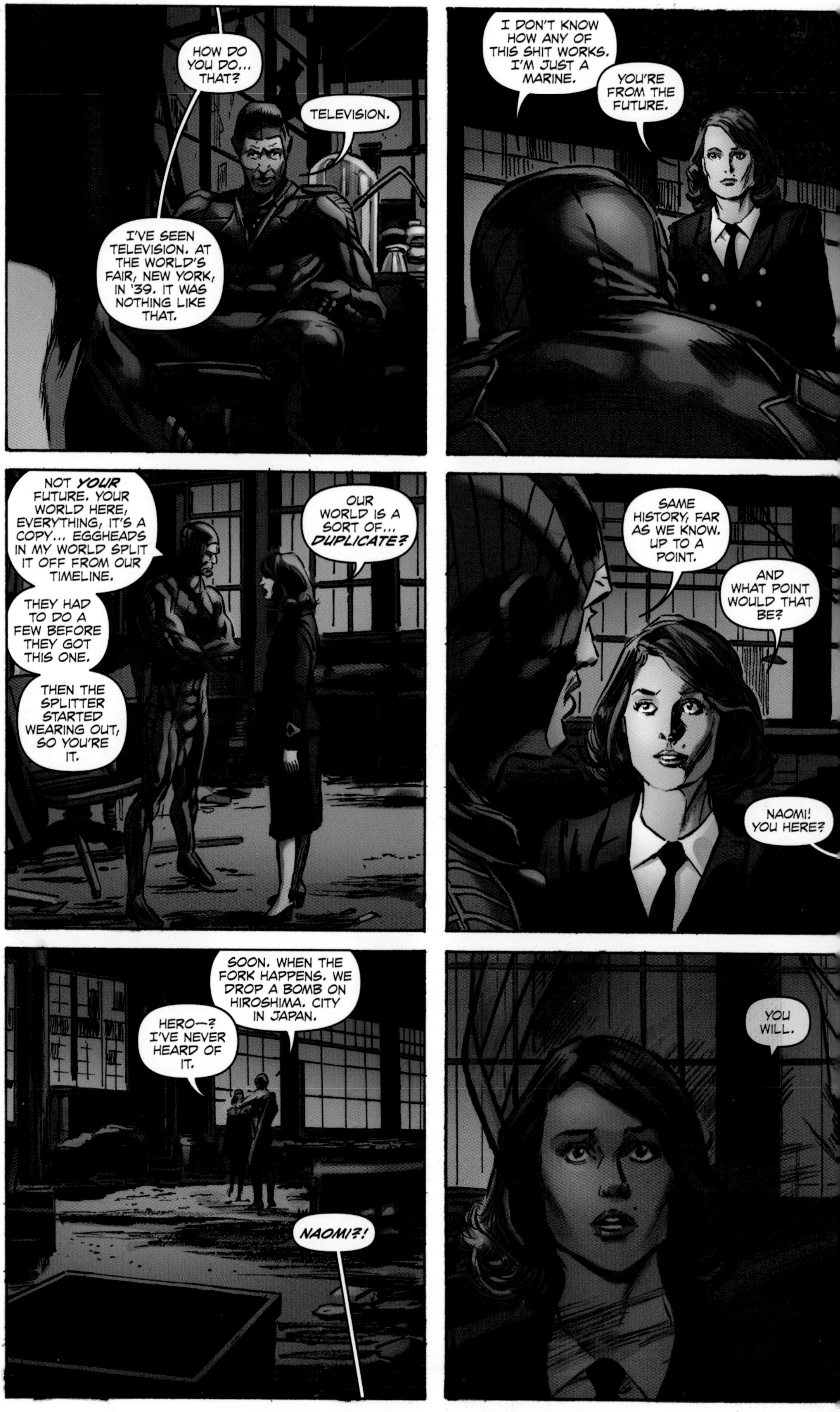

HOW DO YOU DO... THAT?
TELEVISION.
I'VE SEEN TELEVISION. AT THE WORLD'S FAIR, NEW YORK, IN '39. IT WAS NOTHING LIKE THAT.
I DON'T KNOW HOW ANY OF THIS SHIT WORKS. I'M JUST A MARINE.
YOU'RE FROM THE FUTURE.
NOT *YOUR* FUTURE. YOUR WORLD HERE, EVERYTHING, IT'S A COPY... EGGHEADS IN MY WORLD SPLIT IT OFF FROM OUR TIMELINE.
THEY HAD TO DO A FEW BEFORE THEY GOT THIS ONE.
THEN THE SPLITTER STARTED WEARING OUT, SO YOU'RE IT.
OUR WORLD IS A SORT OF... *DUPLICATE?*
SAME HISTORY, FAR AS WE KNOW. UP TO A POINT.
AND WHAT POINT WOULD THAT BE?
NAOMI! YOU HERE?
SOON. WHEN THE FORK HAPPENS. WE DROP A BOMB ON HIROSHIMA. CITY IN JAPAN.
HERO--? I'VE NEVER HEARD OF IT.
NAOMI?!
YOU WILL.

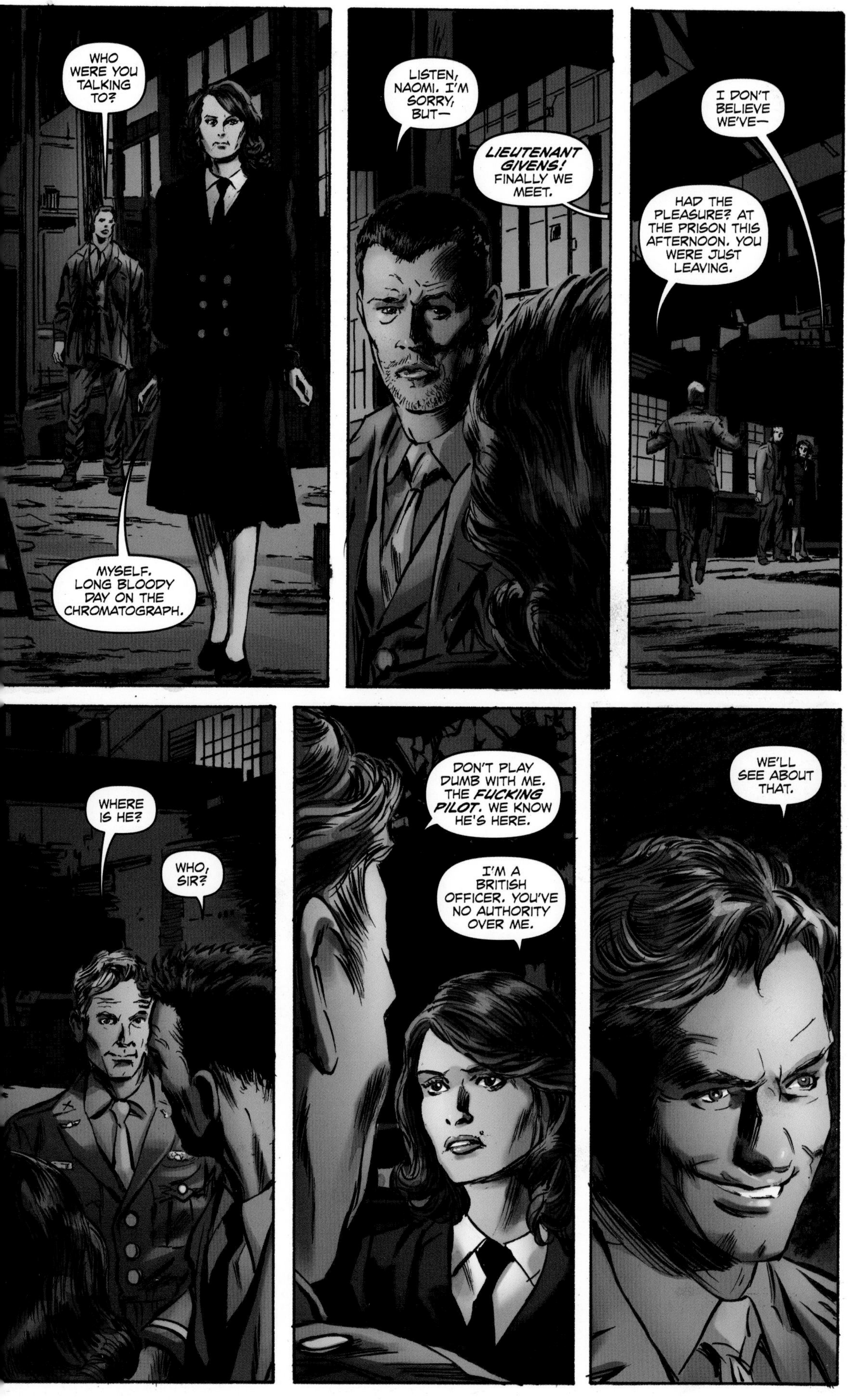
WHO WERE YOU TALKING TO?
MYSELF. LONG BLOODY DAY ON THE CHROMATOGRAPH.
LISTEN, NAOMI. I'M SORRY, BUT—
LIEUTENANT GIVENS! FINALLY WE MEET.
I DON'T BELIEVE WE'VE—
HAD THE PLEASURE? AT THE PRISON THIS AFTERNOON. YOU WERE JUST LEAVING.
WHERE IS HE?
WHO, SIR?
DON'T PLAY DUMB WITH ME. THE FUCKING PILOT. WE KNOW HE'S HERE.
I'M A BRITISH OFFICER. YOU'VE NO AUTHORITY OVER ME.
WE'LL SEE ABOUT THAT.

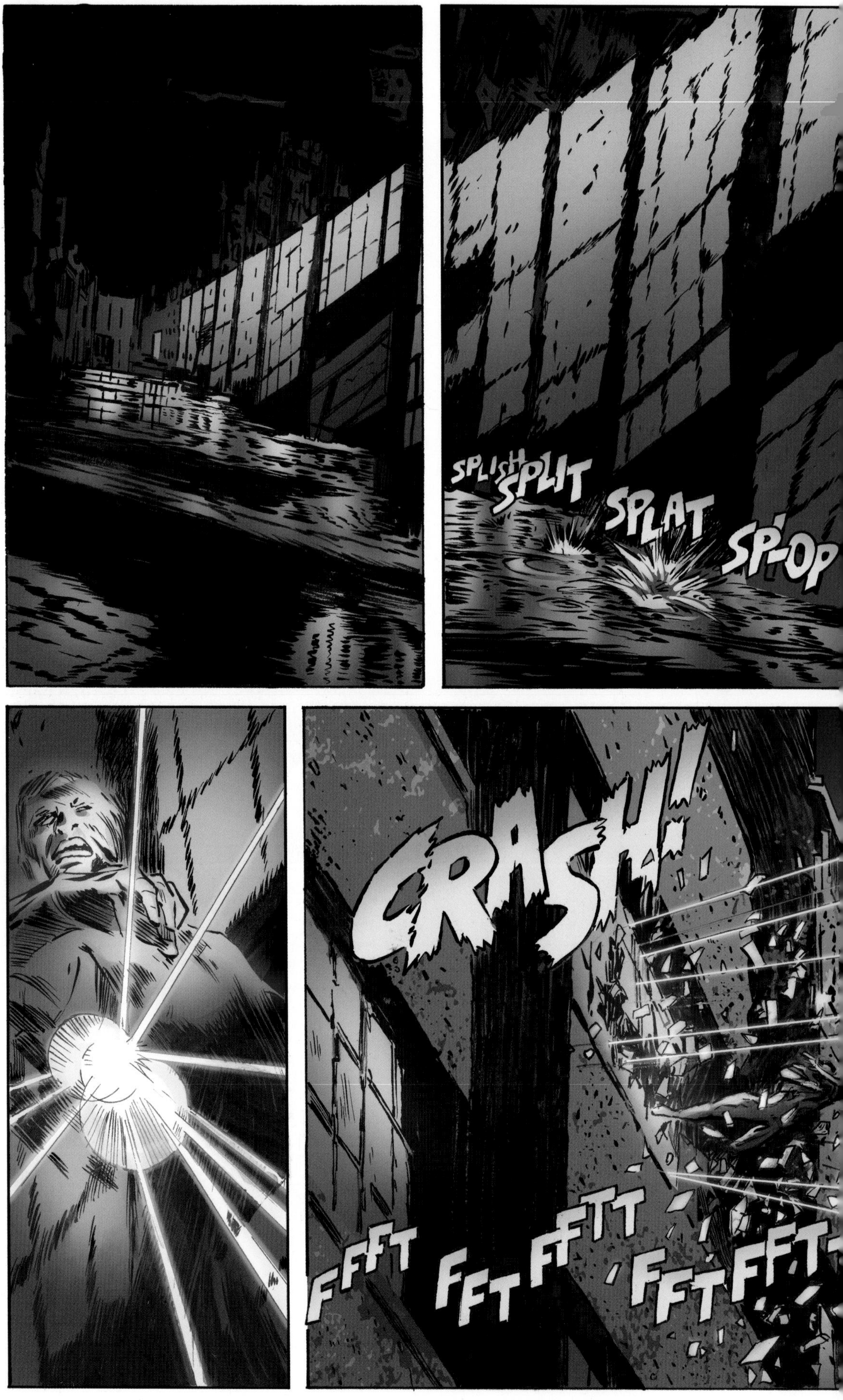
SPLISH
SPLIT
SPLAT
SP-OP
CRASH!
FFFT
FFT FFTT
FFT FFT-

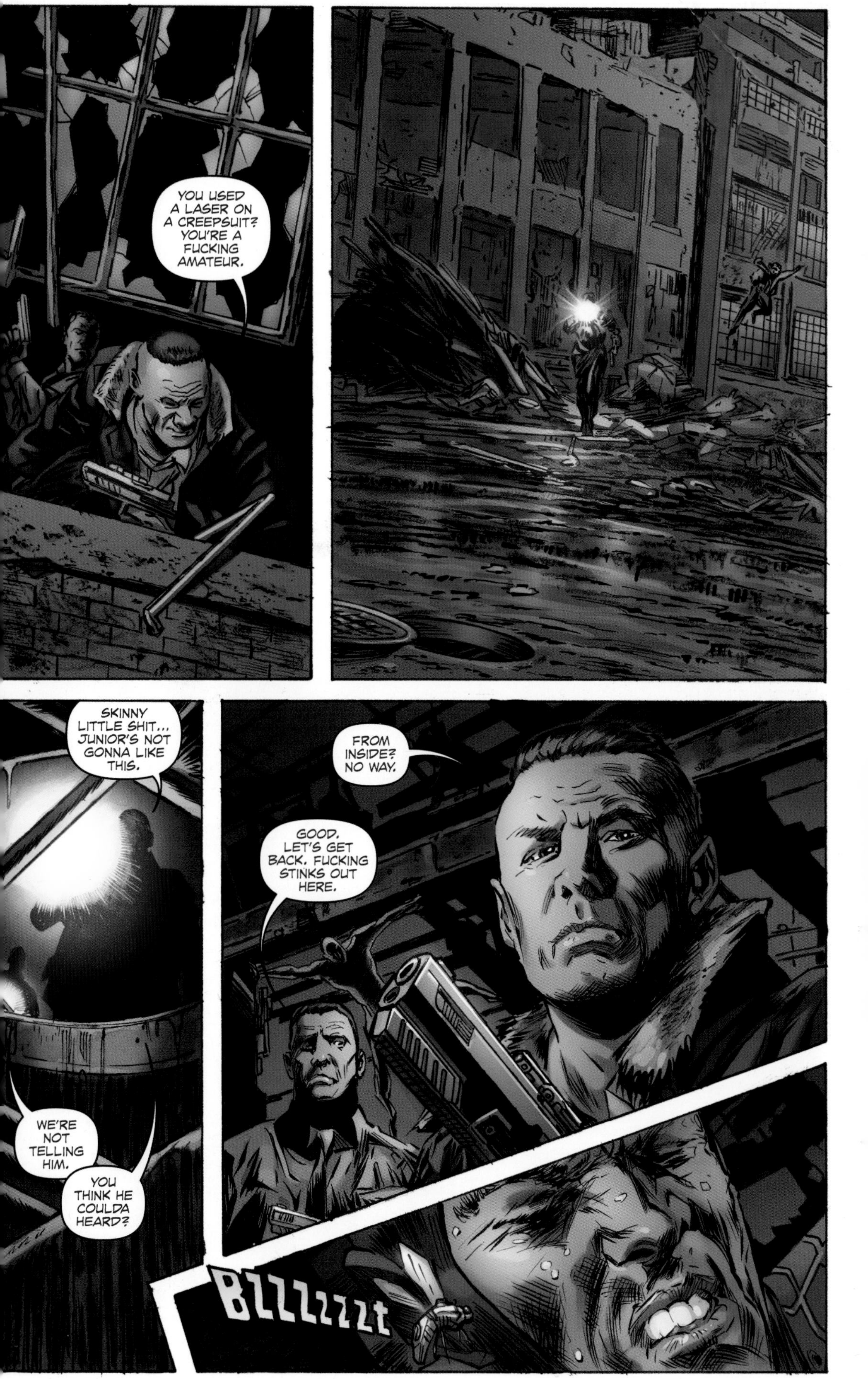
YOU USED A LASER ON A CREEPSUIT? YOU'RE A FUCKING AMATEUR.
SKINNY LITTLE SHIT... JUNIOR'S NOT GONNA LIKE THIS.
FROM INSIDE? NO WAY.
GOOD. LET'S GET BACK. FUCKING STINKS OUT HERE.
WE'RE NOT TELLING HIM.
YOU THINK HE COULDA HEARD?
BZZZzzzt

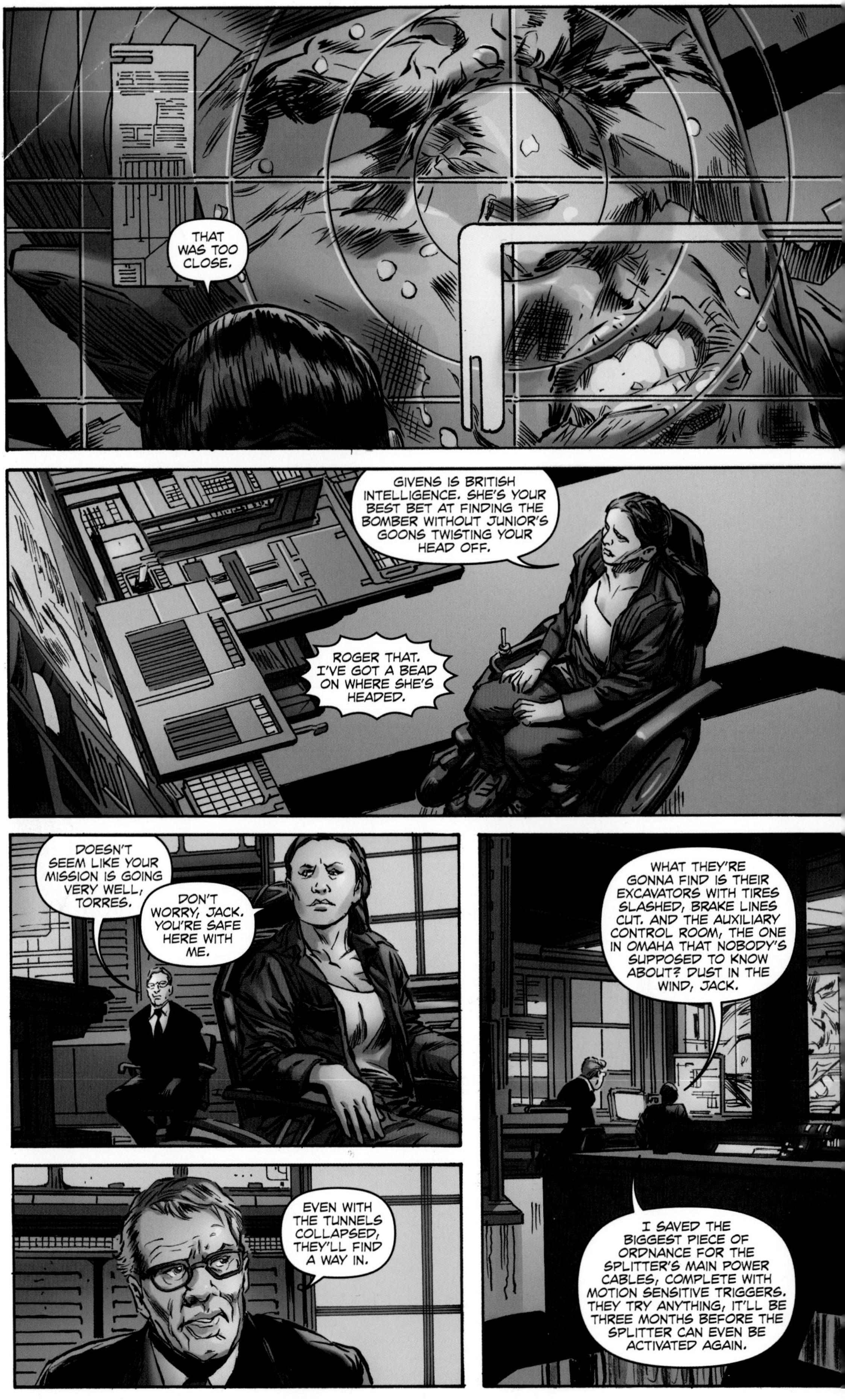
THAT WAS TOO CLOSE.
GIVENS IS BRITISH INTELLIGENCE. SHE'S YOUR BEST BET AT FINDING THE BOMBER WITHOUT JUNIOR'S GOONS TWISTING YOUR HEAD OFF.
ROGER THAT. I'VE GOT A BEAD ON WHERE SHE'S HEADED.
DOESN'T SEEM LIKE YOUR MISSION IS GOING VERY WELL, TORRES.
DON'T WORRY, JACK. YOU'RE SAFE HERE WITH ME.
EVEN WITH THE TUNNELS COLLAPSED, THEY'LL FIND A WAY IN.
WHAT THEY'RE GONNA FIND IS THEIR EXCAVATORS WITH TIRES SLASHED, BRAKE LINES CUT. AND THE AUXILIARY CONTROL ROOM, THE ONE IN OMAHA THAT NOBODY'S SUPPOSED TO KNOW ABOUT? DUST IN THE WIND, JACK.
I SAVED THE BIGGEST PIECE OF ORDNANCE FOR THE SPLITTER'S MAIN POWER CABLES, COMPLETE WITH MOTION SENSITIVE TRIGGERS. THEY TRY ANYTHING, IT'LL BE THREE MONTHS BEFORE THE SPLITTER CAN EVEN BE ACTIVATED AGAIN.

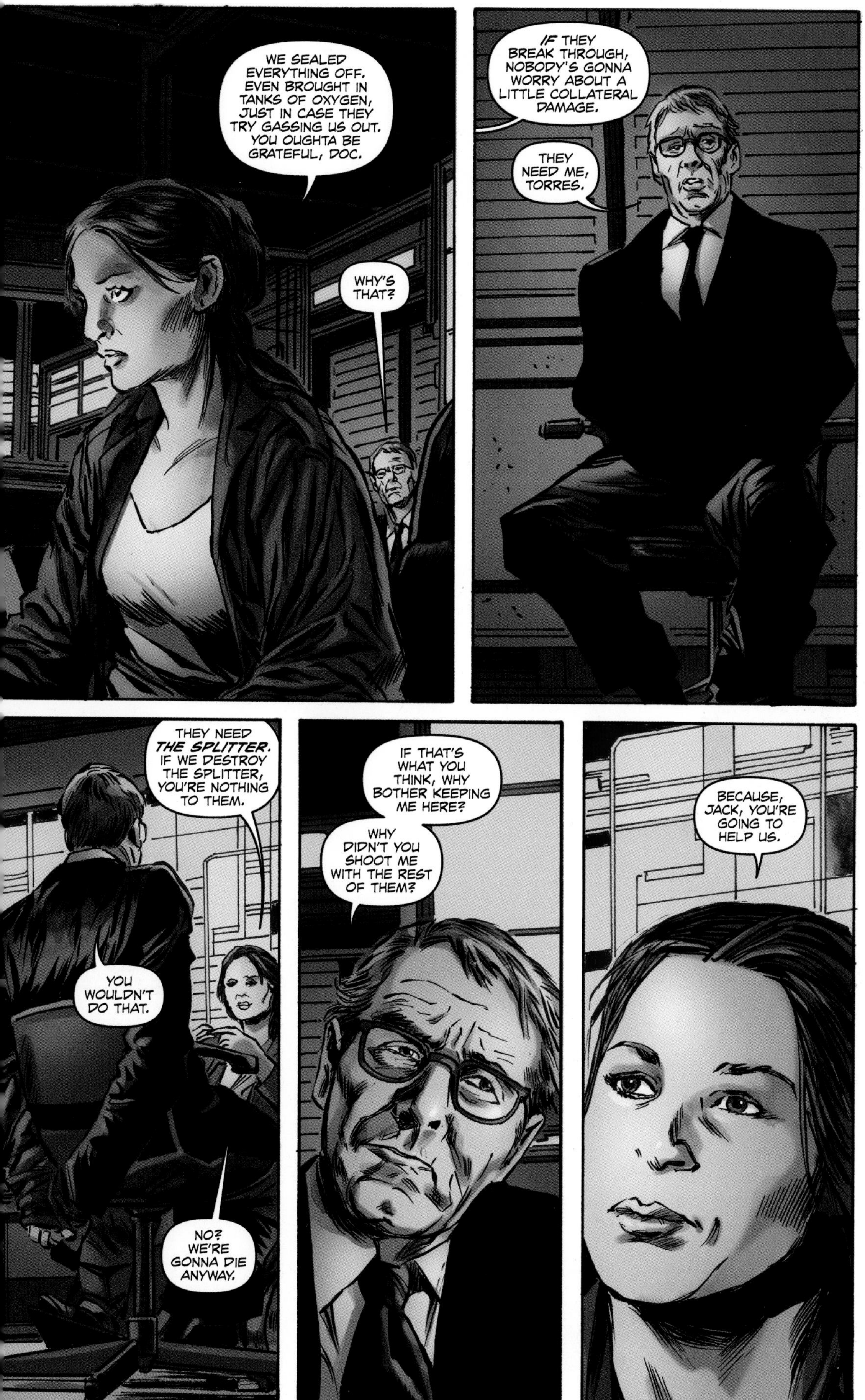

WE SEALED EVERYTHING OFF. EVEN BROUGHT IN TANKS OF OXYGEN, JUST IN CASE THEY TRY GASSING US OUT. YOU OUGHTA BE GRATEFUL, DOC.
WHY'S THAT?
IF THEY BREAK THROUGH, NOBODY'S GONNA WORRY ABOUT A LITTLE COLLATERAL DAMAGE.
THEY NEED ME, TORRES.
THEY NEED THE SPLITTER. IF WE DESTROY THE SPLITTER, YOU'RE NOTHING TO THEM.
YOU WOULDN'T DO THAT.
NO? WE'RE GONNA DIE ANYWAY.
IF THAT'S WHAT YOU THINK, WHY BOTHER KEEPING ME HERE?
WHY DIDN'T YOU SHOOT ME WITH THE REST OF THEM?
BECAUSE, JACK, YOU'RE GOING TO HELP US.

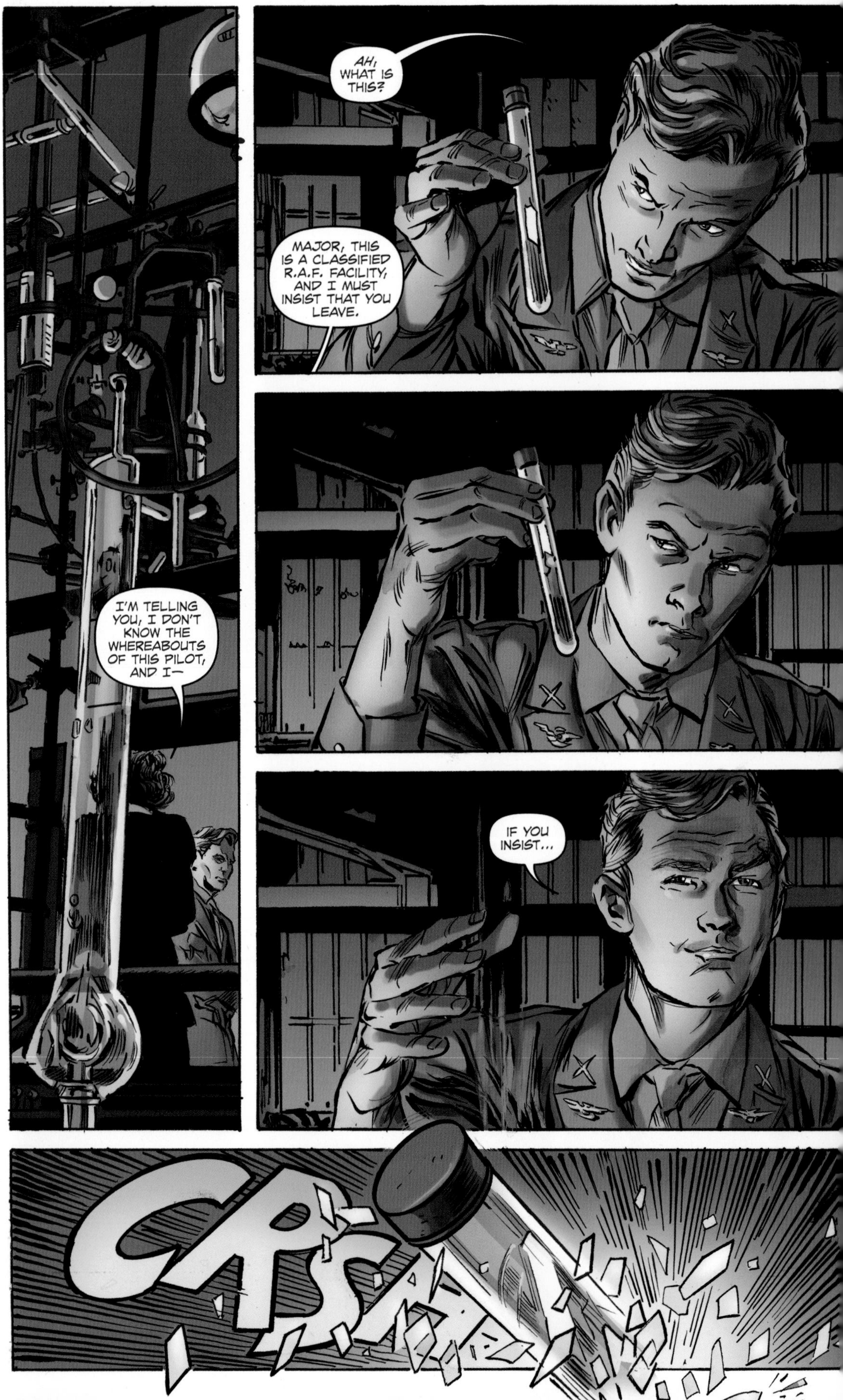
AH, WHAT IS THIS?
MAJOR, THIS IS A CLASSIFIED R.A.F. FACILITY, AND I MUST INSIST THAT YOU LEAVE.
I'M TELLING YOU, I DON'T KNOW THE WHEREABOUTS OF THIS PILOT, AND I—
IF YOU INSIST...
CRSSH

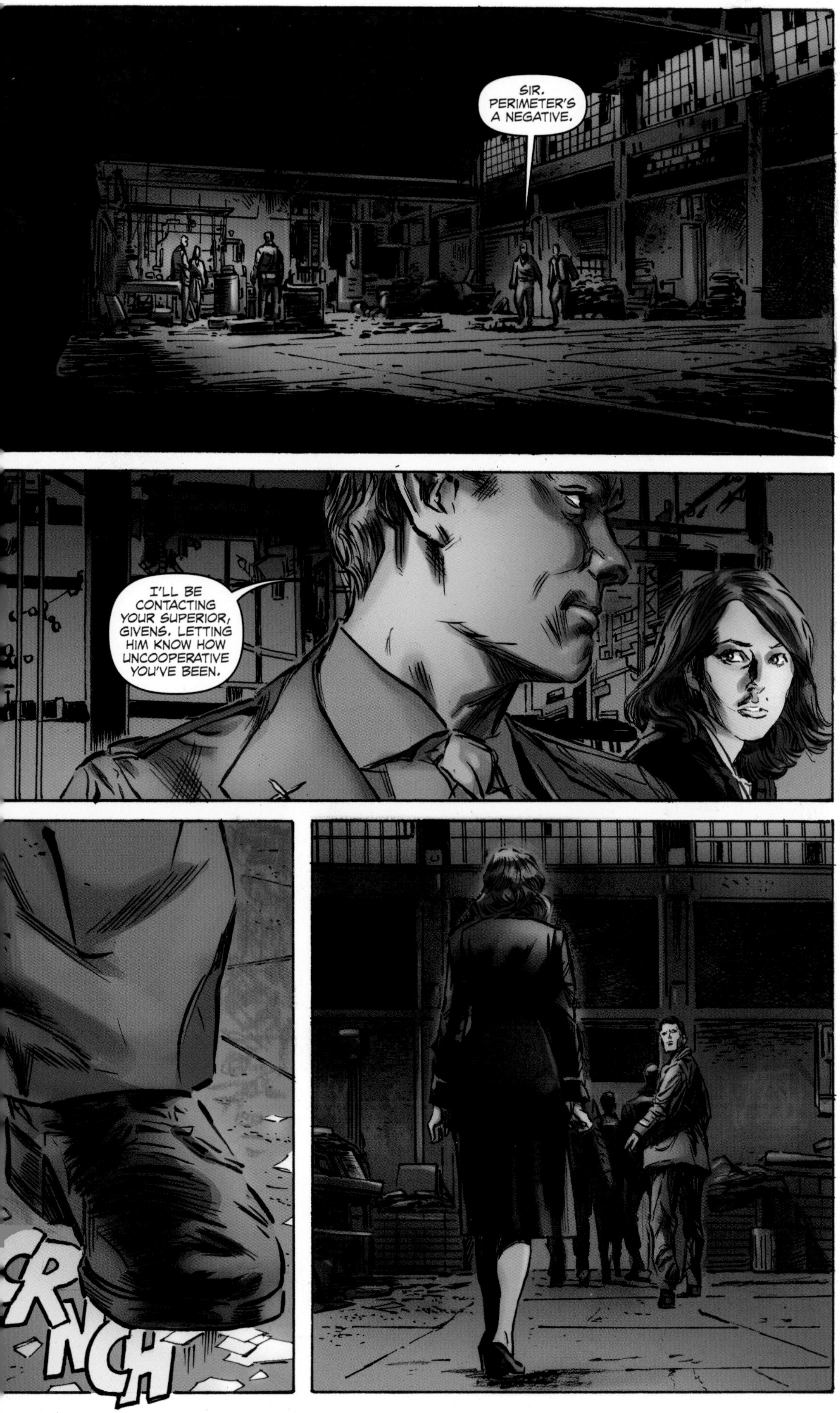
SIR. PERIMETER'S A NEGATIVE.
I'LL BE CONTACTING YOUR SUPERIOR, GIVENS. LETTING HIM KNOW HOW UNCOOPERATIVE YOU'VE BEEN.
CRNCH

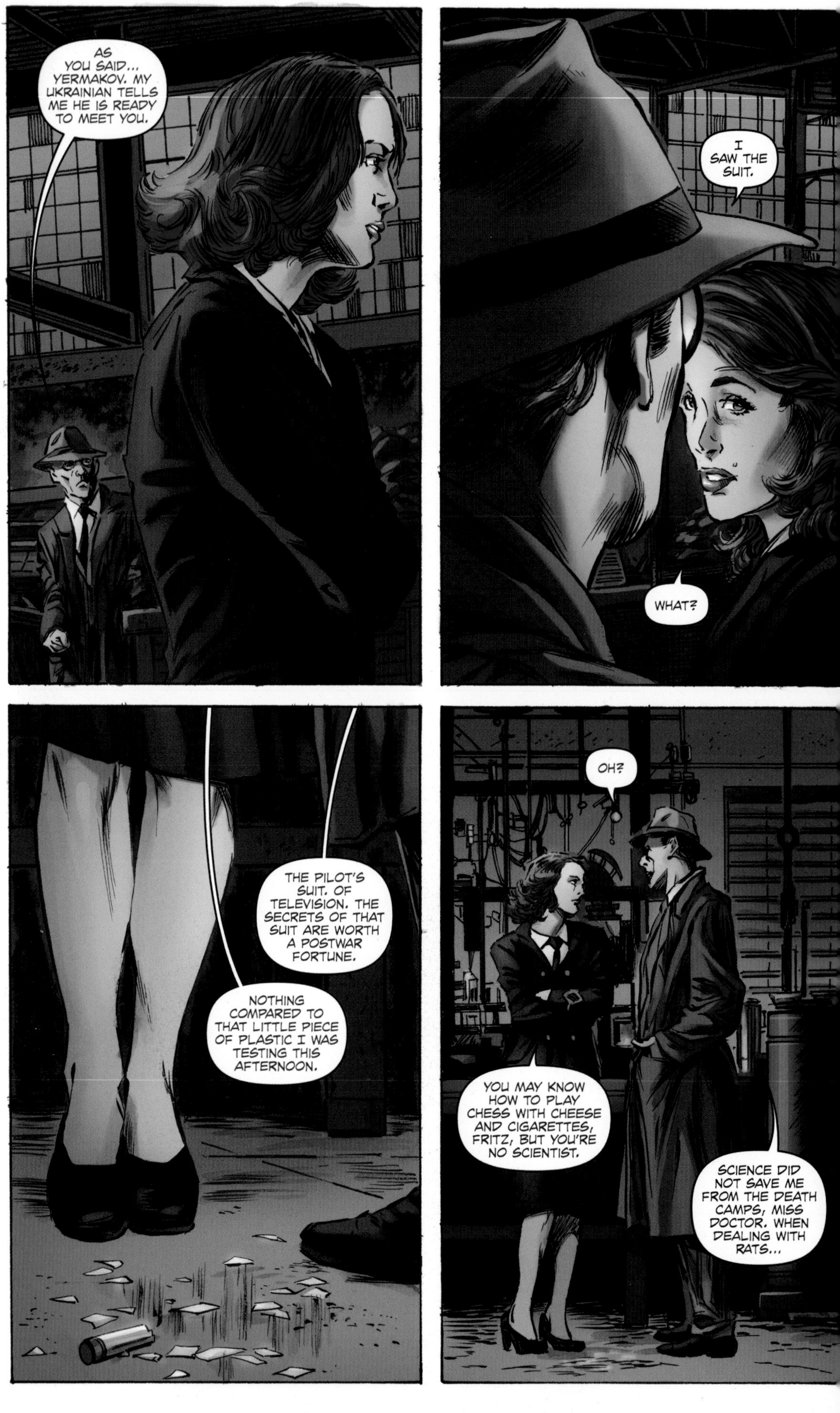
AS YOU SAID... YERMAKOV. MY UKRAINIAN TELLS ME HE IS READY TO MEET YOU.
I SAW THE SUIT.
WHAT?
THE PILOT'S SUIT. OF TELEVISION. THE SECRETS OF THAT SUIT ARE WORTH A POSTWAR FORTUNE.
NOTHING COMPARED TO THAT LITTLE PIECE OF PLASTIC I WAS TESTING THIS AFTERNOON.
OH?
YOU MAY KNOW HOW TO PLAY CHESS WITH CHEESE AND CIGARETTES, FRITZ, BUT YOU'RE NO SCIENTIST.
SCIENCE DID NOT SAVE ME FROM THE DEATH CAMPS, MISS DOCTOR. WHEN DEALING WITH RATS...

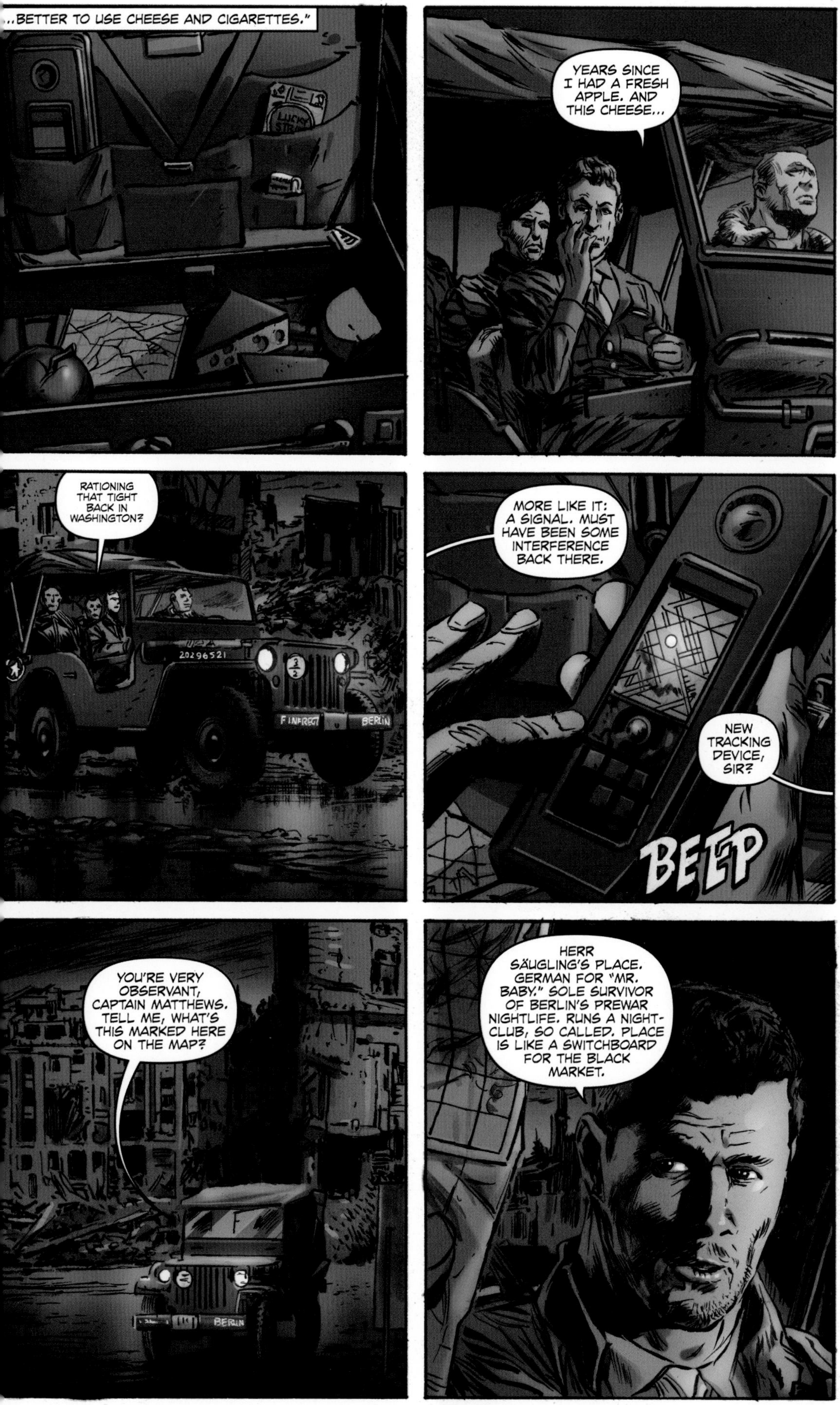

...BETTER TO USE CHEESE AND CIGARETTES."
LUCKY STRIKE
YEARS SINCE I HAD A FRESH APPLE. AND THIS CHEESE...
RATIONING THAT TIGHT BACK IN WASHINGTON?
20296521
BERLIN
MORE LIKE IT: A SIGNAL. MUST HAVE BEEN SOME INTERFERENCE BACK THERE.
NEW TRACKING DEVICE, SIR?
BEEP
YOU'RE VERY OBSERVANT, CAPTAIN MATTHEWS. TELL ME, WHAT'S THIS MARKED HERE ON THE MAP?
BERLIN
HERR SÄUGLING'S PLACE. GERMAN FOR "MR. BABY." SOLE SURVIVOR OF BERLIN'S PREWAR NIGHTLIFE. RUNS A NIGHT-CLUB, SO CALLED. PLACE IS LIKE A SWITCHBOARD FOR THE BLACK MARKET.

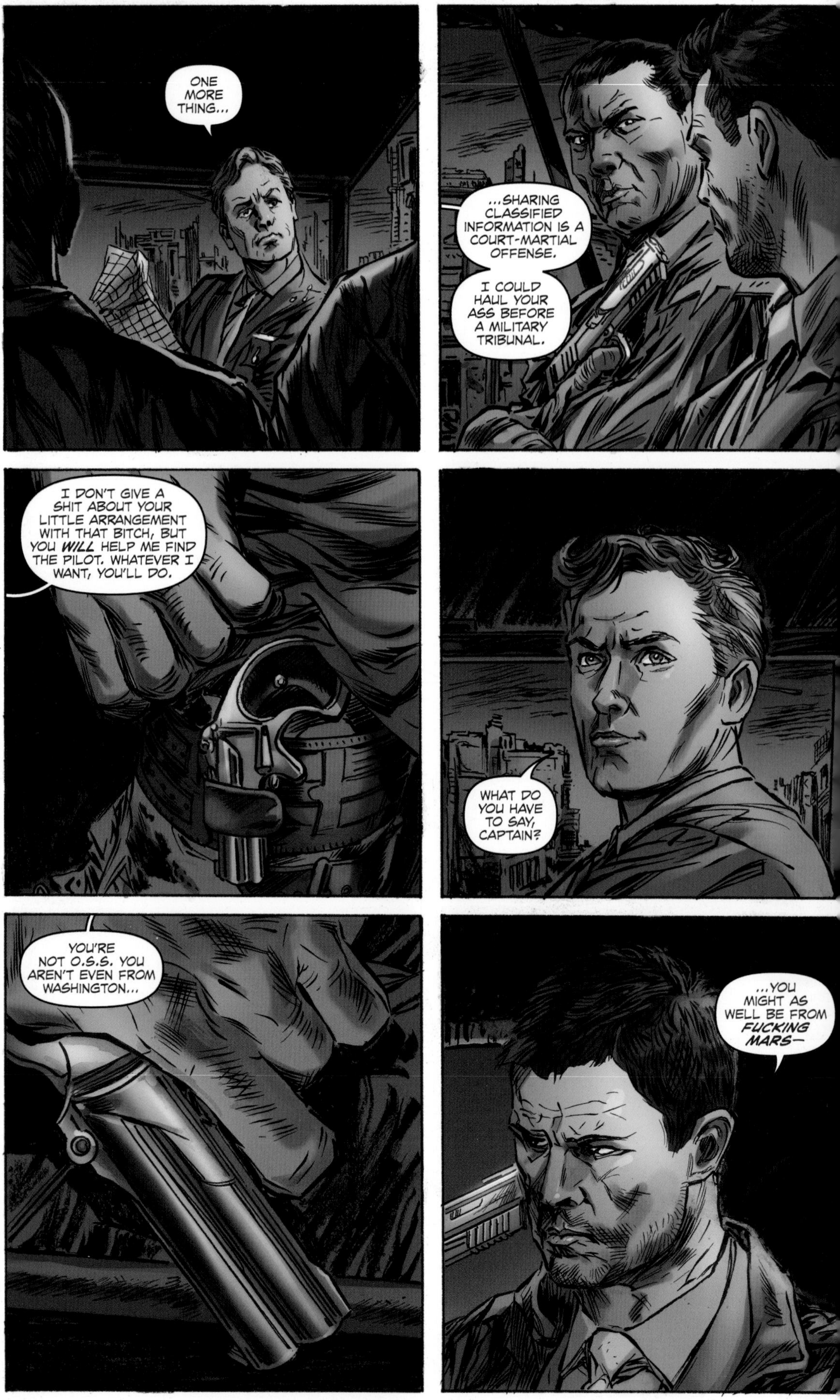
ONE MORE THING...
...SHARING CLASSIFIED INFORMATION IS A COURT-MARTIAL OFFENSE.
I COULD HAUL YOUR ASS BEFORE A MILITARY TRIBUNAL.
I DON'T GIVE A SHIT ABOUT YOUR LITTLE ARRANGEMENT WITH THAT BITCH, BUT YOU *WILL* HELP ME FIND THE PILOT. WHATEVER I WANT, YOU'LL DO.
WHAT DO YOU HAVE TO SAY, CAPTAIN?
YOU'RE NOT O.S.S. YOU AREN'T EVEN FROM WASHINGTON...
...YOU MIGHT AS WELL BE FROM ***FUCKING MARS***—

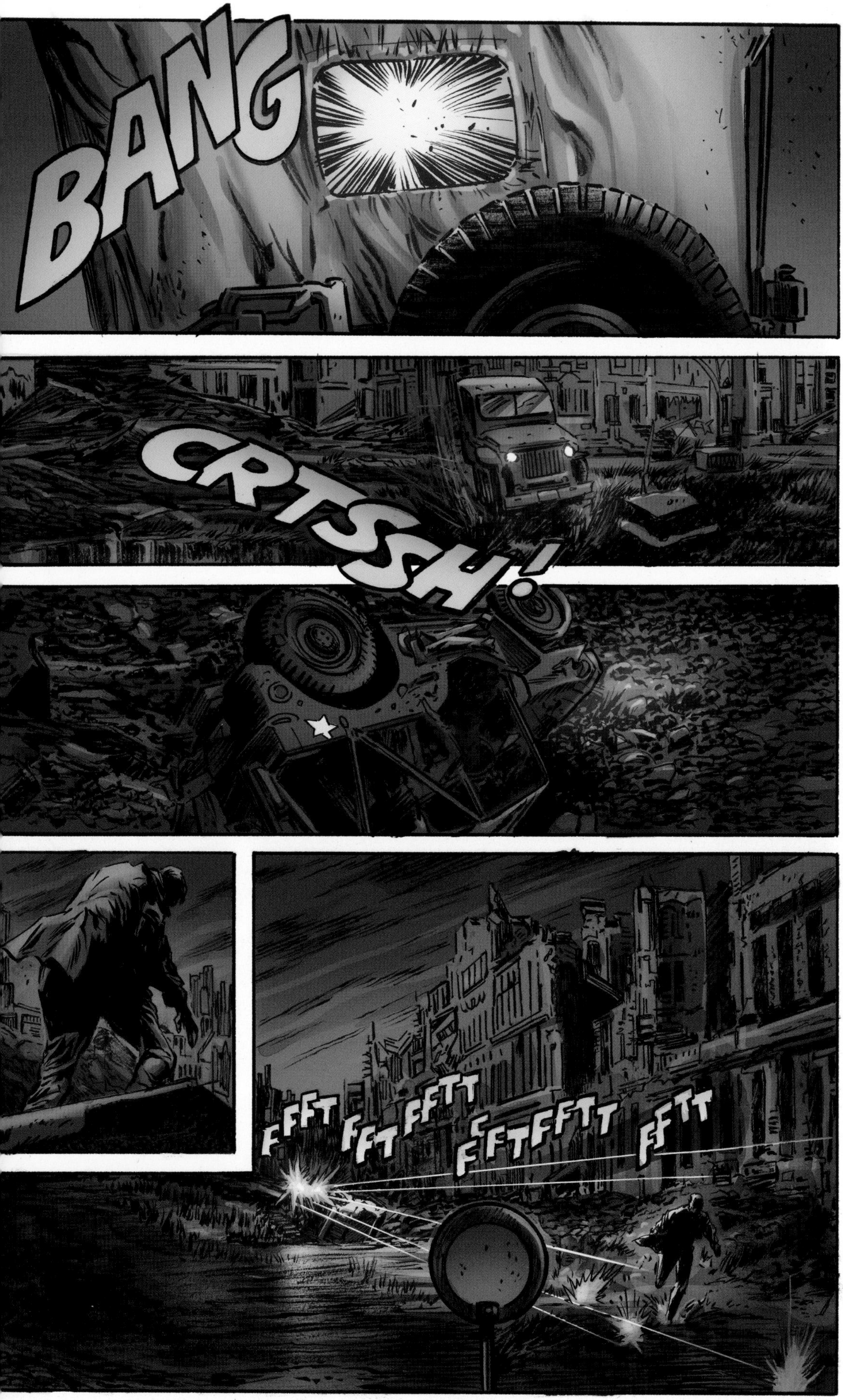

BANG
CRTSH!
FFFT FFT FFTT FFTFFTT FFTT

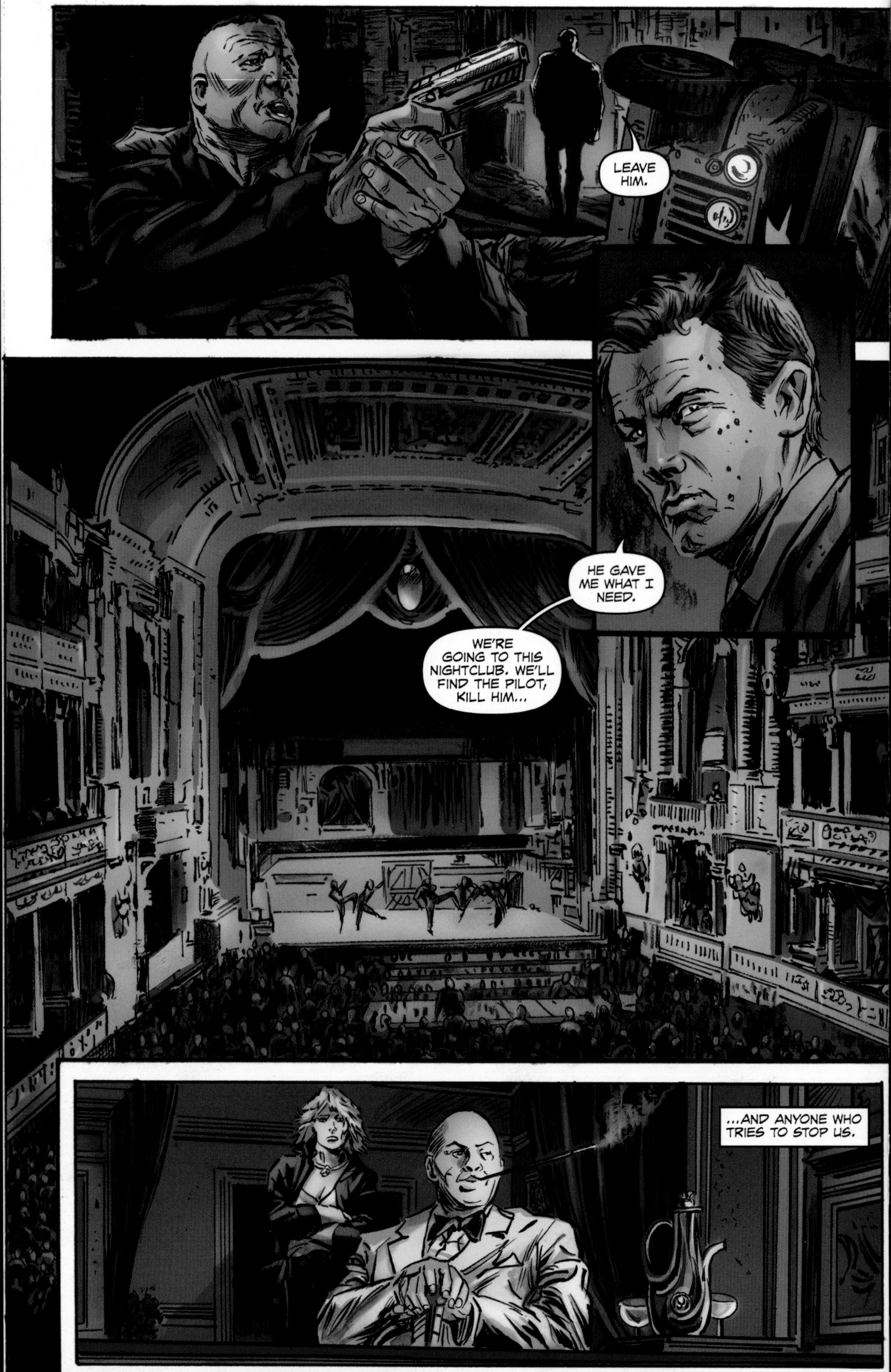
LEAVE HIM.
HE GAVE ME WHAT I NEED.
WE'RE GOING TO THIS NIGHTCLUB. WE'LL FIND THE PILOT, KILL HIM...
...AND ANYONE WHO TRIES TO STOP US.

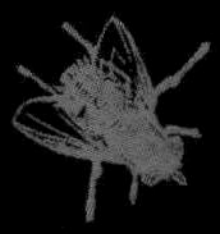

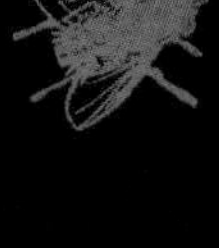

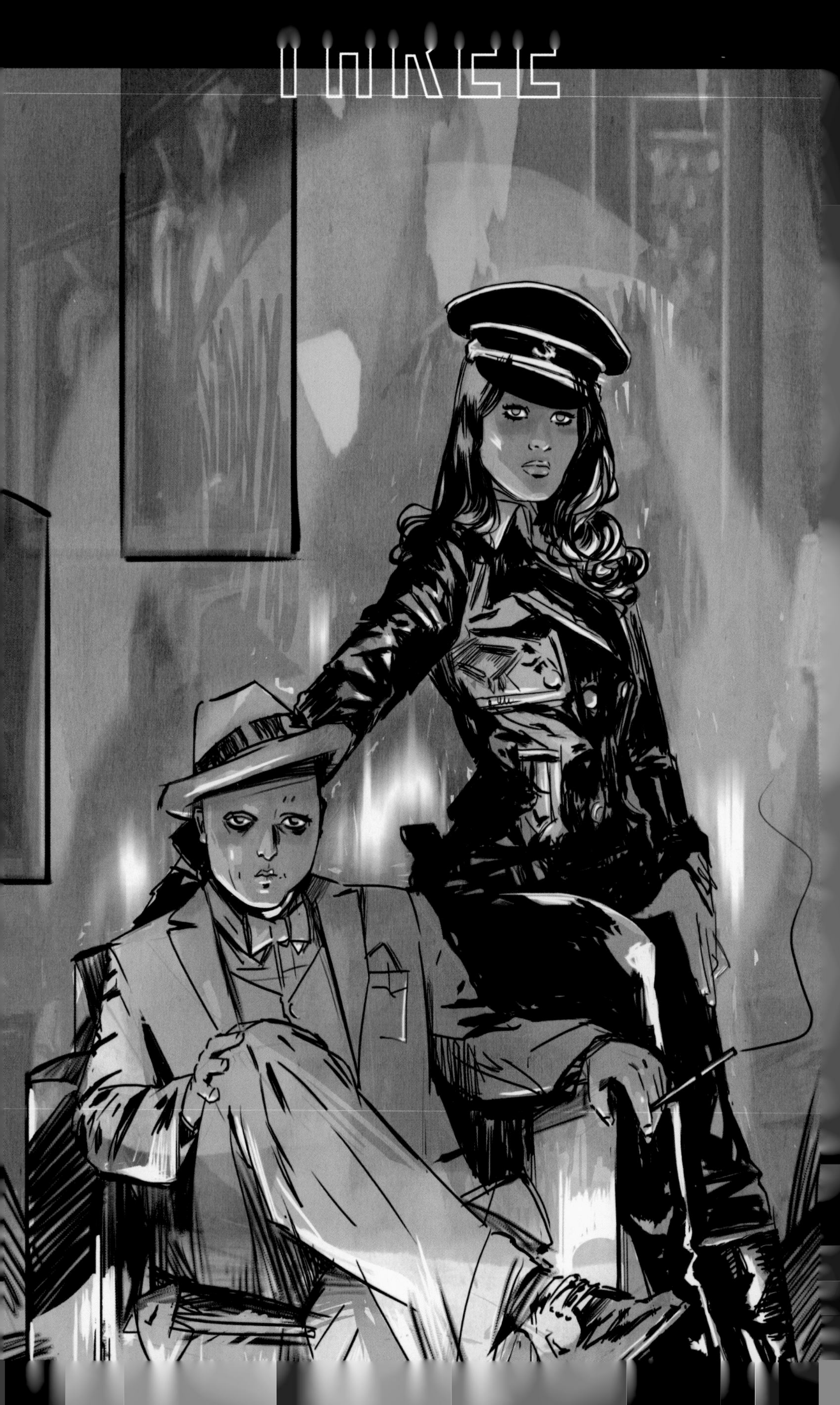

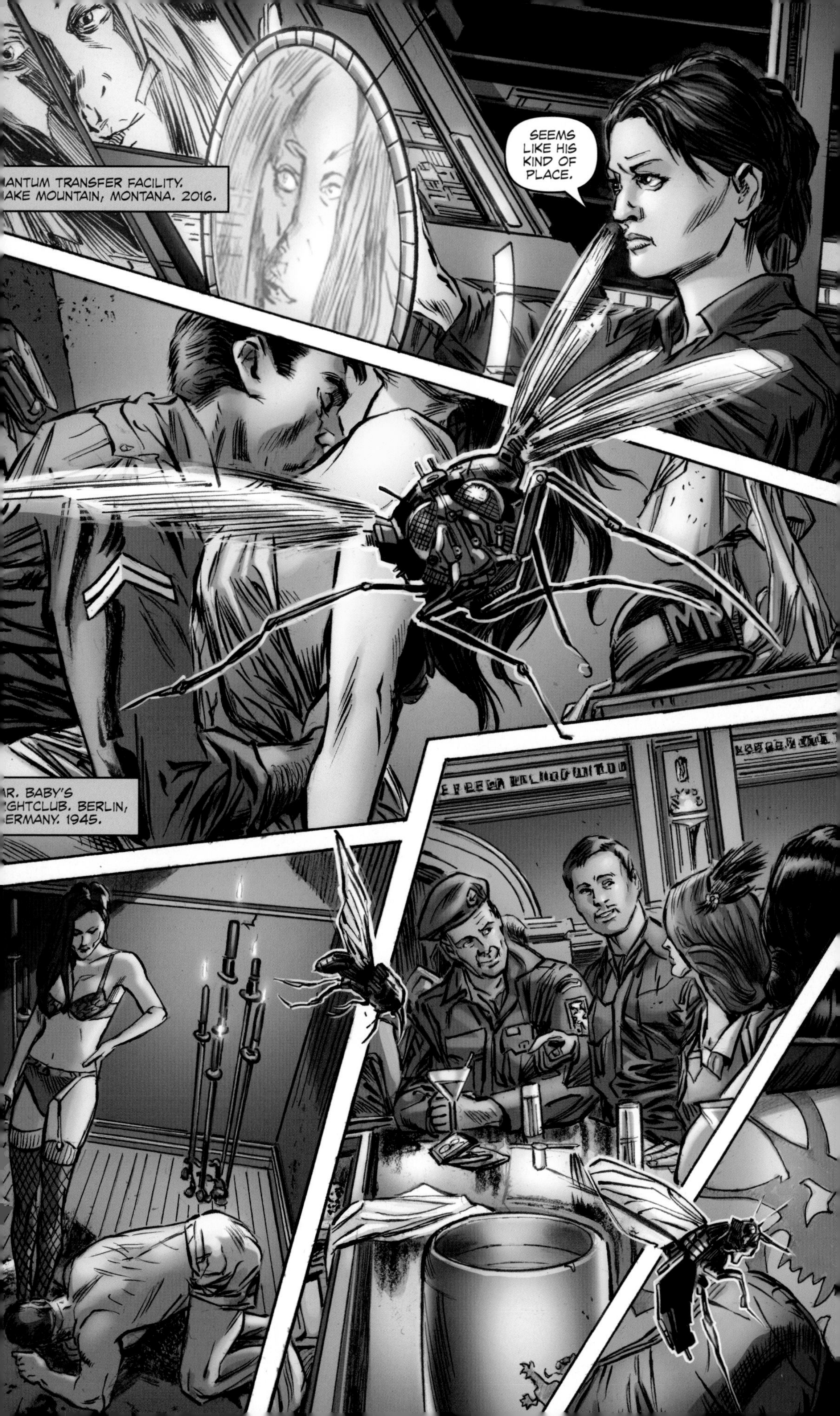
ANTUM TRANSFER FACILITY.
AKE MOUNTAIN, MONTANA. 2016.
SEEMS LIKE HIS KIND OF PLACE.
MP
R. BABY'S
GHTCLUB. BERLIN,
ERMANY. 1945.

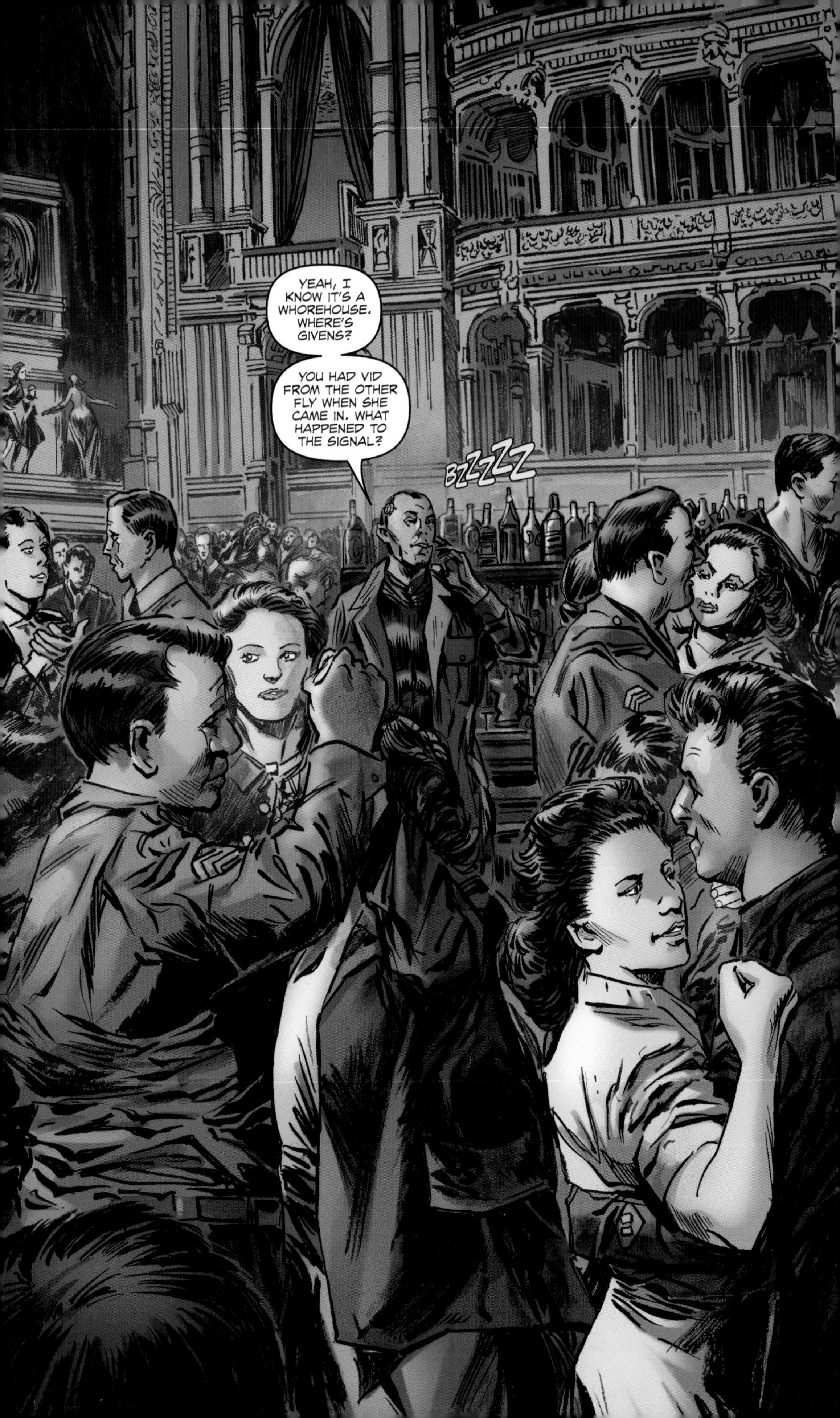

YEAH, I KNOW IT'S A WHOREHOUSE. WHERE'S GIVENS?
YOU HAD VID FROM THE OTHER FLY WHEN SHE CAME IN. WHAT HAPPENED TO THE SIGNAL?
BZZZZZ

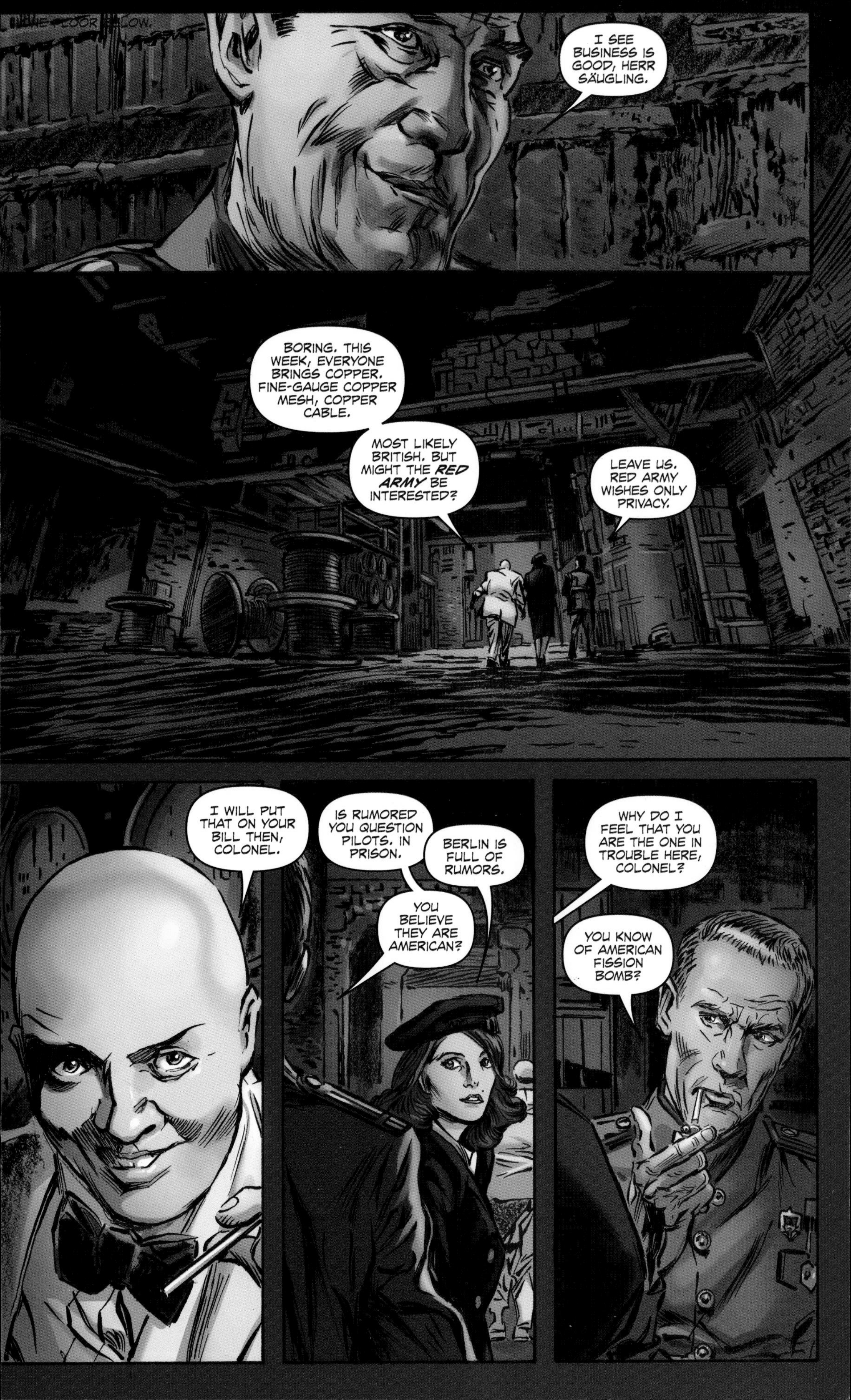
I SEE BUSINESS IS GOOD, HERR SÄUGLING.
BORING. THIS WEEK, EVERYONE BRINGS COPPER. FINE-GAUGE COPPER MESH, COPPER CABLE.
MOST LIKELY BRITISH. BUT MIGHT THE RED ARMY BE INTERESTED?
LEAVE US. RED ARMY WISHES ONLY PRIVACY.
I WILL PUT THAT ON YOUR BILL THEN, COLONEL.
IS RUMORED YOU QUESTION PILOTS. IN PRISON.
BERLIN IS FULL OF RUMORS.
YOU BELIEVE THEY ARE AMERICAN?
WHY DO I FEEL THAT YOU ARE THE ONE IN TROUBLE HERE, COLONEL?
YOU KNOW OF AMERICAN FISSION BOMB?

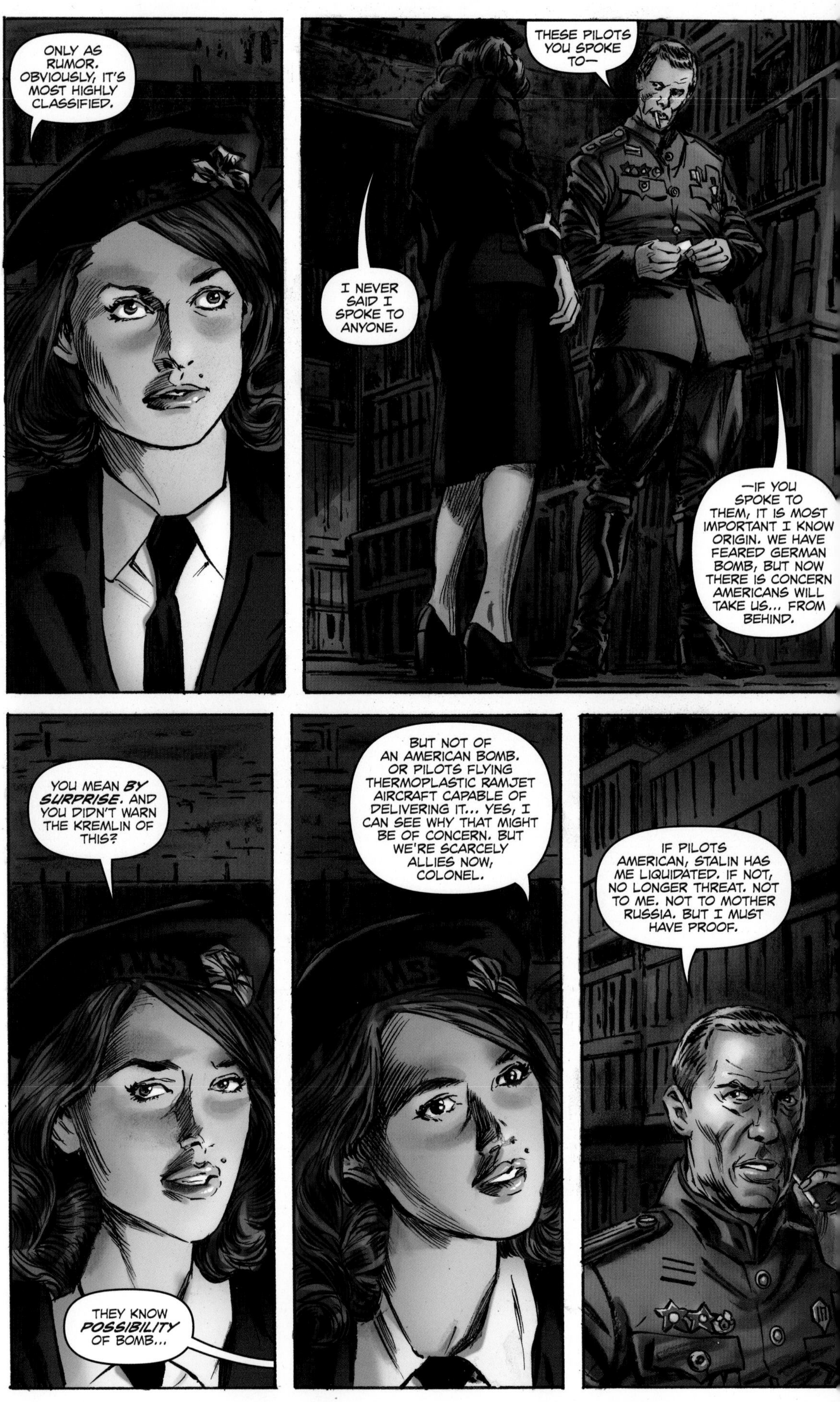
ONLY AS RUMOR. OBVIOUSLY, IT'S MOST HIGHLY CLASSIFIED.
THESE PILOTS YOU SPOKE TO—
I NEVER SAID I SPOKE TO ANYONE.
—IF YOU SPOKE TO THEM, IT IS MOST IMPORTANT I KNOW ORIGIN. WE HAVE FEARED GERMAN BOMB, BUT NOW THERE IS CONCERN AMERICANS WILL TAKE US... FROM BEHIND.
YOU MEAN *BY SURPRISE*. AND YOU DIDN'T WARN THE KREMLIN OF THIS?
THEY KNOW *POSSIBILITY* OF BOMB...
BUT NOT OF AN AMERICAN BOMB. OR PILOTS FLYING THERMOPLASTIC RAMJET AIRCRAFT CAPABLE OF DELIVERING IT... YES, I CAN SEE WHY THAT MIGHT BE OF CONCERN. BUT WE'RE SCARCELY ALLIES NOW, COLONEL.
IF PILOTS AMERICAN, STALIN HAS ME LIQUIDATED. IF NOT, NO LONGER THREAT. NOT TO ME. NOT TO MOTHER RUSSIA. BUT I MUST HAVE PROOF.

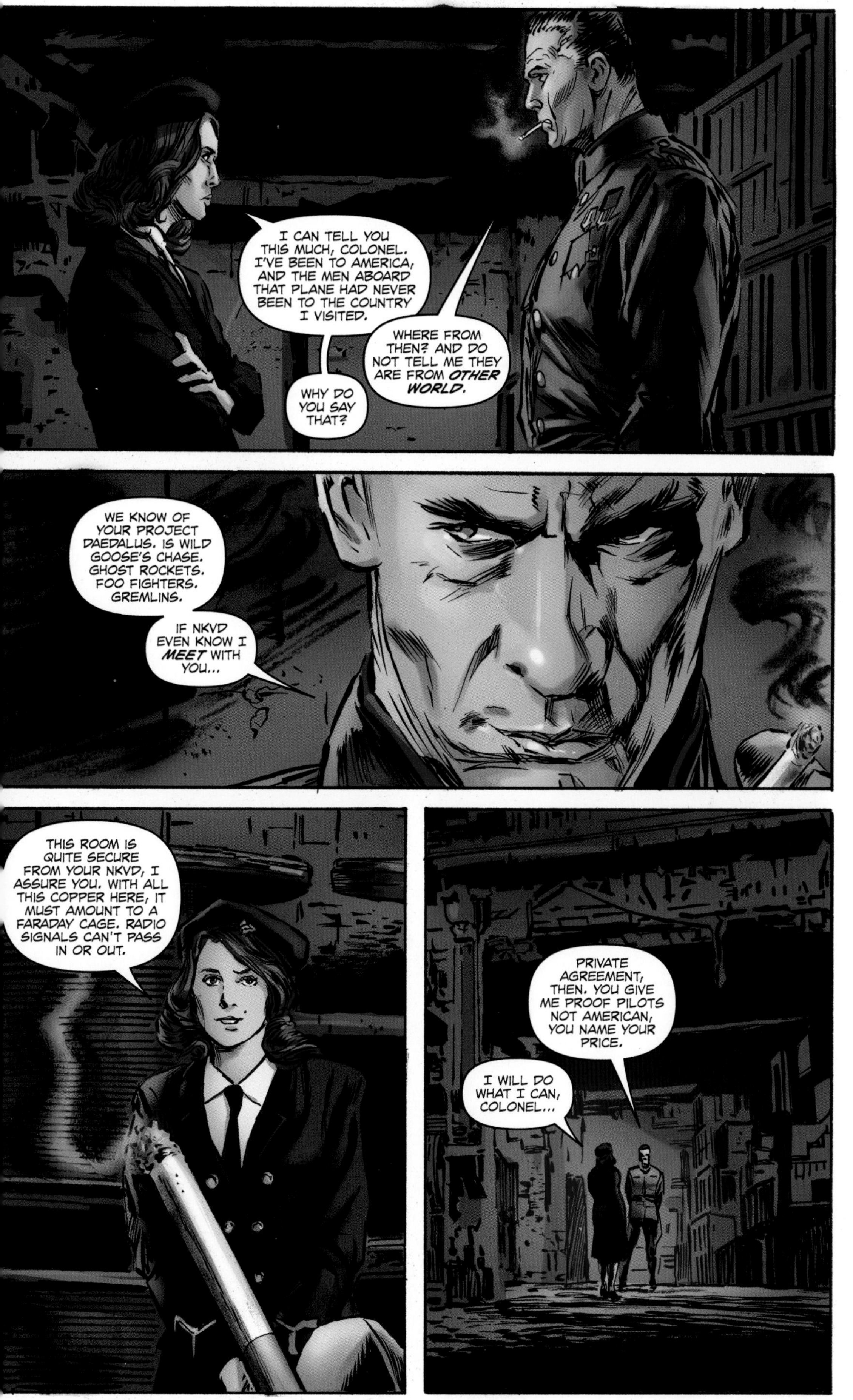
I CAN TELL YOU THIS MUCH, COLONEL. I'VE BEEN TO AMERICA, AND THE MEN ABOARD THAT PLANE HAD NEVER BEEN TO THE COUNTRY I VISITED.
WHY DO YOU SAY THAT?
WHERE FROM THEN? AND DO NOT TELL ME THEY ARE FROM *OTHER WORLD.*
WE KNOW OF YOUR PROJECT DAEDALUS. IS WILD GOOSE'S CHASE. GHOST ROCKETS. FOO FIGHTERS. GREMLINS.
IF NKVD EVEN KNOW I *MEET* WITH YOU...
THIS ROOM IS QUITE SECURE FROM YOUR NKVD, I ASSURE YOU. WITH ALL THIS COPPER HERE, IT MUST AMOUNT TO A FARADAY CAGE. RADIO SIGNALS CAN'T PASS IN OR OUT.
PRIVATE AGREEMENT, THEN. YOU GIVE ME PROOF PILOTS NOT AMERICAN, YOU NAME YOUR PRICE.
I WILL DO WHAT I CAN, COLONEL...

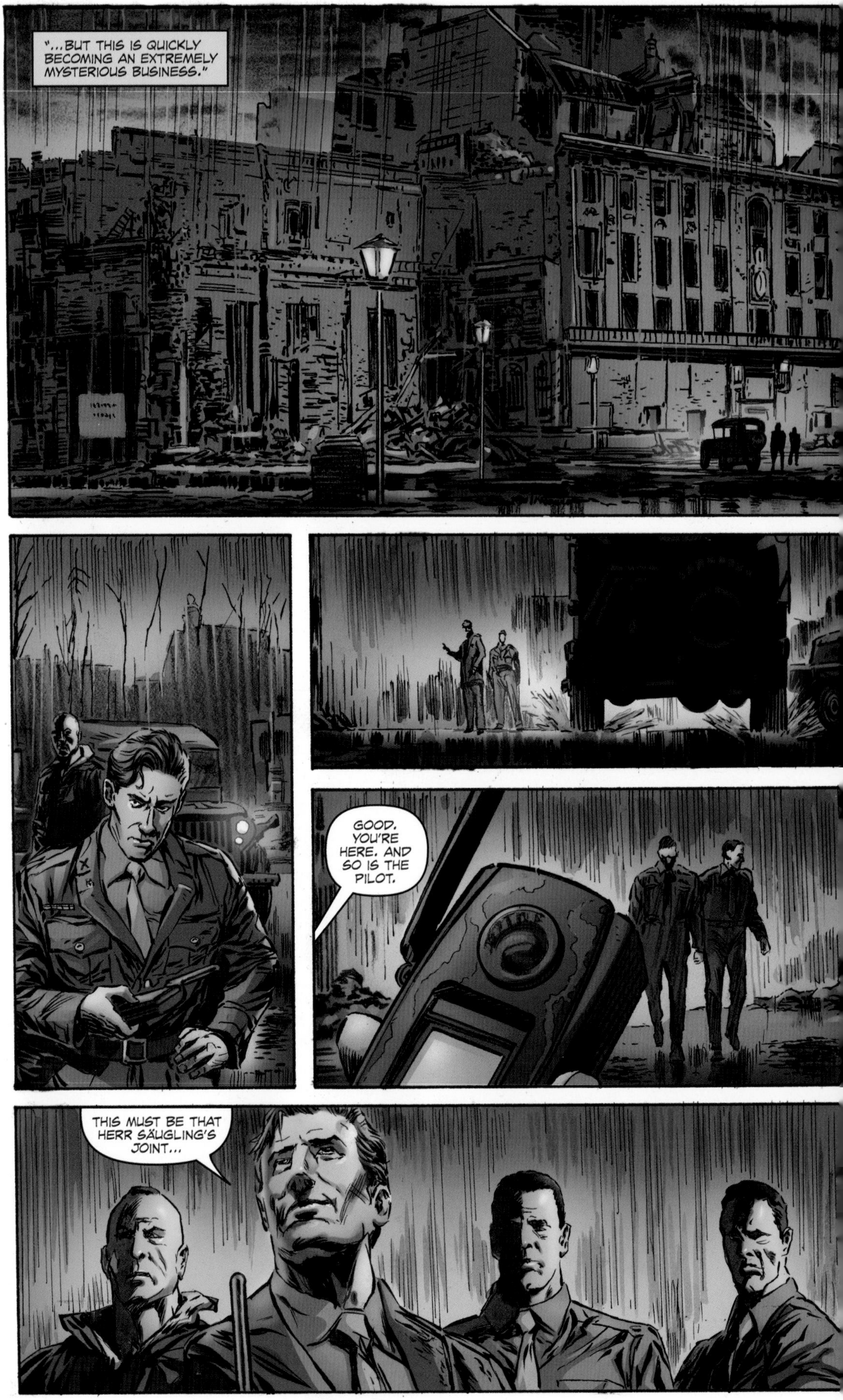
"...BUT THIS IS QUICKLY BECOMING AN EXTREMELY MYSTERIOUS BUSINESS."
GOOD. YOU'RE HERE. AND SO IS THE PILOT.
THIS MUST BE THAT HERR SÄUGLING'S JOINT...

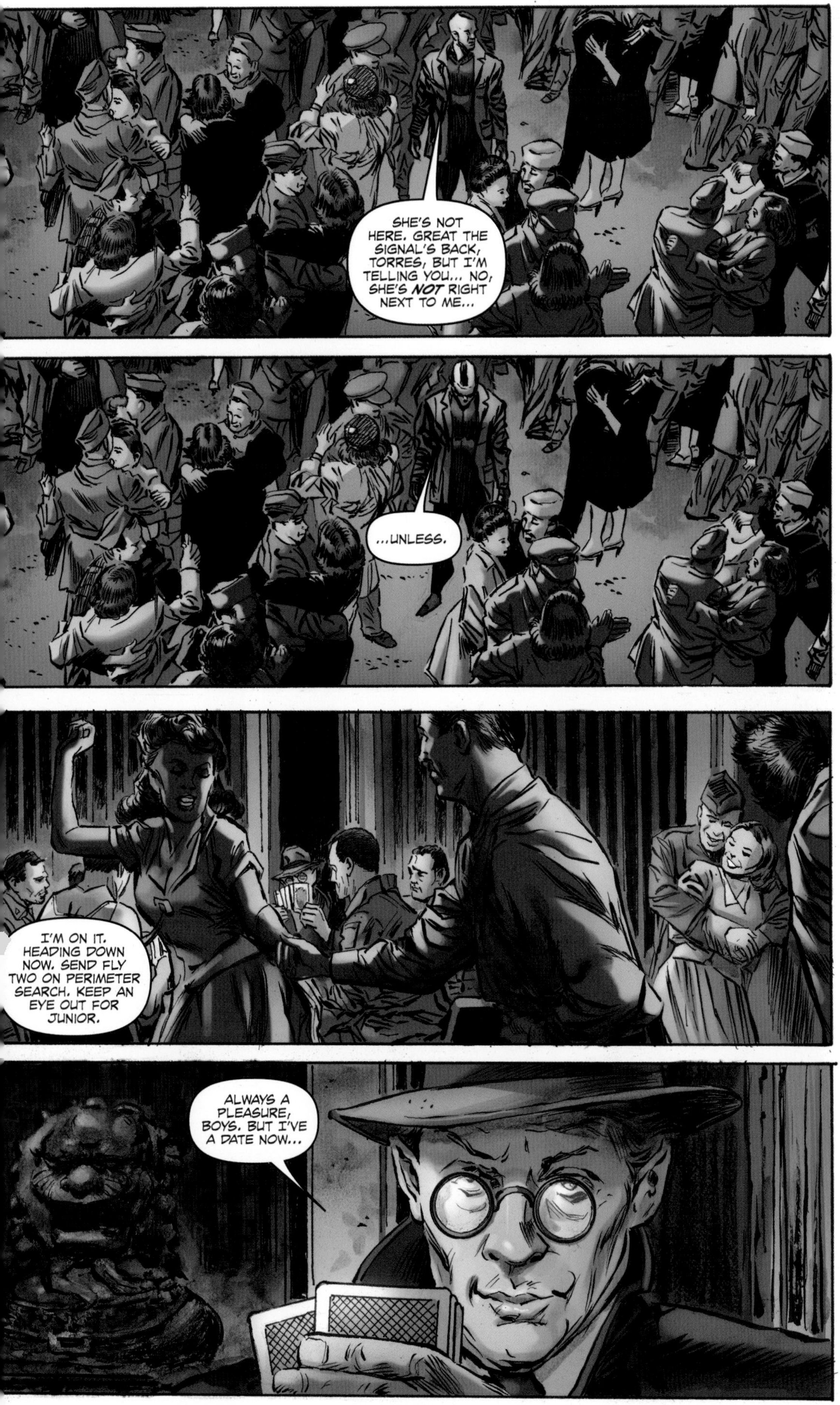
SHE'S NOT HERE. GREAT THE SIGNAL'S BACK, TORRES, BUT I'M TELLING YOU... NO, SHE'S **NOT** RIGHT NEXT TO ME...
...UNLESS.
I'M ON IT. HEADING DOWN NOW. SEND FLY TWO ON PERIMETER SEARCH. KEEP AN EYE OUT FOR JUNIOR.
ALWAYS A PLEASURE, BOYS. BUT I'VE A DATE NOW...

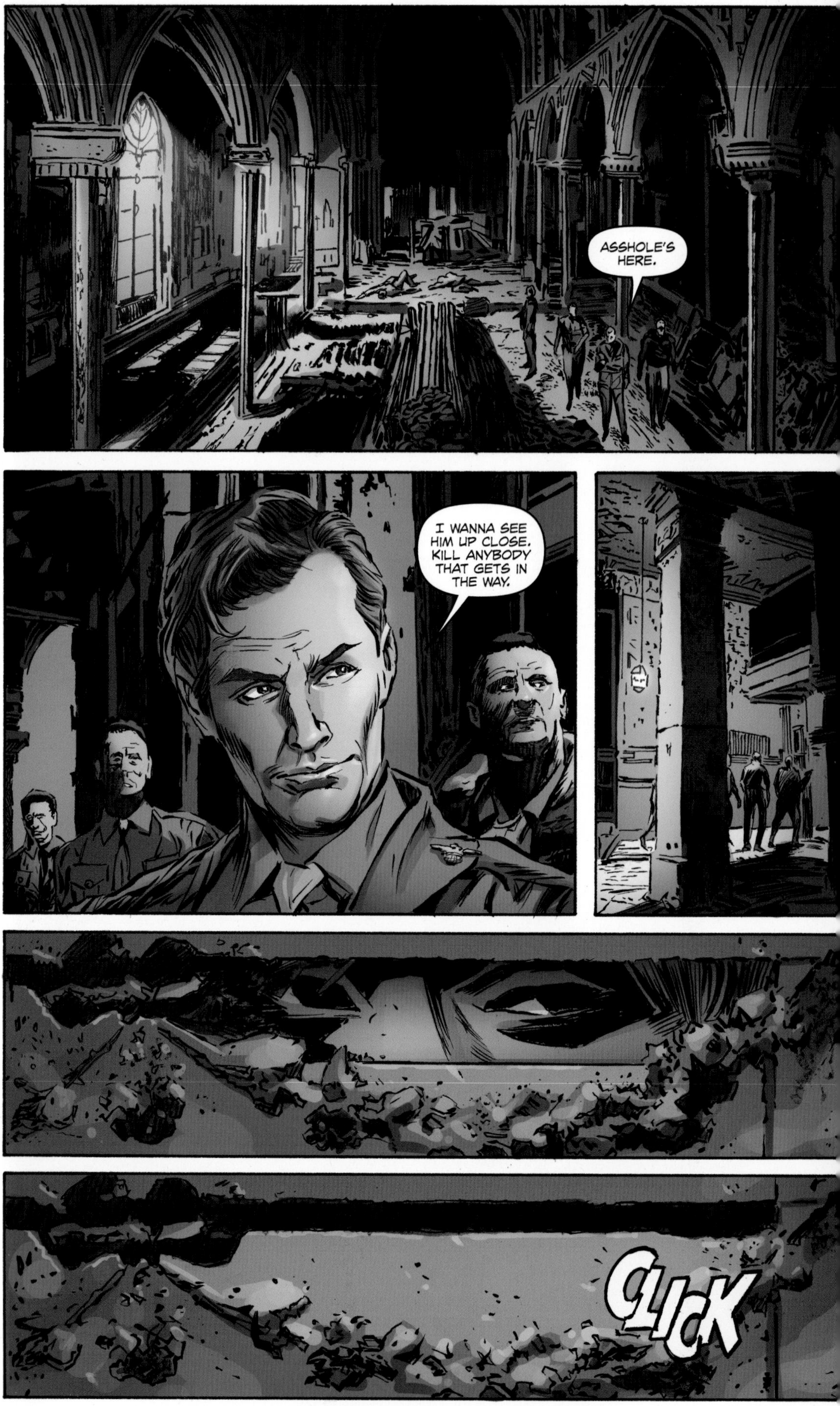
ASSHOLE'S HERE.
I WANNA SEE HIM UP CLOSE. KILL ANYBODY THAT GETS IN THE WAY.
CLICK

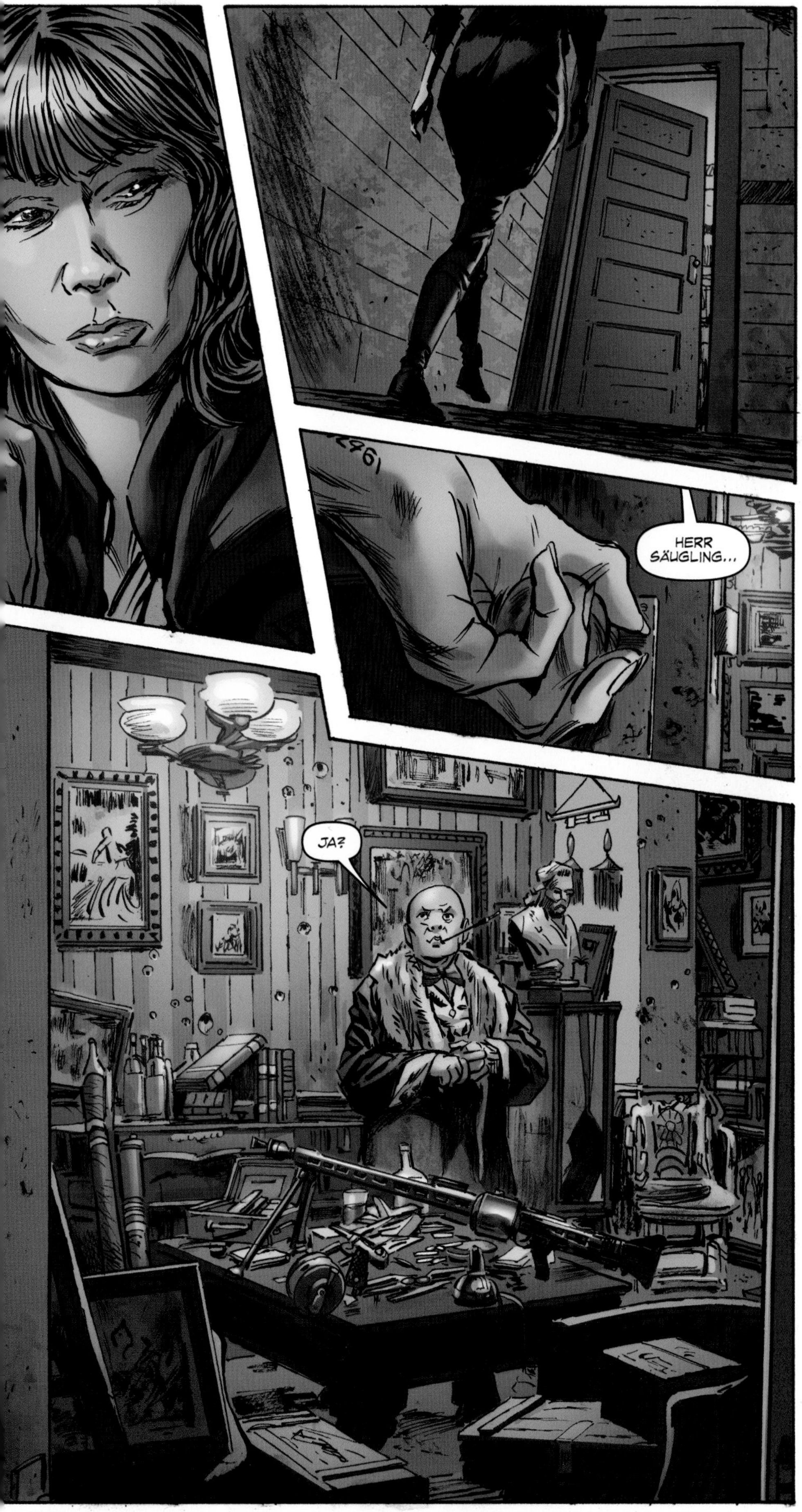
HERR SÄUGLING...
JA?

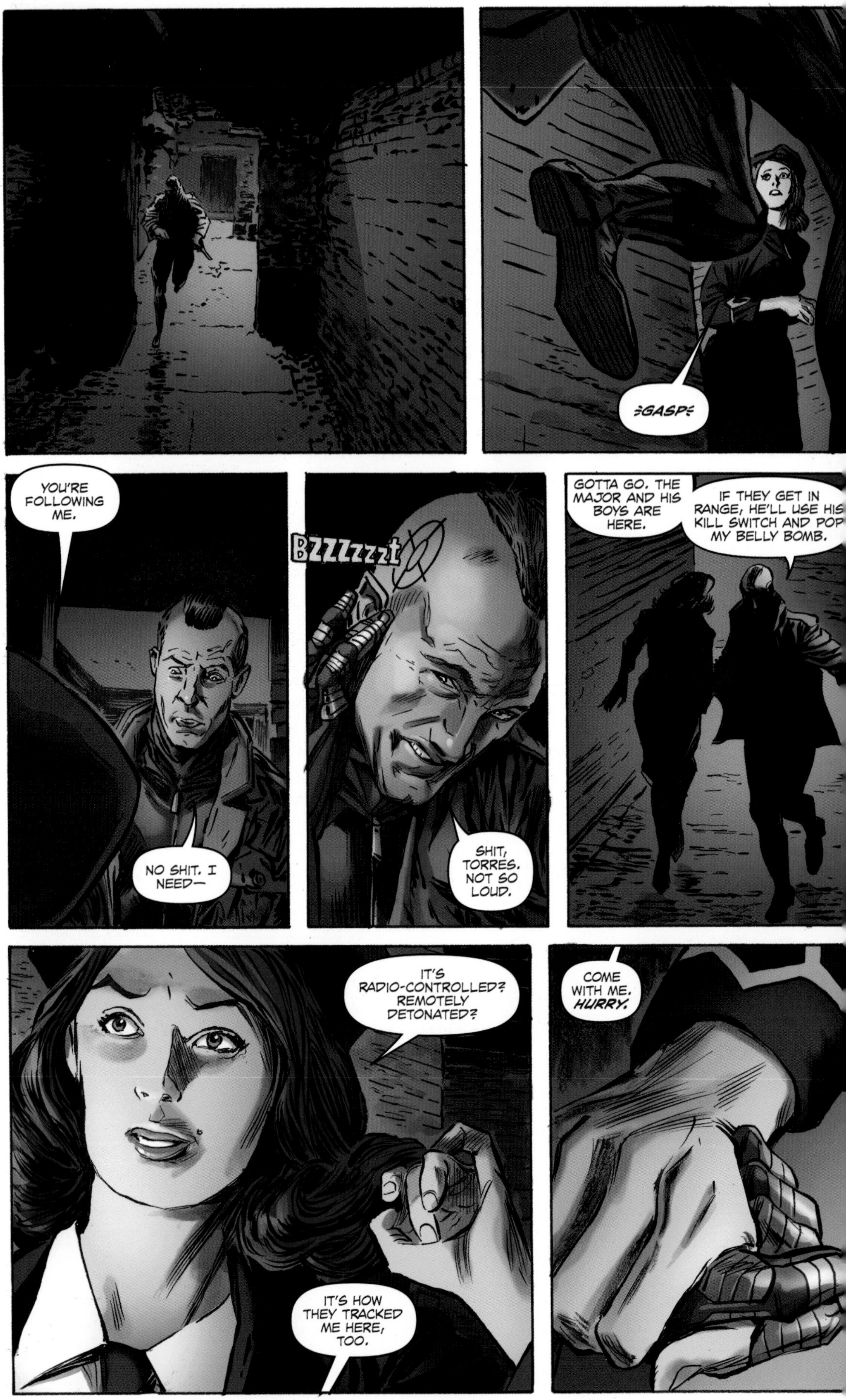

≈GASP≈
YOU'RE FOLLOWING ME.
NO SHIT. I NEED—
BZZZzzzt
SHIT, TORRES. NOT SO LOUD.
GOTTA GO. THE MAJOR AND HIS BOYS ARE HERE.
IF THEY GET IN RANGE, HE'LL USE HIS KILL SWITCH AND POP MY BELLY BOMB.
IT'S RADIO-CONTROLLED? REMOTELY DETONATED?
IT'S HOW THEY TRACKED ME HERE, TOO.
COME WITH ME. HURRY.

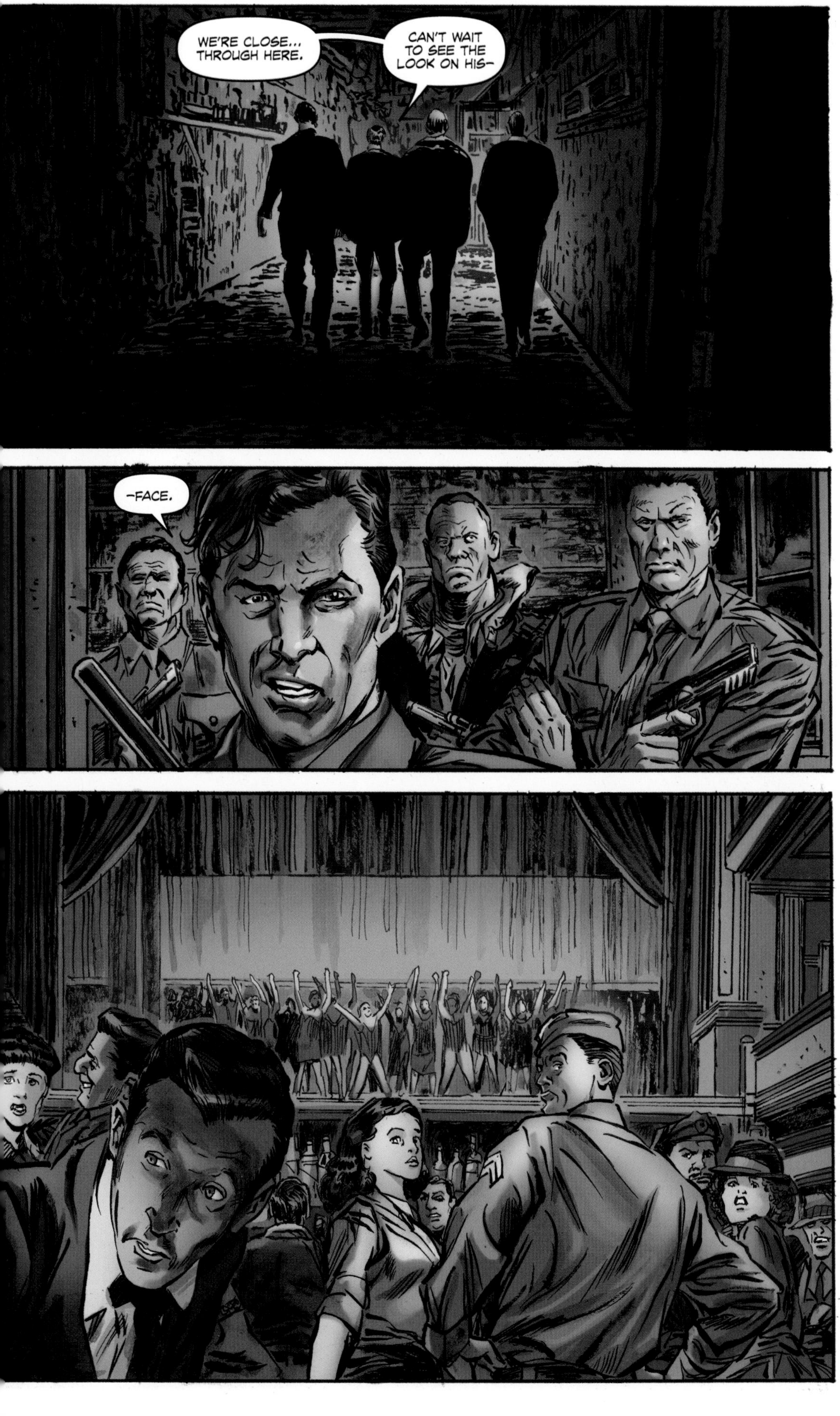

WE'RE CLOSE... THROUGH HERE.
CAN'T WAIT TO SEE THE LOOK ON HIS–
–FACE.

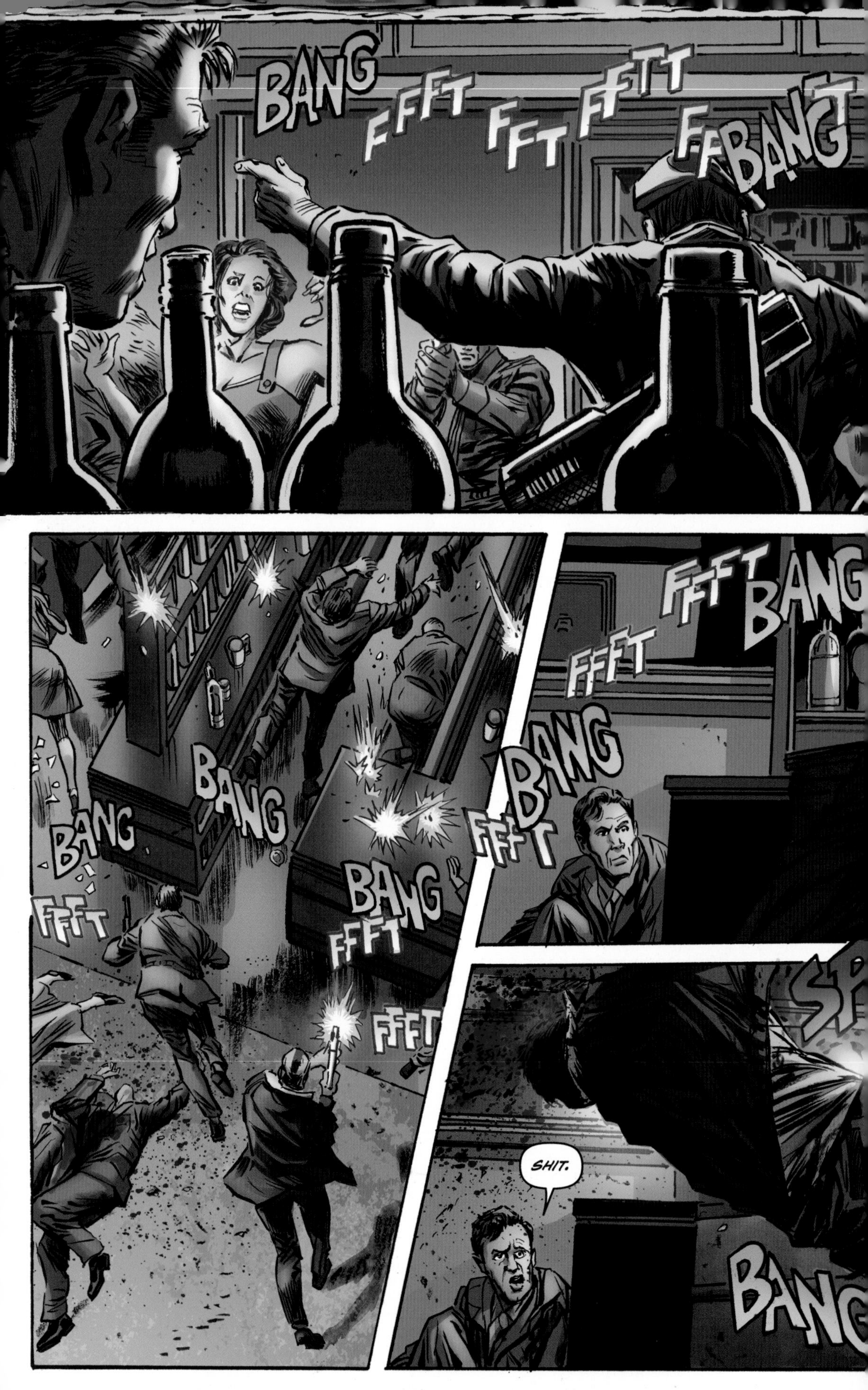
BANG
FFFT
FFT
FFTT
FFBANGT
BANG
BANG
BANG
FFFT
FFFT
FFFT
FFFT
BANG
FFFT
BANG
FFFT
SHIT.
BANG

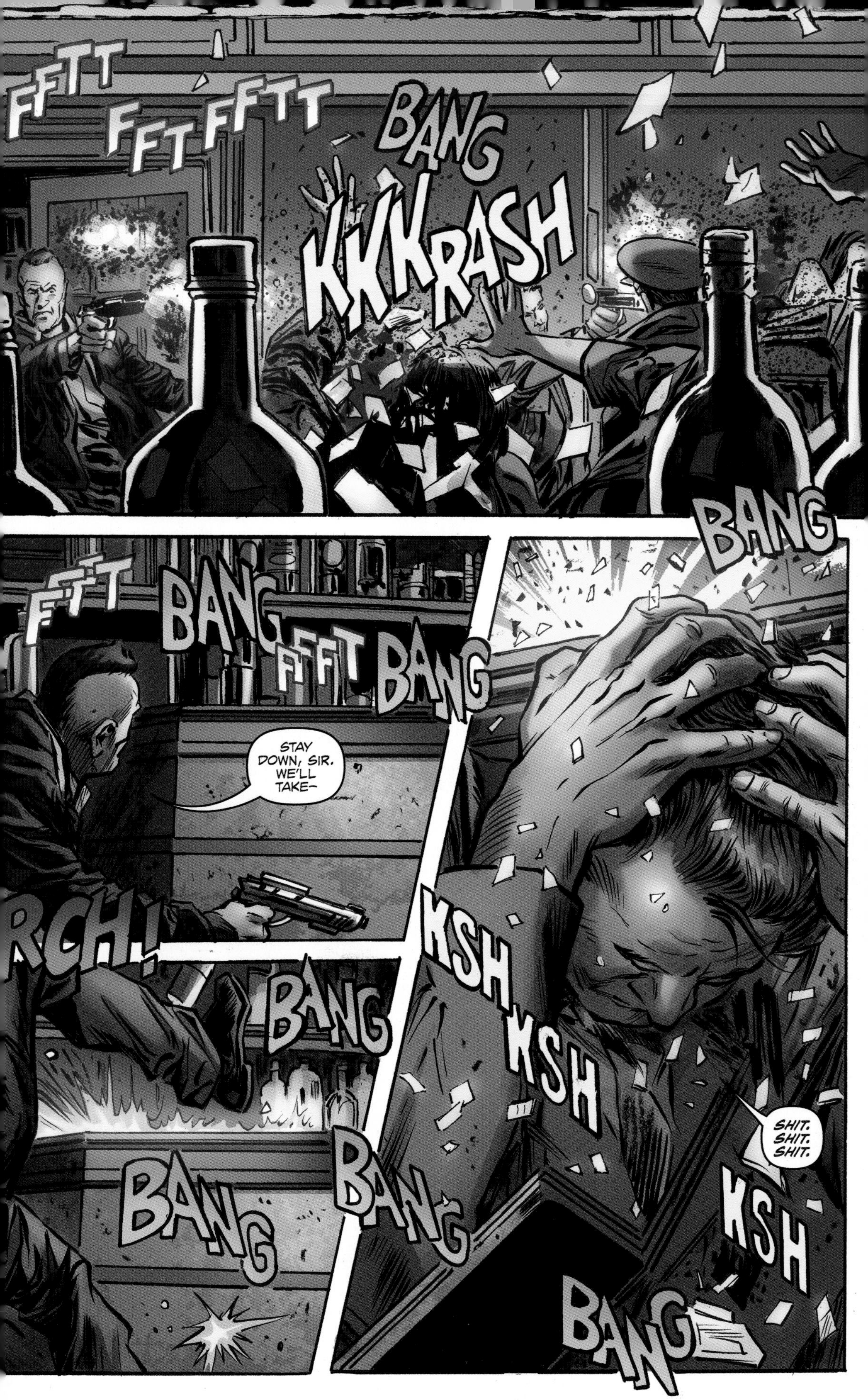
FFTT
FFT FFTT
BANG
KKKRASH
BANG
FFTT
BANG
FFFT BANG
STAY DOWN, SIR. WE'LL TAKE–
RCH!
BANG
BANG
BANG
KSH
KSH
SHIT. SHIT. SHIT.
KSH
BANG

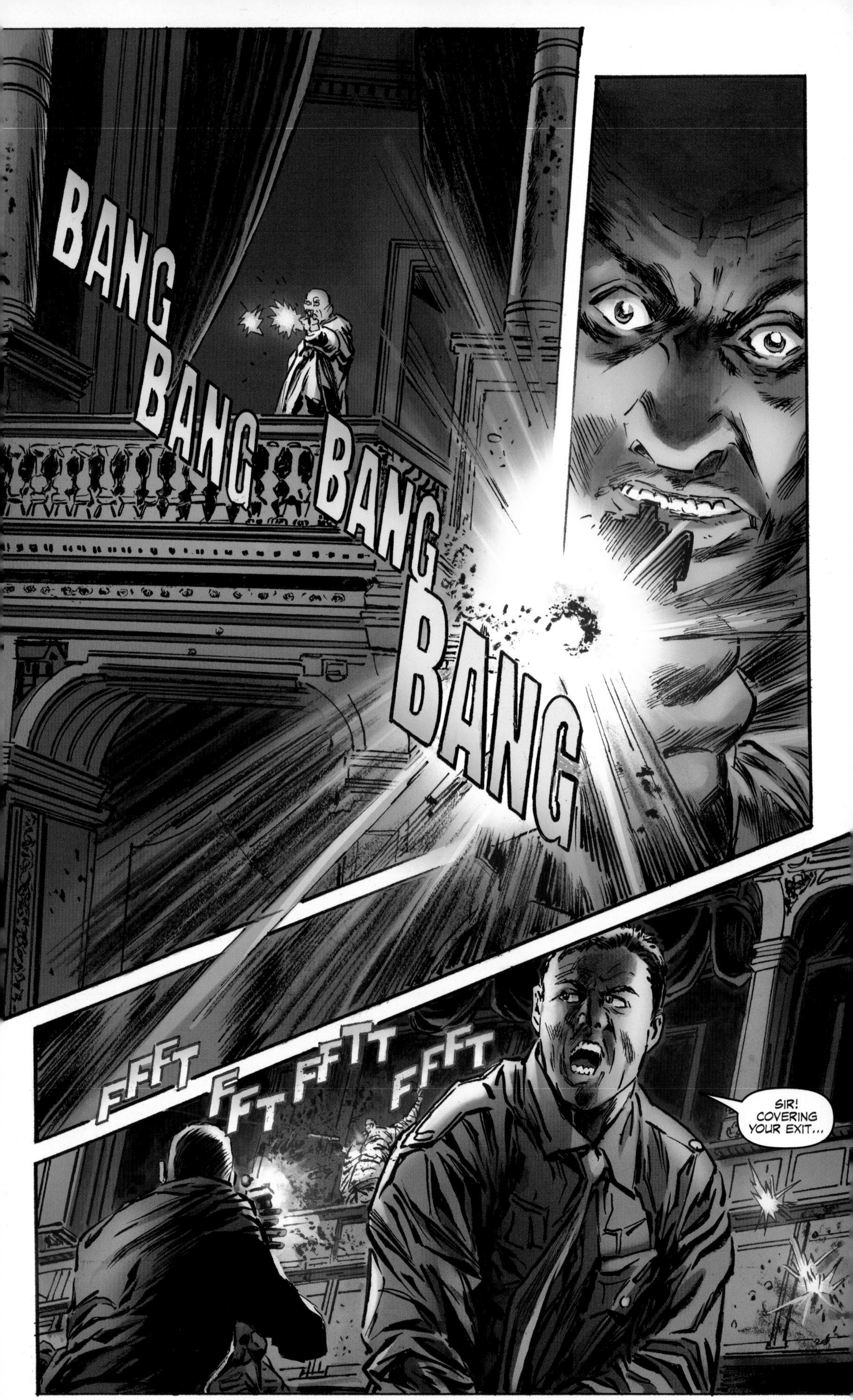
BANG
BANG
BANG
BANG
FFFT
FFT
FFTT
FFFT
SIR! COVERING YOUR EXIT...

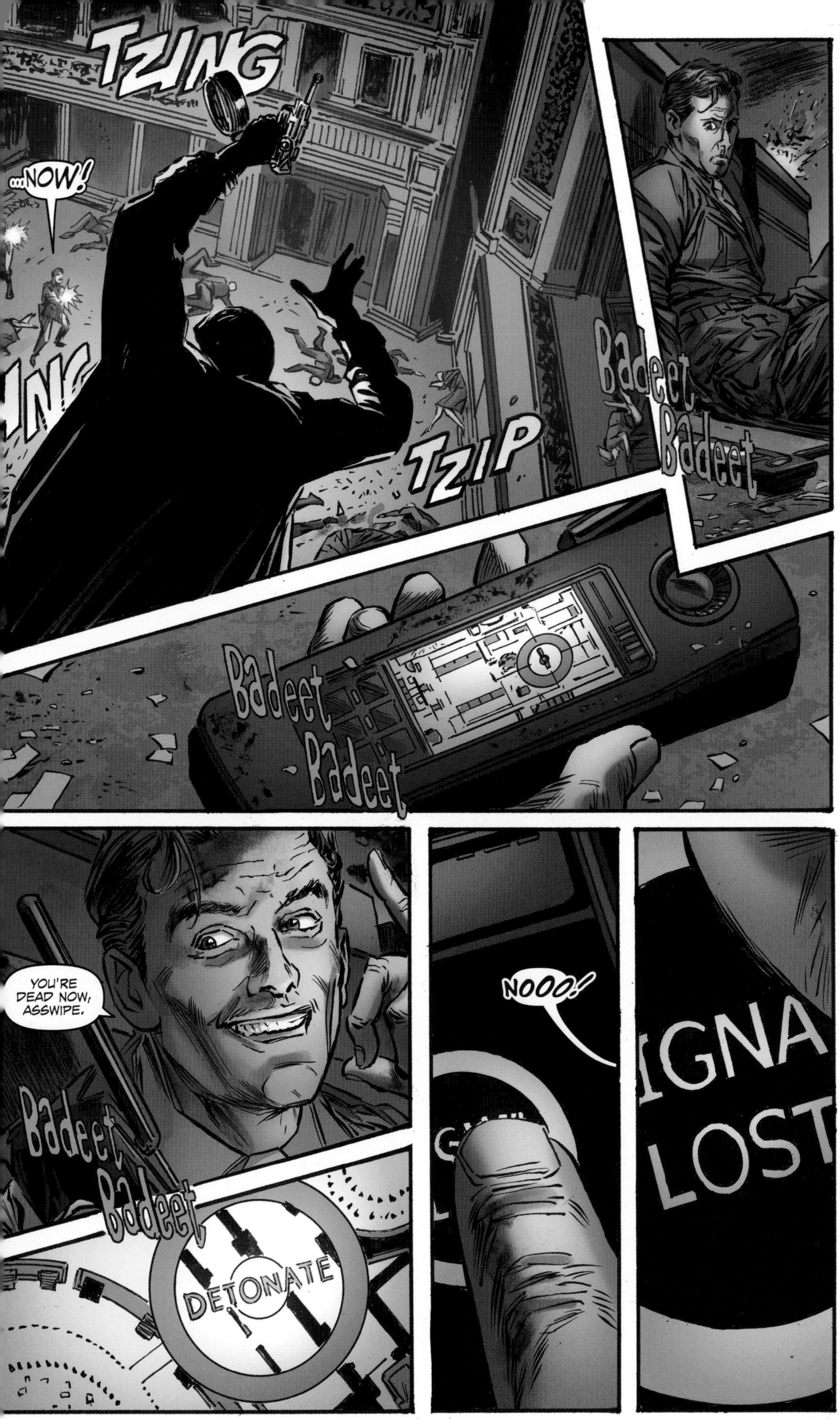
TZING
...NOW!
TZIP
Badeet
Badeet
Badeet
Badeet
YOU'RE DEAD NOW, ASSWIPE.
Badeet
Badeet
DETONATE
NOOO!
IGNA
LOST

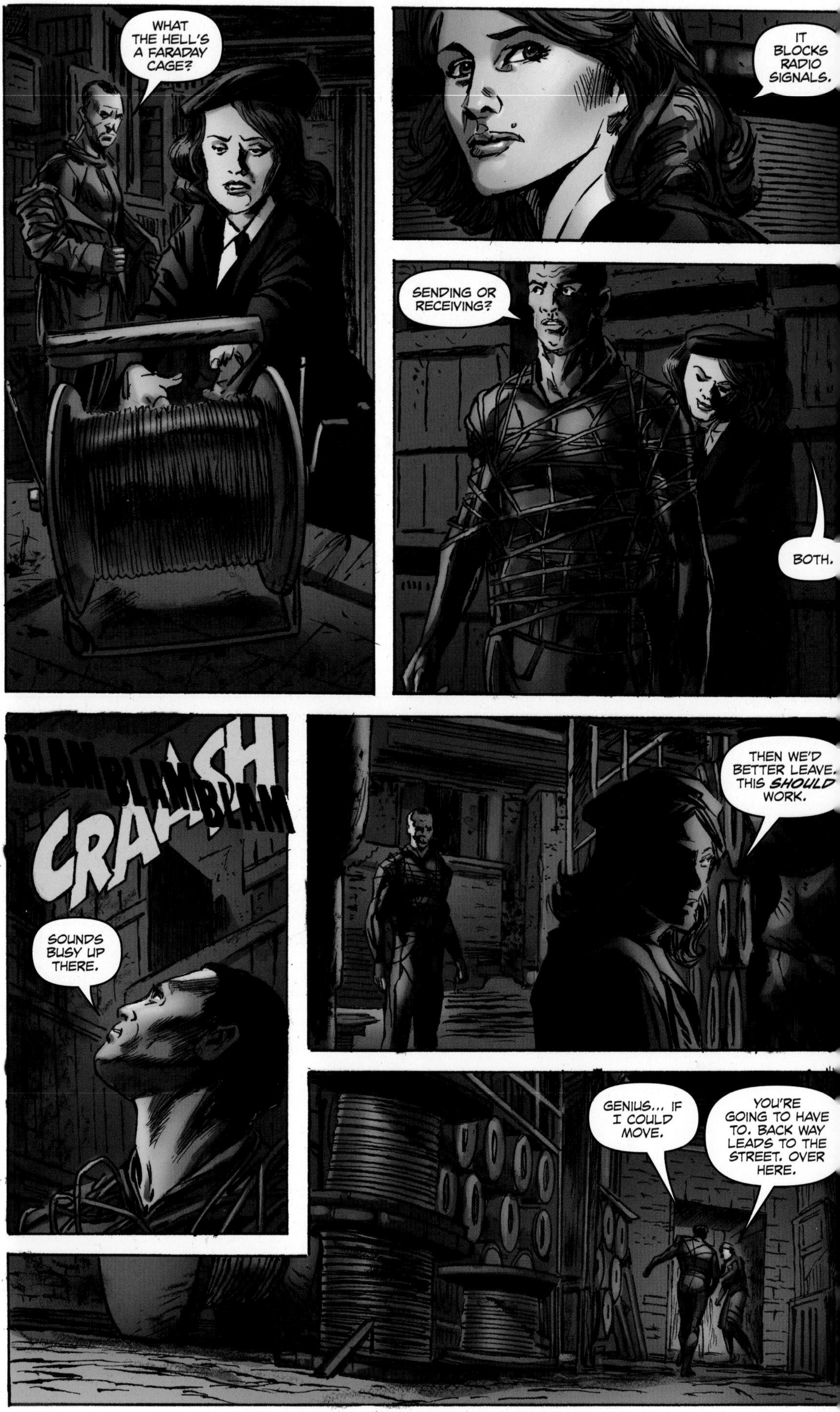
WHAT THE HELL'S A FARADAY CAGE?
IT BLOCKS RADIO SIGNALS.
SENDING OR RECEIVING?
BOTH.
BLAM BLAM BLAM BLAM
CRASH
SOUNDS BUSY UP THERE.
THEN WE'D BETTER LEAVE. THIS SHOULD WORK.
GENIUS... IF I COULD MOVE.
YOU'RE GOING TO HAVE TO. BACK WAY LEADS TO THE STREET. OVER HERE.

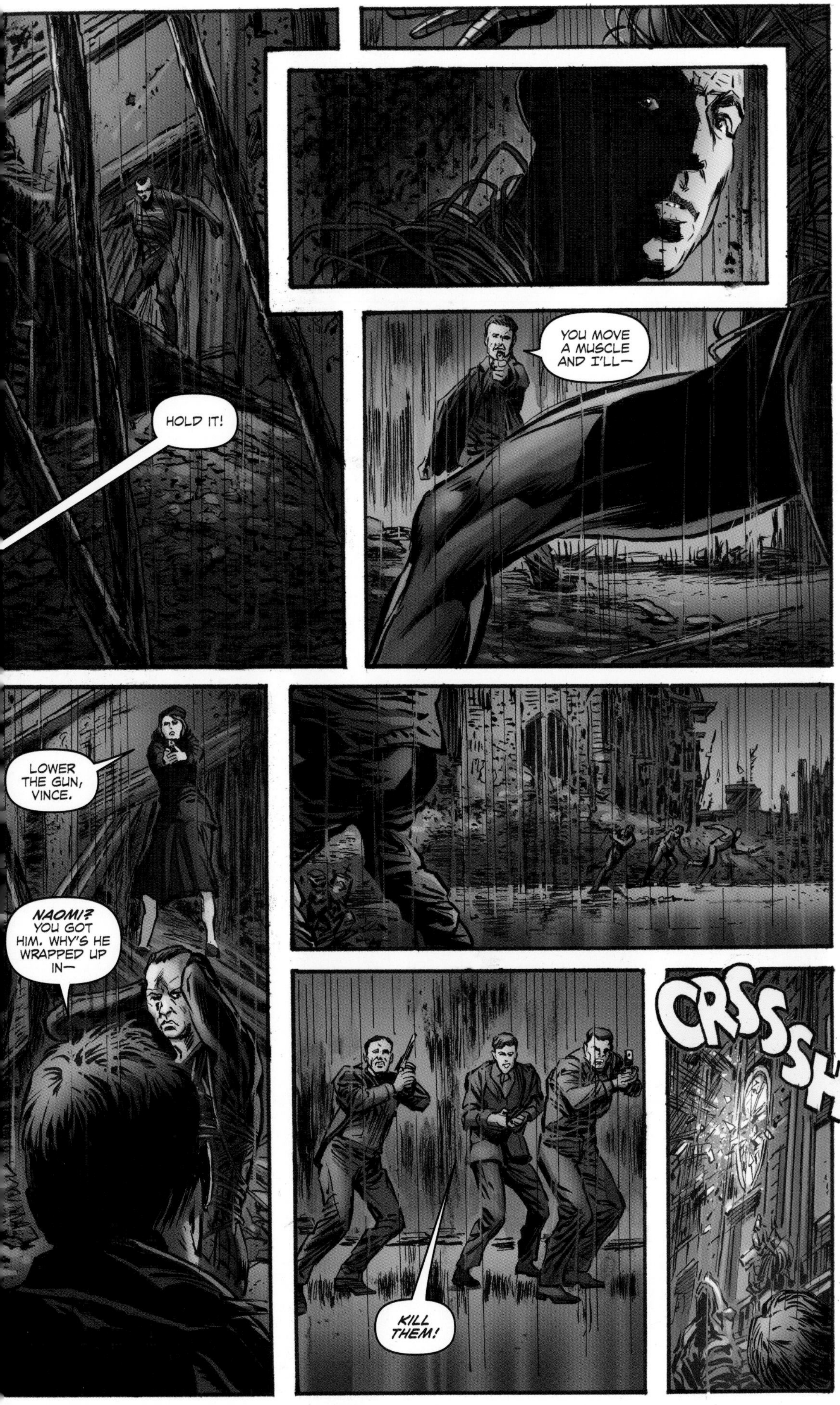
YOU MOVE A MUSCLE AND I'LL—
HOLD IT!
LOWER THE GUN, VINCE.
NAOMI? YOU GOT HIM. WHY'S HE WRAPPED UP IN—
KILL THEM!
CRSSSH

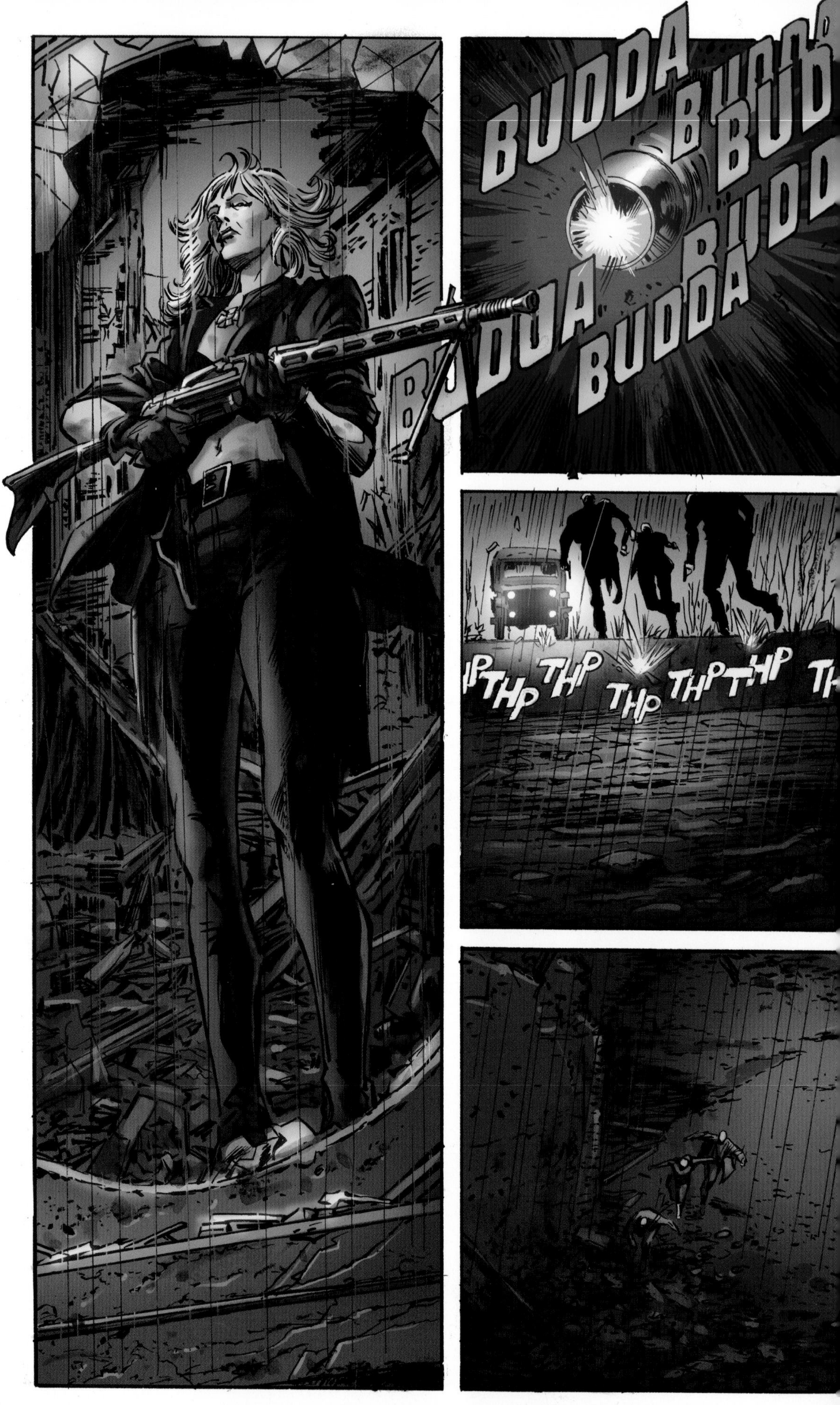
BUDDA
BUDDA
BUDDA
BUDDA
THP THP THP
THP THP THP

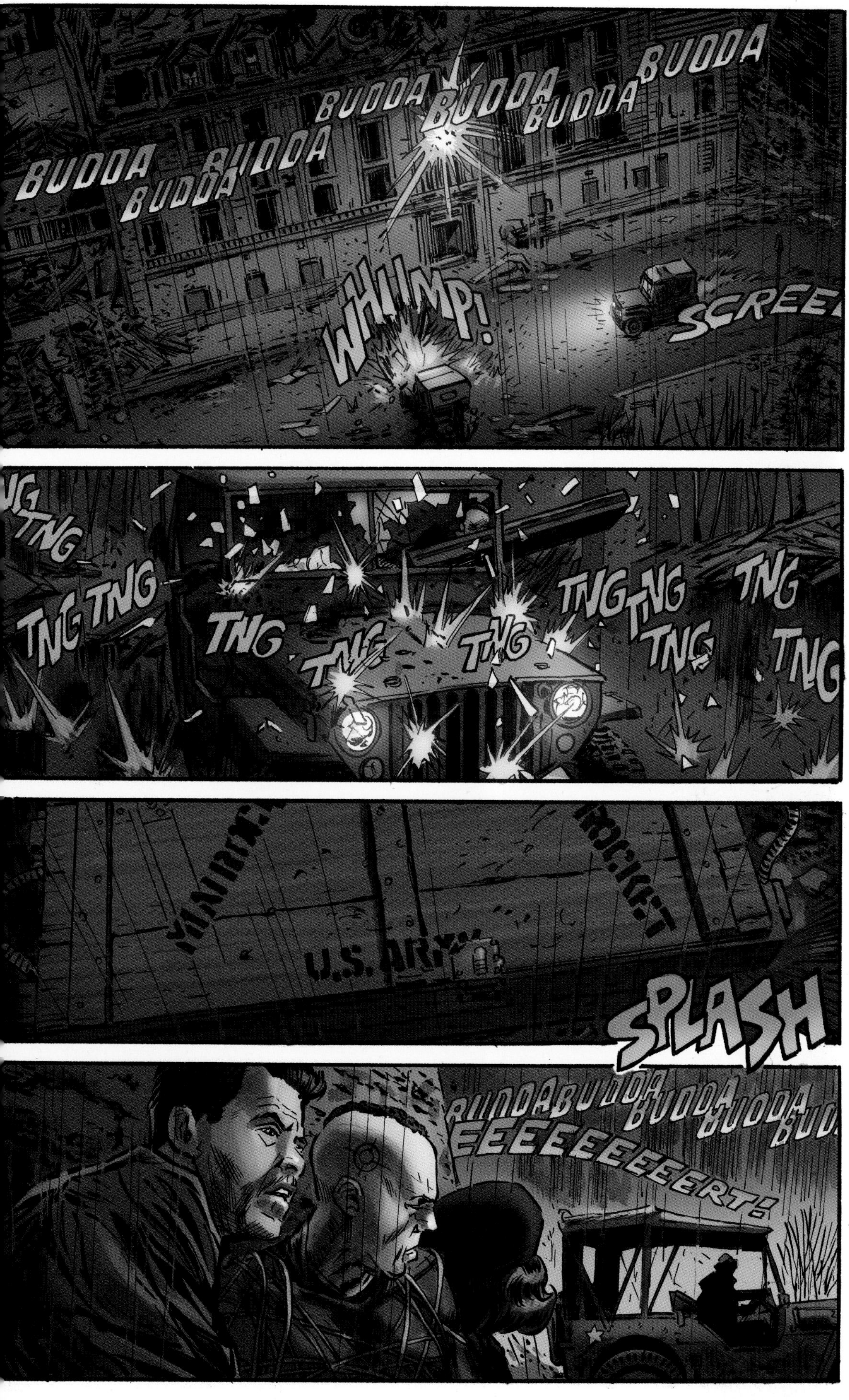
BUDDA BUDDA BUDDA BUDDA BUDDA BUDDA BUDDA
WHUMP!
SCREE
TNG TNG TNG TNG TNG TNG TNG TNG TNG TNG TNG TNG TNG
SPLASH
BUDDA BUDDA BUDDA BUDDA
EEEEEEEEEEEERT!

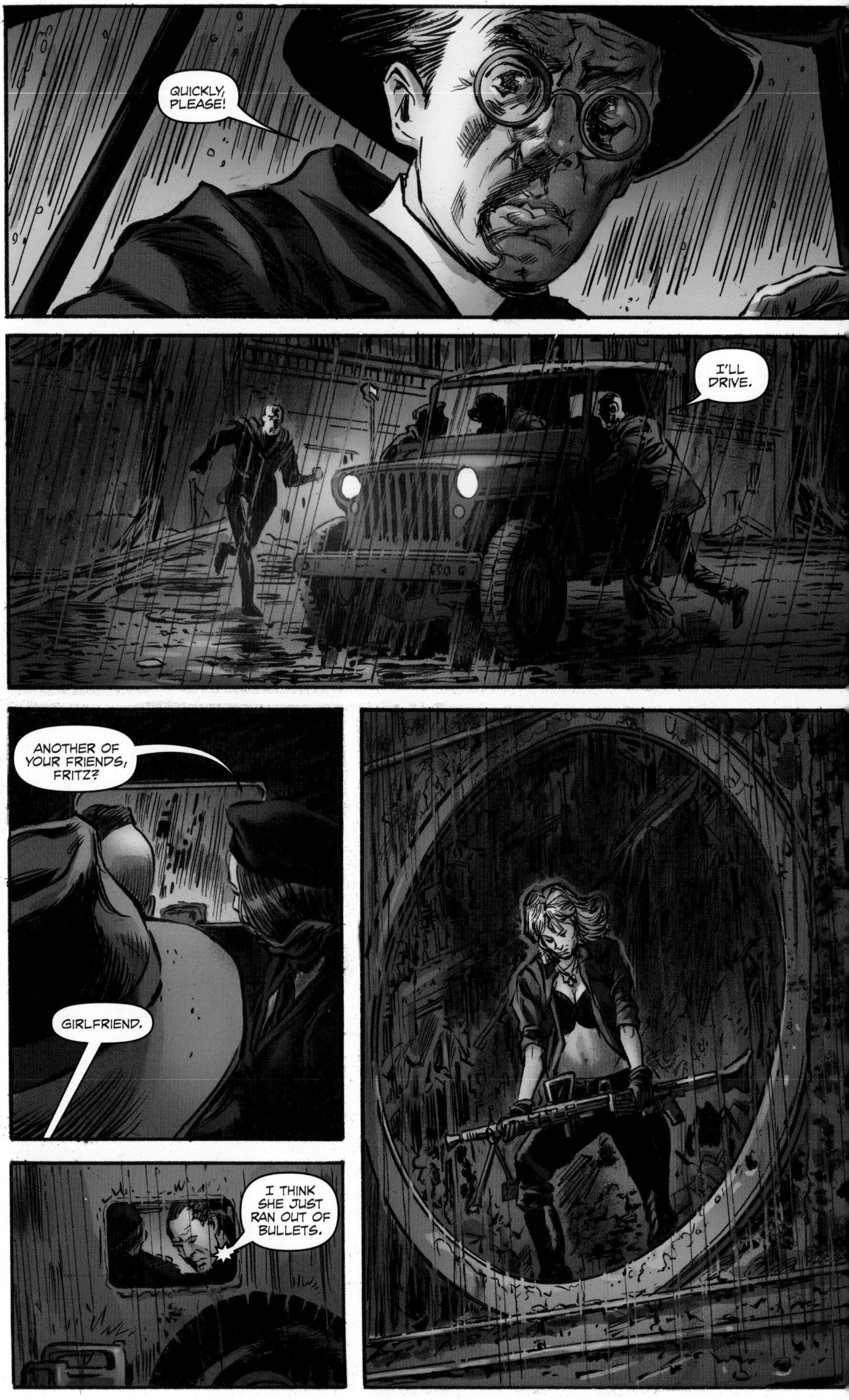
QUICKLY, PLEASE!
I'LL DRIVE.
ANOTHER OF YOUR FRIENDS, FRITZ?
GIRLFRIEND.
I THINK SHE JUST RAN OUT OF BULLETS.

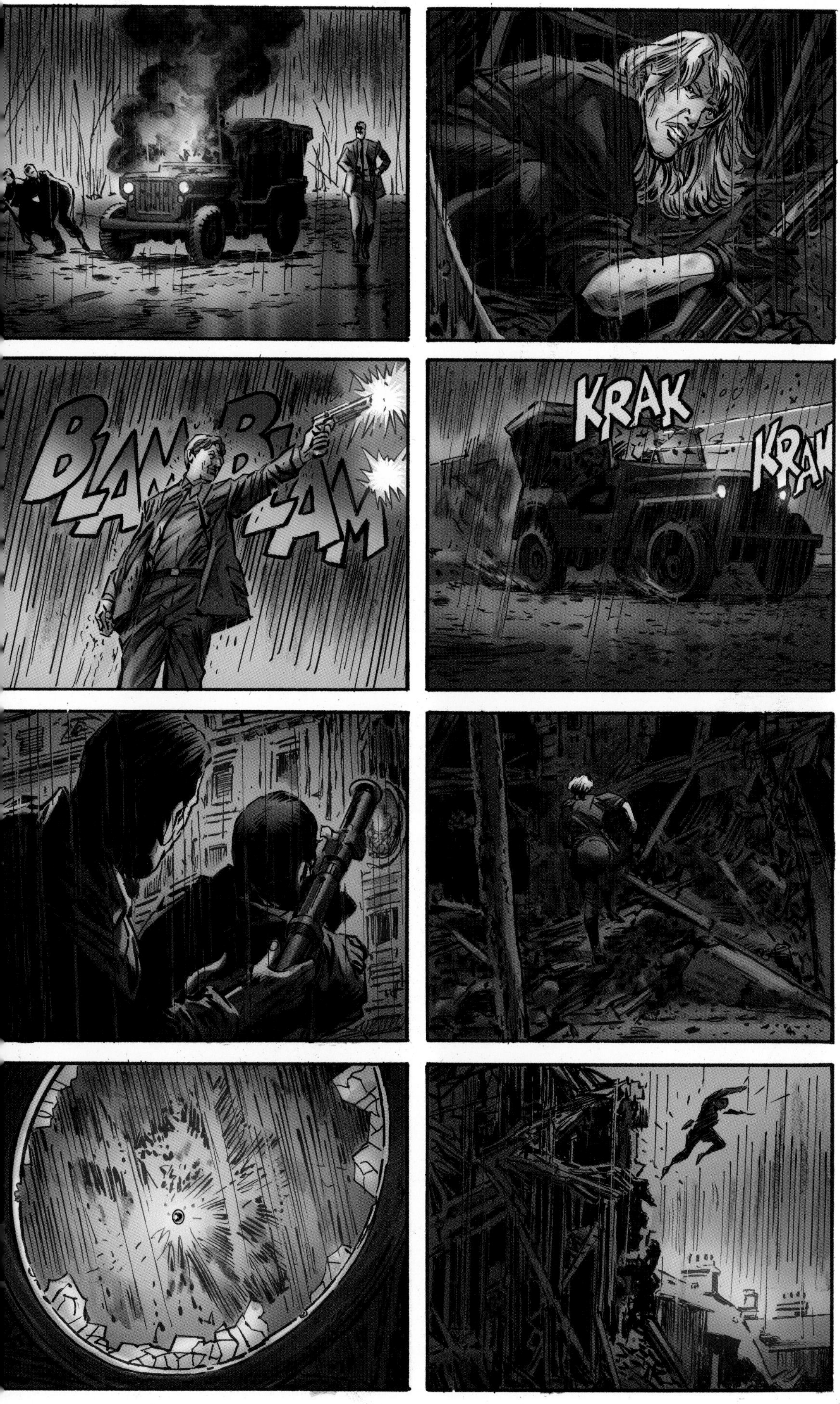

BLAM BLAM
KRAK
KRAK

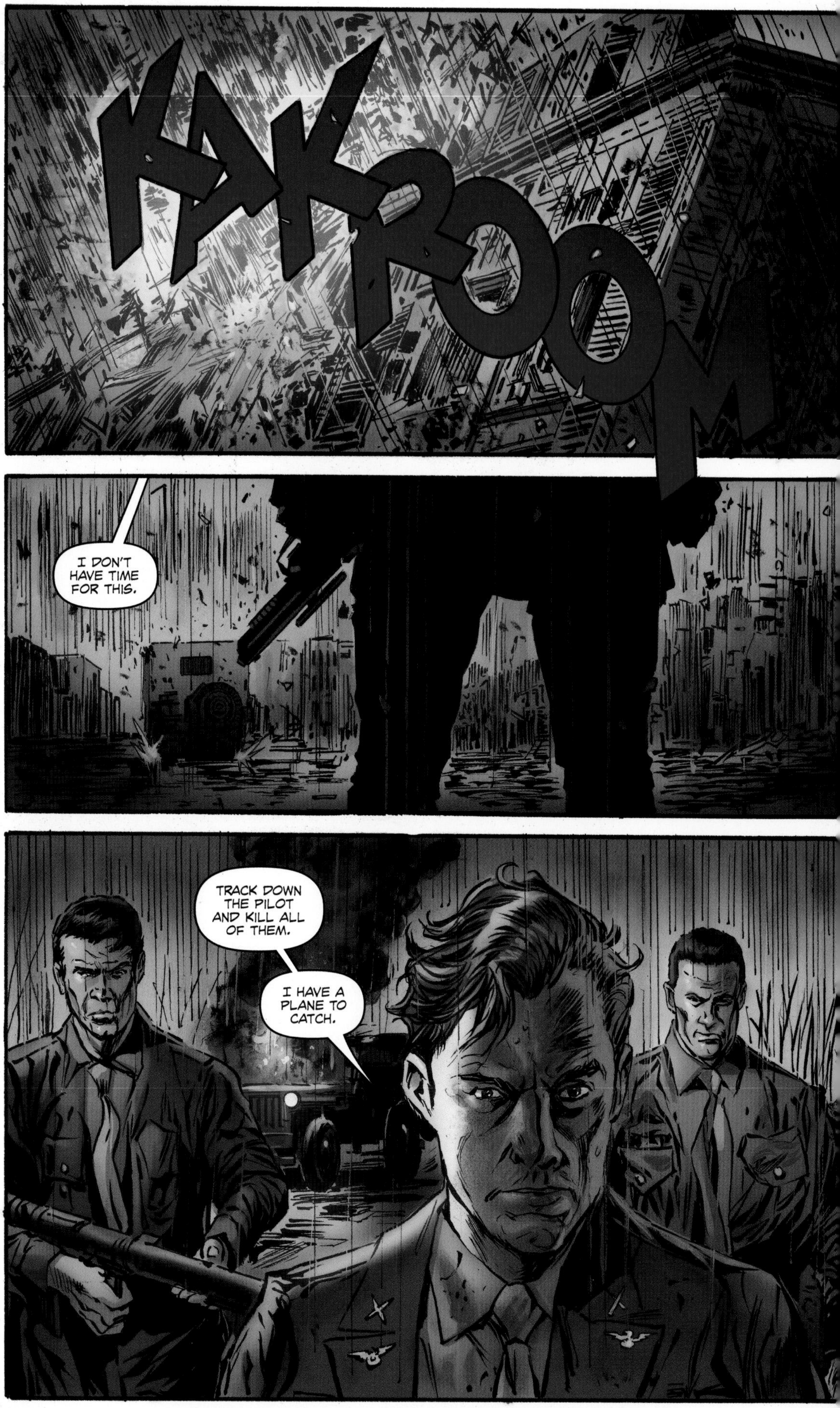
KAKROOM
I DON'T HAVE TIME FOR THIS.
TRACK DOWN THE PILOT AND KILL ALL OF THEM.
I HAVE A PLANE TO CATCH.

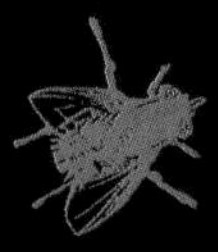

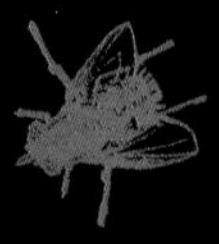

FOUR

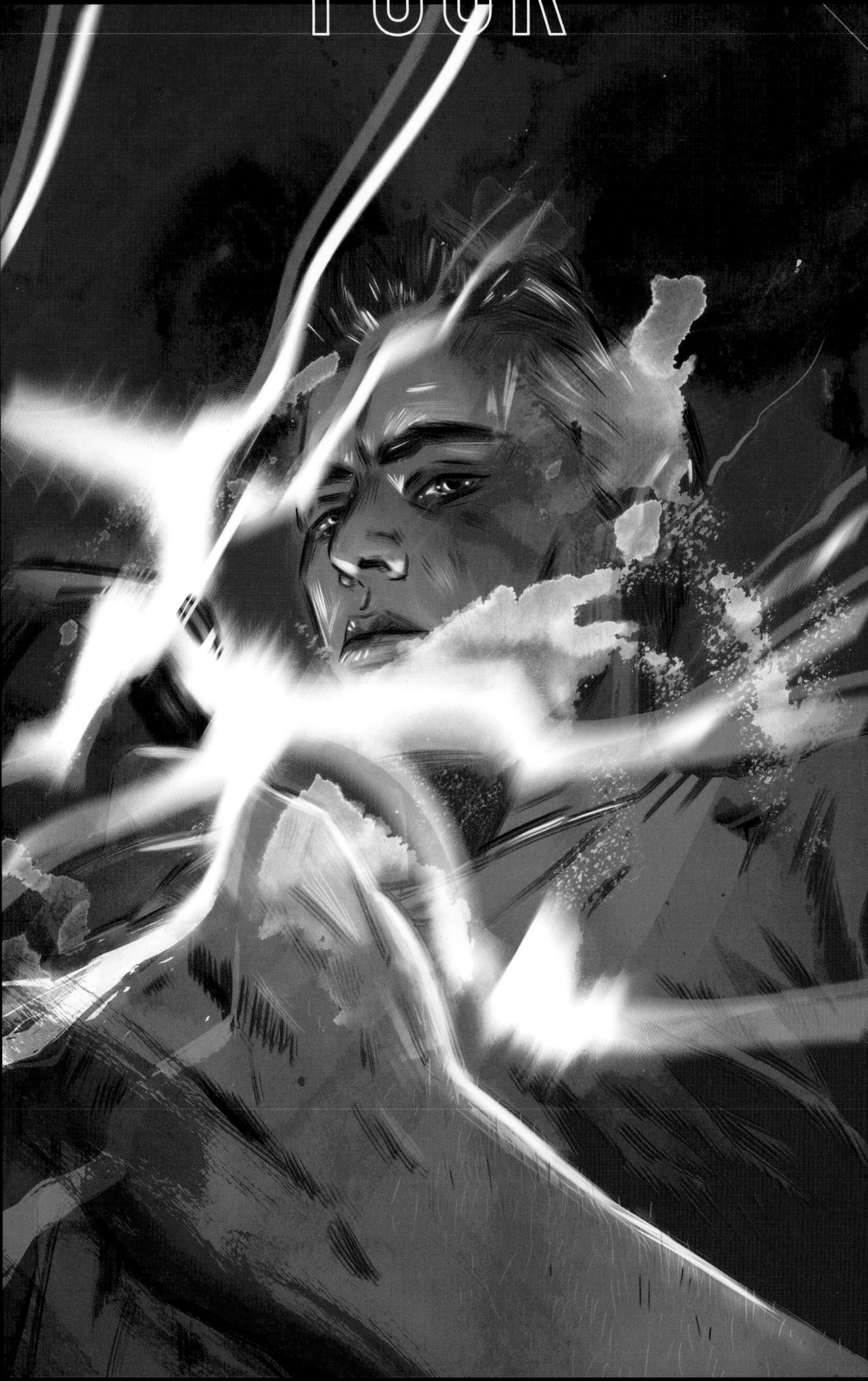

Art by **TULA LOTAY**

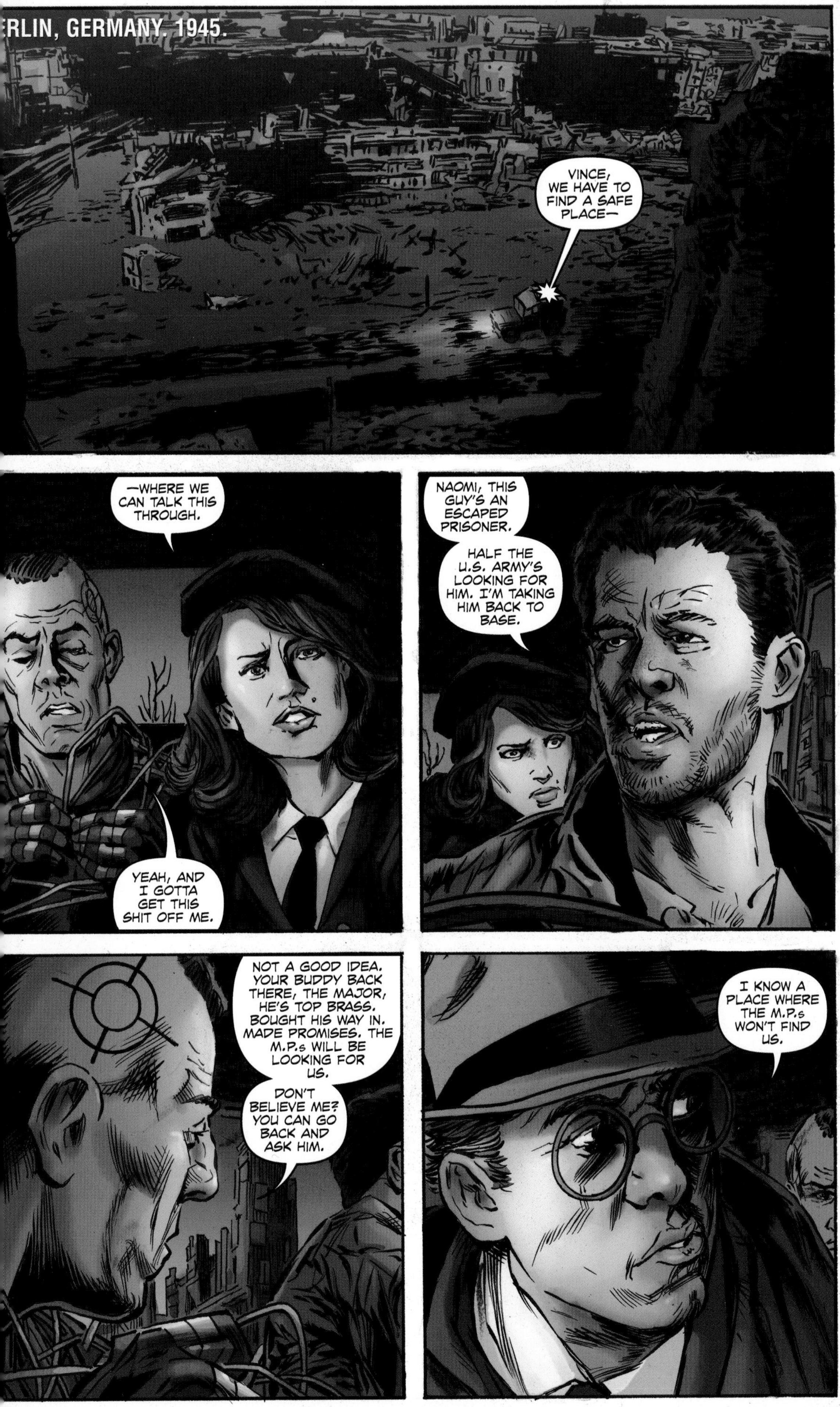

ERLIN, GERMANY. 1945.
VINCE, WE HAVE TO FIND A SAFE PLACE—
—WHERE WE CAN TALK THIS THROUGH.
YEAH, AND I GOTTA GET THIS SHIT OFF ME.
NAOMI, THIS GUY'S AN ESCAPED PRISONER.
HALF THE U.S. ARMY'S LOOKING FOR HIM. I'M TAKING HIM BACK TO BASE.
NOT A GOOD IDEA. YOUR BUDDY BACK THERE, THE MAJOR, HE'S TOP BRASS. BOUGHT HIS WAY IN. MADE PROMISES. THE M.P.s WILL BE LOOKING FOR US.
DON'T BELIEVE ME? YOU CAN GO BACK AND ASK HIM.
I KNOW A PLACE WHERE THE M.P.s WON'T FIND US.

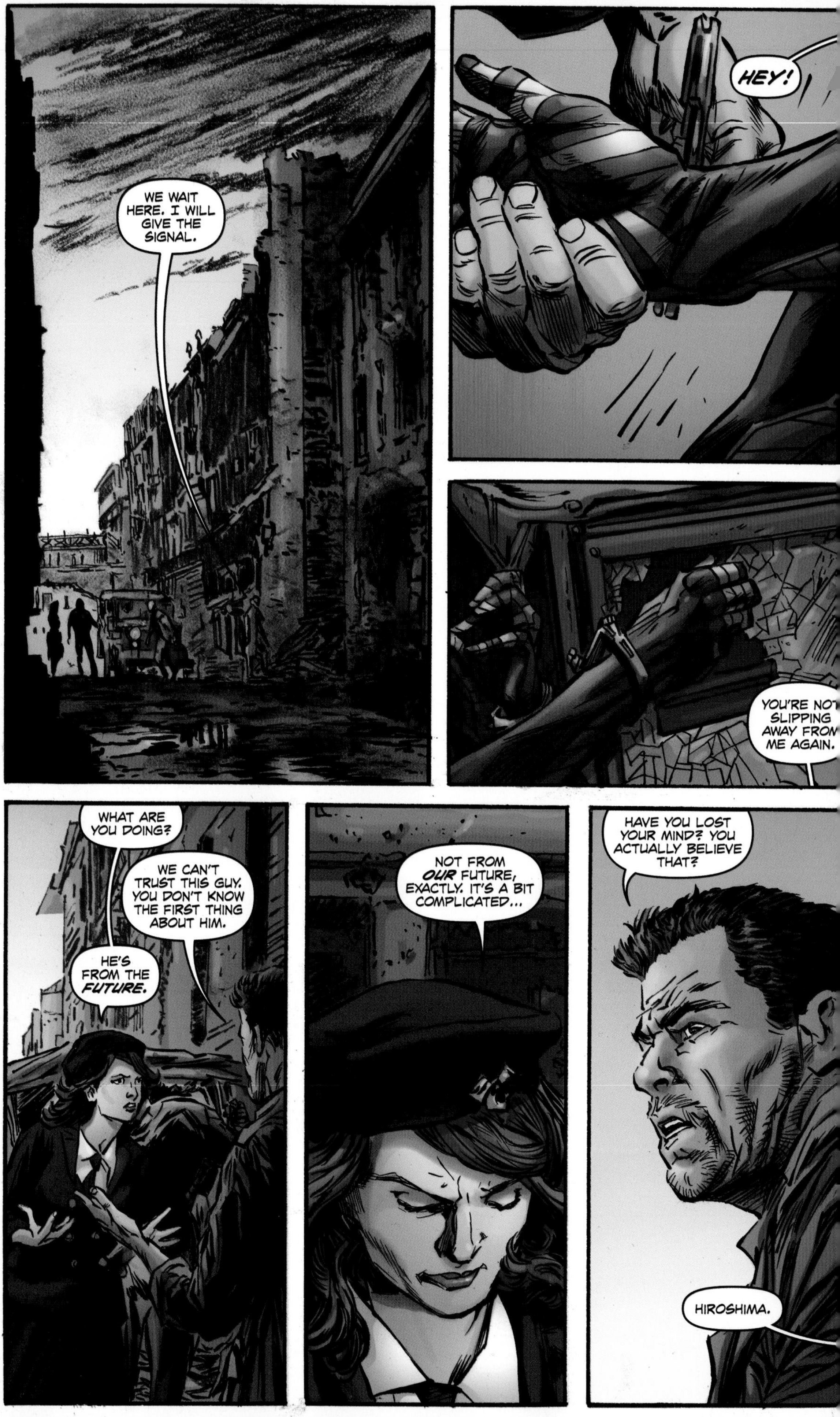
WE WAIT HERE. I WILL GIVE THE SIGNAL.
HEY!
YOU'RE NOT SLIPPING AWAY FROM ME AGAIN.
WHAT ARE YOU DOING?
WE CAN'T TRUST THIS GUY. YOU DON'T KNOW THE FIRST THING ABOUT HIM.
HE'S FROM THE *FUTURE.*
NOT FROM *OUR* FUTURE, EXACTLY. IT'S A BIT COMPLICATED...
HAVE YOU LOST YOUR MIND? YOU ACTUALLY BELIEVE THAT?
HIROSHIMA.

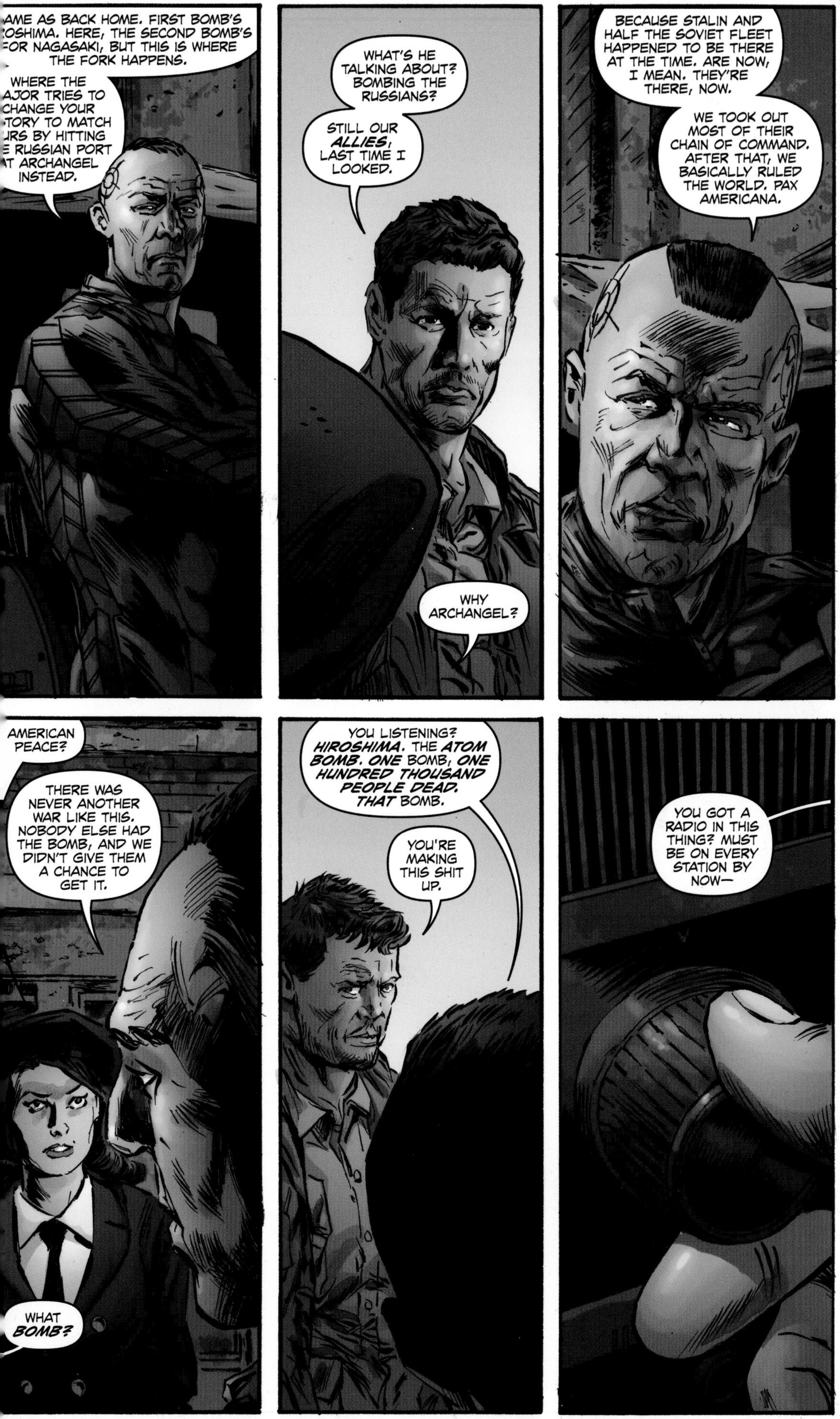
AME AS BACK HOME. FIRST BOMB'S
ROSHIMA. HERE, THE SECOND BOMB'S
FOR NAGASAKI, BUT THIS IS WHERE
THE FORK HAPPENS.
WHERE THE
AJOR TRIES TO
CHANGE YOUR
STORY TO MATCH
URS BY HITTING
E RUSSIAN PORT
AT ARCHANGEL
INSTEAD.
WHAT'S HE TALKING ABOUT? BOMBING THE RUSSIANS?
STILL OUR *ALLIES*, LAST TIME I LOOKED.
WHY ARCHANGEL?
BECAUSE STALIN AND HALF THE SOVIET FLEET HAPPENED TO BE THERE AT THE TIME. ARE NOW, I MEAN. THEY'RE THERE, NOW.
WE TOOK OUT MOST OF THEIR CHAIN OF COMMAND. AFTER THAT, WE BASICALLY RULED THE WORLD. PAX AMERICANA.
AMERICAN PEACE?
THERE WAS NEVER ANOTHER WAR LIKE THIS. NOBODY ELSE HAD THE BOMB, AND WE DIDN'T GIVE THEM A CHANCE TO GET IT.
WHAT *BOMB*?
YOU LISTENING? ***HIROSHIMA***. THE ***ATOM BOMB***. ***ONE*** BOMB, ***ONE HUNDRED THOUSAND PEOPLE DEAD***. ***THAT*** BOMB.
YOU'RE MAKING THIS SHIT UP.
YOU GOT A RADIO IN THIS THING? MUST BE ON EVERY STATION BY NOW—

—MUSHROOM-SHAPED CLOUD RISING 40,000 FEET INTO THE SKY ABOVE THE CITY.

NO WORD HAS YET BEEN RECEIVED FROM JAPANESE AUTHORITIES REGARDING THE EXTENT OF THE DAMAGE OR THE NUMBER OF CASUALTIES, BUT IT IS BELIEVED THAT NEARLY TWO THIRDS OF HIROSHIMA HAS BEEN LEVELED.

THE DESTRUCTIVE POWER OF THE BOMB IS ESTIMATED AT 20,000 TONNES OF TNT, ROUGHLY 500 TIMES MORE POWERFUL THAN THE LARGEST AERIAL BOMB USED DURING THE WAR SO FAR—

TORRES. THE CUFFS, TAKE 'EM OFF.

THIS IS NOT YOUR SHIT, SEE? NOT YOUR TIME. NOT YOUR WORLD.

CLAN

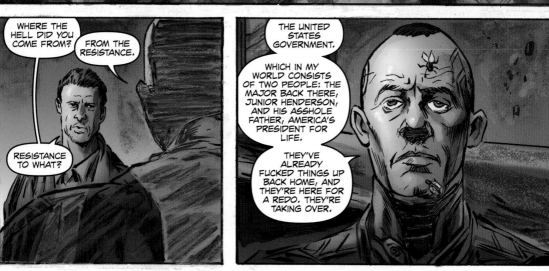

WHERE THE HELL DID YOU COME FROM?

FROM THE RESISTANCE.

RESISTANCE TO WHAT?

THE UNITED STATES GOVERNMENT.

WHICH IN MY WORLD CONSISTS OF TWO PEOPLE: THE MAJOR BACK THERE, JUNIOR HENDERSON, AND HIS ASSHOLE FATHER, AMERICA'S PRESIDENT FOR LIFE.

THEY'VE ALREADY FUCKED THINGS UP BACK HOME, AND THEY'RE HERE FOR A REDO. THEY'RE TAKING OVER.

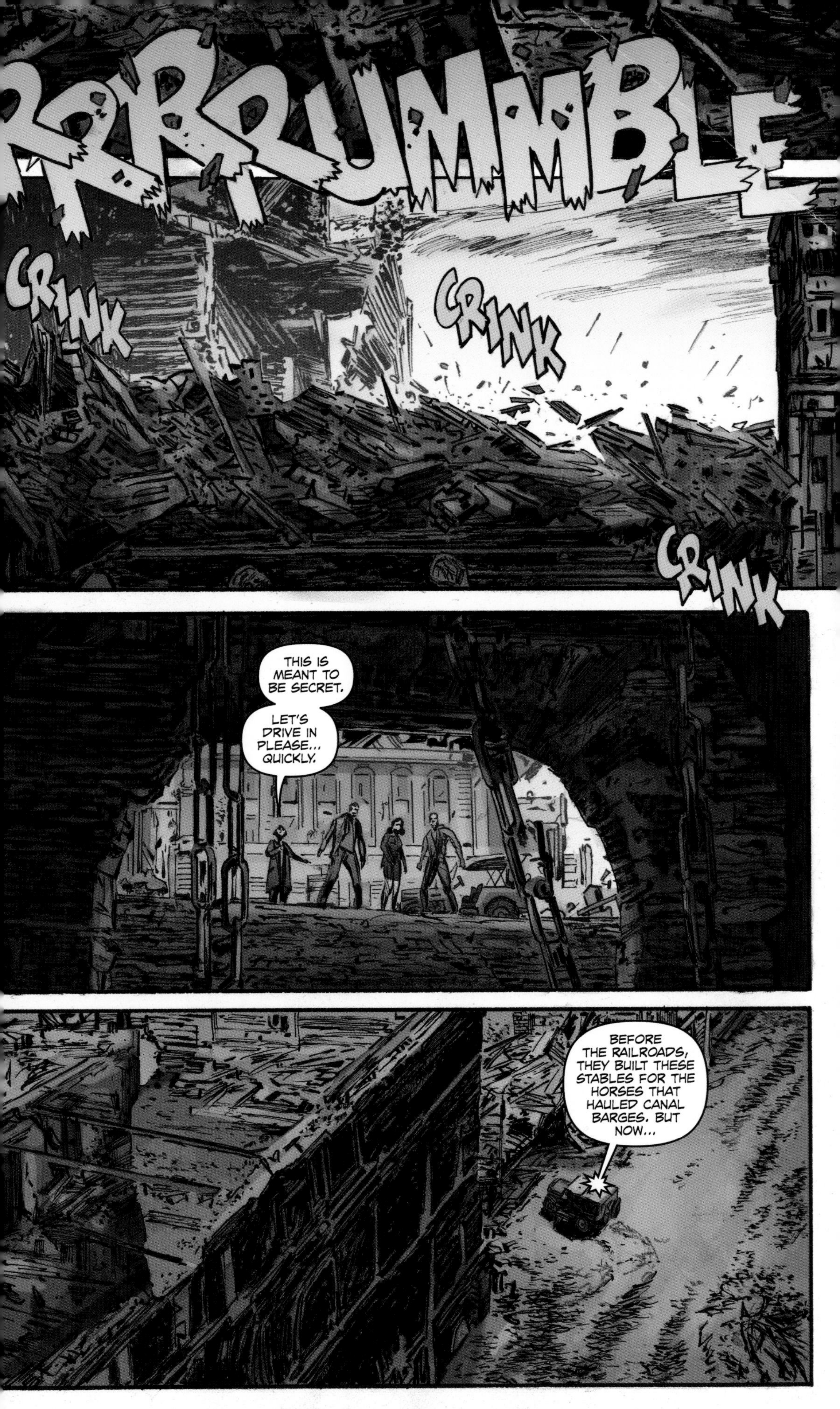
RRRUMMBLE
CRINK
CRINK
CRINK
THIS IS MEANT TO BE SECRET.
LET'S DRIVE IN PLEASE... QUICKLY.
BEFORE THE RAILROADS, THEY BUILT THESE STABLES FOR THE HORSES THAT HAULED CANAL BARGES. BUT NOW...

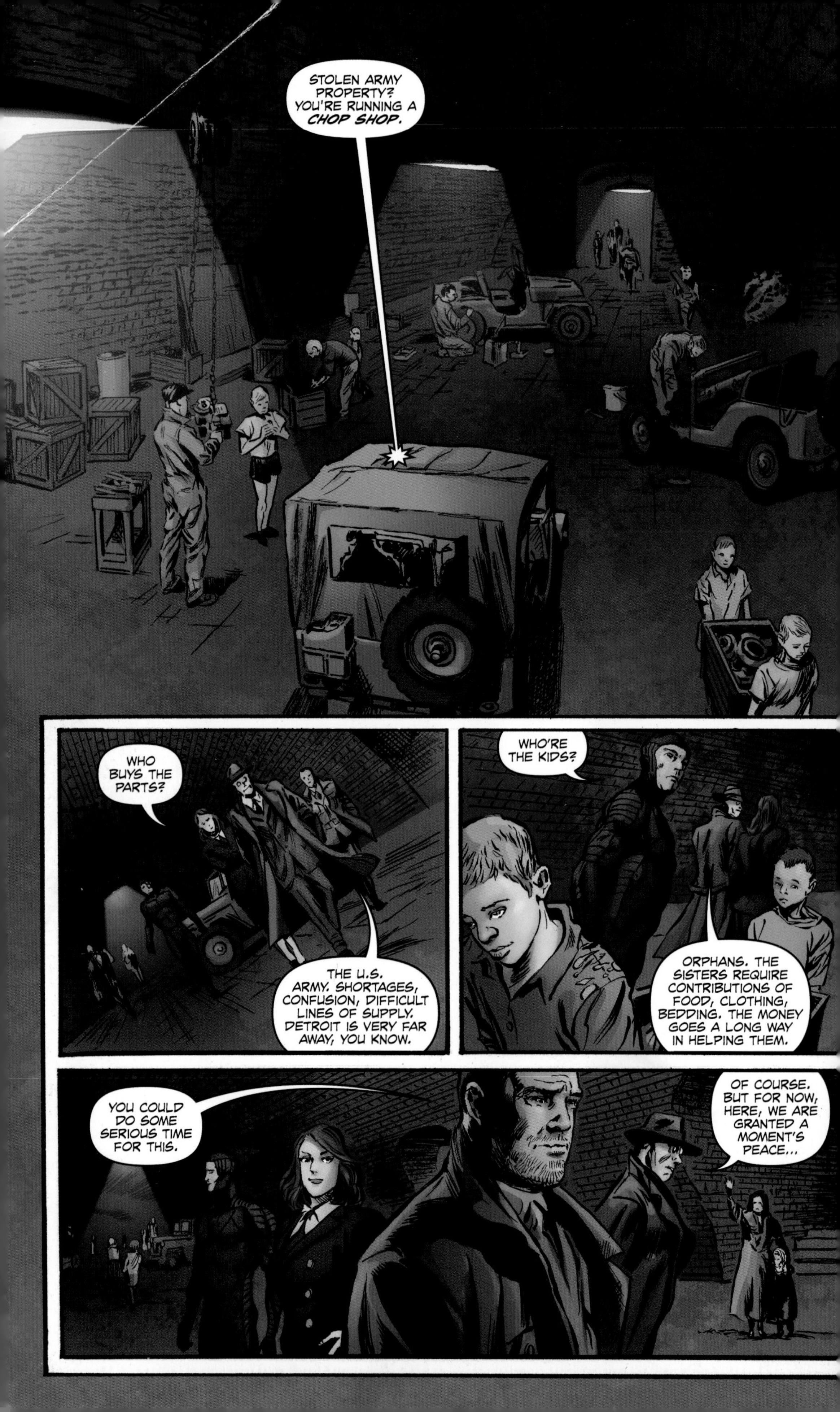
STOLEN ARMY PROPERTY? YOU'RE RUNNING A *CHOP SHOP*.
WHO BUYS THE PARTS?
THE U.S. ARMY. SHORTAGES, CONFUSION, DIFFICULT LINES OF SUPPLY. DETROIT IS VERY FAR AWAY, YOU KNOW.
WHO'RE THE KIDS?
ORPHANS. THE SISTERS REQUIRE CONTRIBUTIONS OF FOOD, CLOTHING, BEDDING. THE MONEY GOES A LONG WAY IN HELPING THEM.
YOU COULD DO SOME SERIOUS TIME FOR THIS.
OF COURSE. BUT FOR NOW, HERE, WE ARE GRANTED A MOMENT'S PEACE...

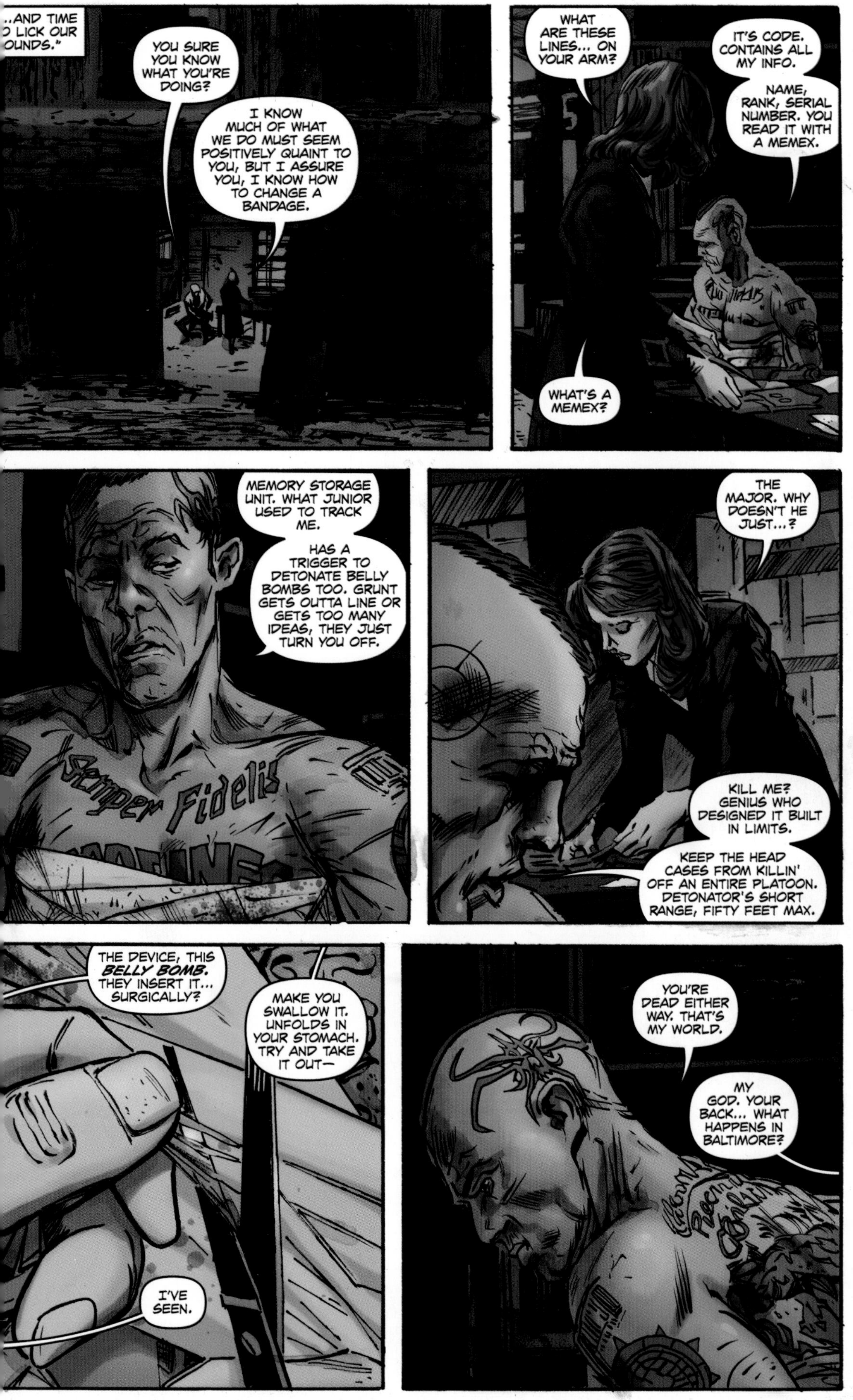

..AND TIME
O LICK OUR
OUNDS."
YOU SURE YOU KNOW WHAT YOU'RE DOING?
I KNOW MUCH OF WHAT WE DO MUST SEEM POSITIVELY QUAINT TO YOU, BUT I ASSURE YOU, I KNOW HOW TO CHANGE A BANDAGE.
WHAT ARE THESE LINES... ON YOUR ARM?
IT'S CODE. CONTAINS ALL MY INFO.
NAME, RANK, SERIAL NUMBER. YOU READ IT WITH A MEMEX.
WHAT'S A MEMEX?
MEMORY STORAGE UNIT. WHAT JUNIOR USED TO TRACK ME.
HAS A TRIGGER TO DETONATE BELLY BOMBS TOO. GRUNT GETS OUTTA LINE OR GETS TOO MANY IDEAS, THEY JUST TURN YOU OFF.
Semper Fidelis
THE MAJOR. WHY DOESN'T HE JUST...?
KILL ME? GENIUS WHO DESIGNED IT BUILT IN LIMITS.
KEEP THE HEAD CASES FROM KILLIN' OFF AN ENTIRE PLATOON. DETONATOR'S SHORT RANGE, FIFTY FEET MAX.
THE DEVICE, THIS *BELLY BOMB.* THEY INSERT IT... SURGICALLY?
MAKE YOU SWALLOW IT. UNFOLDS IN YOUR STOMACH. TRY AND TAKE IT OUT—
I'VE SEEN.
YOU'RE DEAD EITHER WAY. THAT'S MY WORLD.
MY GOD. YOUR BACK... WHAT HAPPENS IN BALTIMORE?

SOMEBODY SABOTAGED A NUCLEAR POWER PLANT. IT TRIGGERED OUR GLOBAL FAILSAFE SYSTEM. SET OFF THE NUCLEAR BOMBS WE'D BURIED IN EVERY CLIENT NATION...

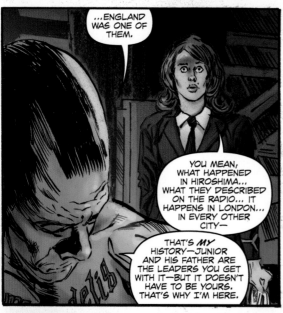

...ENGLAND WAS ONE OF THEM.

YOU MEAN, WHAT HAPPENED IN HIROSHIMA... WHAT THEY DESCRIBED ON THE RADIO... IT HAPPENS IN LONDON... IN EVERY OTHER CITY—

THAT'S *MY* HISTORY—JUNIOR AND HIS FATHER ARE THE LEADERS YOU GET WITH IT—BUT IT DOESN'T HAVE TO BE YOURS. THAT'S WHY I'M HERE.

WHAT DO YOU INTEND TO DO?

STOP HIM. THEY'LL BE USING ONE OF THE NEW B-29S TO DELIVER THE BOMB. SAME AS HIROSHIMA.

IT HAS TO BE CLOSE. FIND THE BOMBER, FIND JUNIOR.

HOW DO YOU HIDE A B-29? HOW COULD HE HAVE ACCOMPLISHED ALL THIS?

THEY DID THEIR HOMEWORK. KNEW WHO WAS CROOKED, WHO TO BLACKMAIL, WHO TO KEEP QUIET.

THERE WERE GENERALS WHO WANTED TO TAKE OUT RUSSIA AFTER THE NAZIS. JUNIOR JUST HELPED THEM DO IT.

I DON'T UNDERSTAND HOW YOUR PRESIDENT, HIS SON... EVERYTHING YOU'VE SAID ABOUT THEM... HOW COULD THEY HAVE THAT MUCH POWER?

IT'S BEEN THAT WAY AS LONG AS I CAN REMEMBER. BUT BALTIMORE...

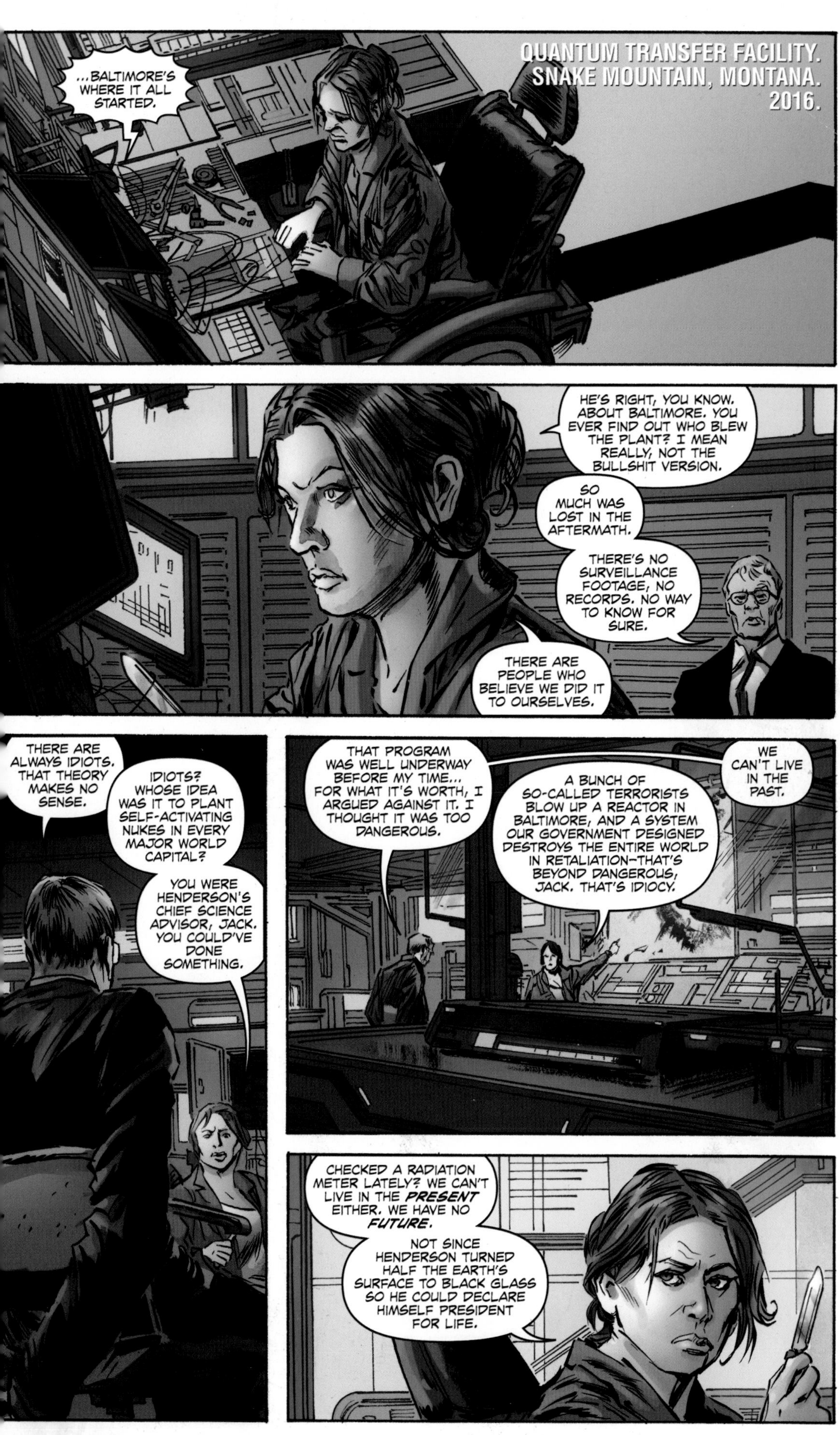

QUANTUM TRANSFER FACILITY. SNAKE MOUNTAIN, MONTANA. 2016.
...BALTIMORE'S WHERE IT ALL STARTED.
HE'S RIGHT, YOU KNOW. ABOUT BALTIMORE. YOU EVER FIND OUT WHO BLEW THE PLANT? I MEAN REALLY, NOT THE BULLSHIT VERSION.
SO MUCH WAS LOST IN THE AFTERMATH.
THERE'S NO SURVEILLANCE FOOTAGE, NO RECORDS. NO WAY TO KNOW FOR SURE.
THERE ARE PEOPLE WHO BELIEVE WE DID IT TO OURSELVES.
THERE ARE ALWAYS IDIOTS. THAT THEORY MAKES NO SENSE.
IDIOTS? WHOSE IDEA WAS IT TO PLANT SELF-ACTIVATING NUKES IN EVERY MAJOR WORLD CAPITAL?
YOU WERE HENDERSON'S CHIEF SCIENCE ADVISOR, JACK. YOU COULD'VE DONE SOMETHING.
THAT PROGRAM WAS WELL UNDERWAY BEFORE MY TIME... FOR WHAT IT'S WORTH, I ARGUED AGAINST IT. I THOUGHT IT WAS TOO DANGEROUS.
A BUNCH OF SO-CALLED TERRORISTS BLOW UP A REACTOR IN BALTIMORE, AND A SYSTEM OUR GOVERNMENT DESIGNED DESTROYS THE ENTIRE WORLD IN RETALIATION–THAT'S BEYOND DANGEROUS, JACK. THAT'S IDIOCY.
WE CAN'T LIVE IN THE PAST.
CHECKED A RADIATION METER LATELY? WE CAN'T LIVE IN THE ***PRESENT*** EITHER. WE HAVE NO ***FUTURE.***
NOT SINCE HENDERSON TURNED HALF THE EARTH'S SURFACE TO BLACK GLASS SO HE COULD DECLARE HIMSELF PRESIDENT FOR LIFE.

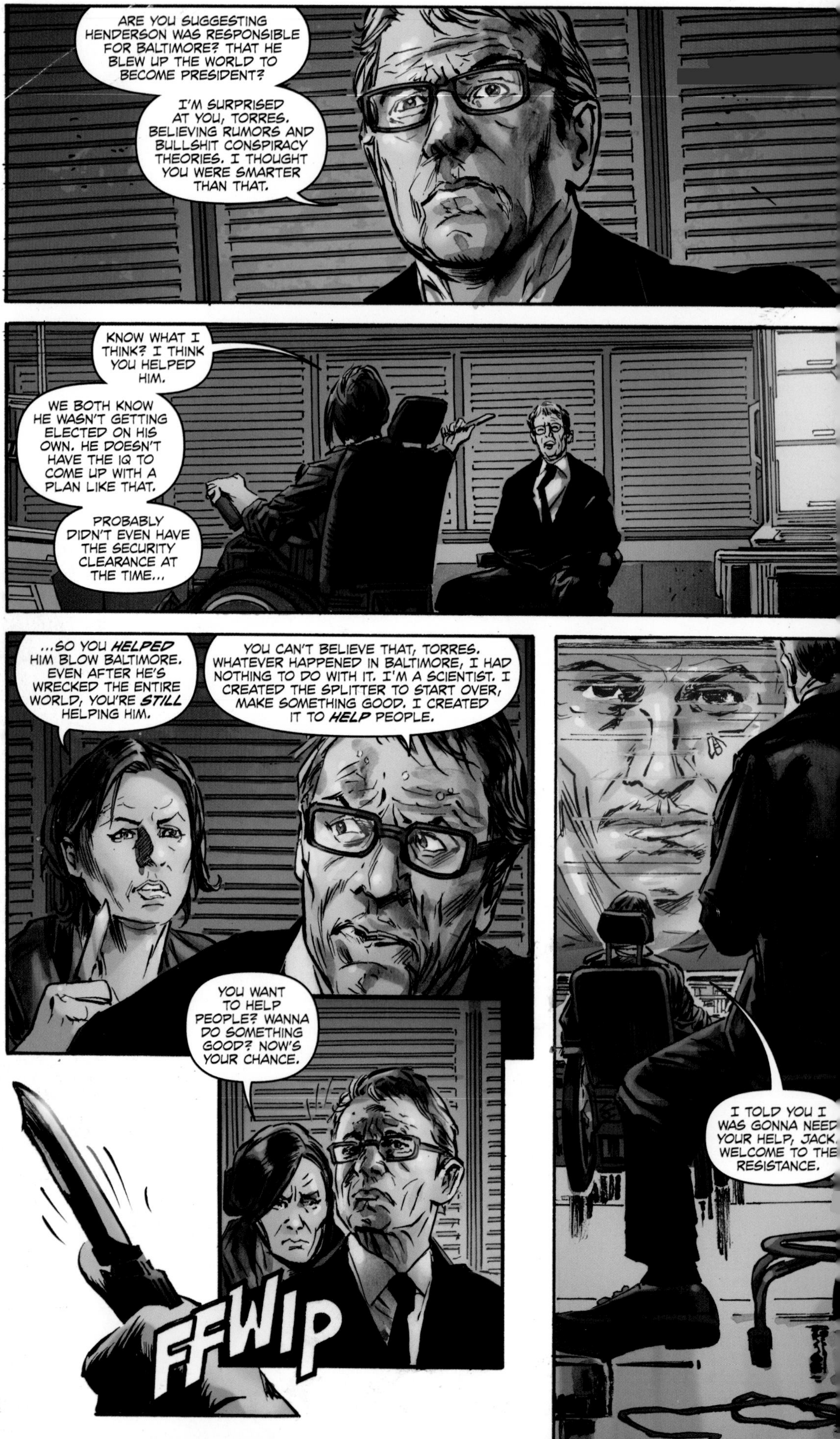
ARE YOU SUGGESTING HENDERSON WAS RESPONSIBLE FOR BALTIMORE? THAT HE BLEW UP THE WORLD TO BECOME PRESIDENT?
I'M SURPRISED AT YOU, TORRES. BELIEVING RUMORS AND BULLSHIT CONSPIRACY THEORIES. I THOUGHT YOU WERE SMARTER THAN THAT.
KNOW WHAT I THINK? I THINK YOU HELPED HIM.
WE BOTH KNOW HE WASN'T GETTING ELECTED ON HIS OWN. HE DOESN'T HAVE THE IQ TO COME UP WITH A PLAN LIKE THAT.
PROBABLY DIDN'T EVEN HAVE THE SECURITY CLEARANCE AT THE TIME...
...SO YOU HELPED HIM BLOW BALTIMORE. EVEN AFTER HE'S WRECKED THE ENTIRE WORLD, YOU'RE STILL HELPING HIM.
YOU CAN'T BELIEVE THAT, TORRES. WHATEVER HAPPENED IN BALTIMORE, I HAD NOTHING TO DO WITH IT. I'M A SCIENTIST. I CREATED THE SPLITTER TO START OVER, MAKE SOMETHING GOOD. I CREATED IT TO HELP PEOPLE.
YOU WANT TO HELP PEOPLE? WANNA DO SOMETHING GOOD? NOW'S YOUR CHANCE.
FFWIP
I TOLD YOU I WAS GONNA NEED YOUR HELP, JACK. WELCOME TO THE RESISTANCE.

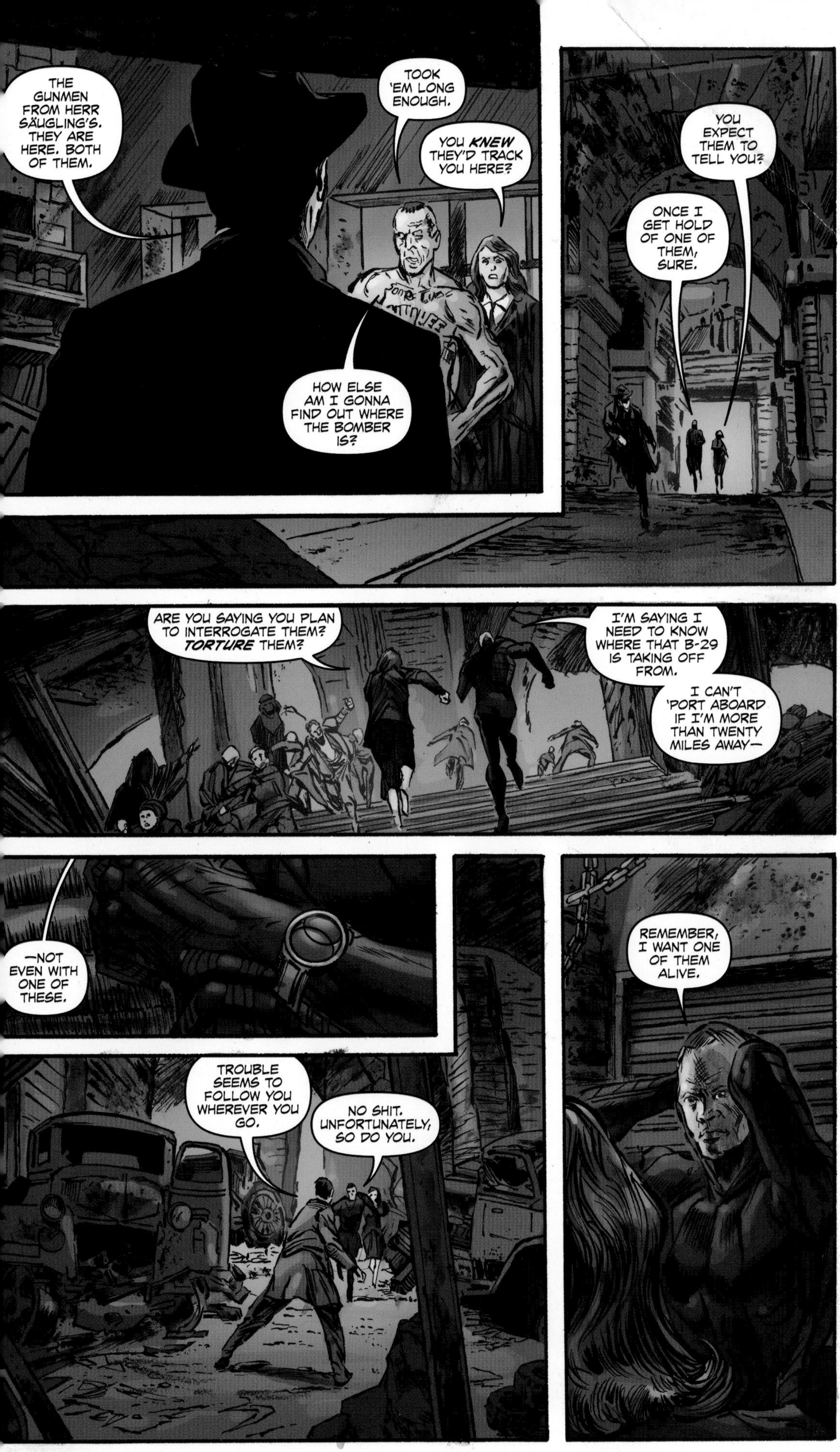
THE GUNMEN FROM HERR SÄUGLING'S. THEY ARE HERE. BOTH OF THEM.
TOOK 'EM LONG ENOUGH.
YOU *KNEW* THEY'D TRACK YOU HERE?
HOW ELSE AM I GONNA FIND OUT WHERE THE BOMBER IS?
YOU EXPECT THEM TO TELL YOU?
ONCE I GET HOLD OF ONE OF THEM, SURE.
ARE YOU SAYING YOU PLAN TO INTERROGATE THEM? *TORTURE* THEM?
I'M SAYING I NEED TO KNOW WHERE THAT B-29 IS TAKING OFF FROM.
I CAN'T 'PORT ABOARD IF I'M MORE THAN TWENTY MILES AWAY—
—NOT EVEN WITH ONE OF THESE.
TROUBLE SEEMS TO FOLLOW YOU WHEREVER YOU GO.
NO SHIT. UNFORTUNATELY, SO DO YOU.
REMEMBER, I WANT ONE OF THEM ALIVE.

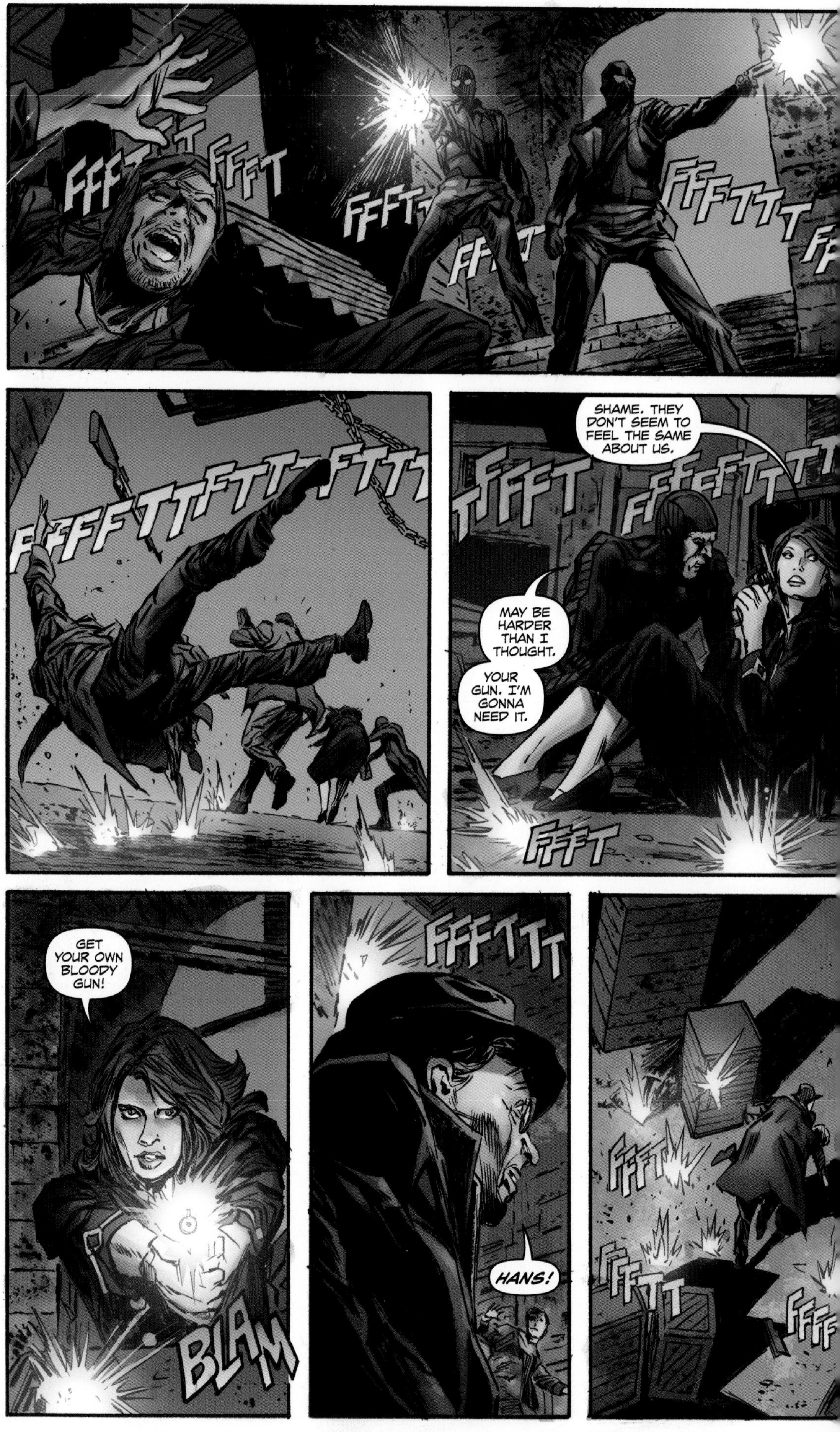

FFFT
FFFT
FFFT
FFFT
FFFFTTTT
FFFFTTTFTTT FTTT
FFFFT
SHAME. THEY DON'T SEEM TO FEEL THE SAME ABOUT US.
FFFFFFTTTTT
MAY BE HARDER THAN I THOUGHT.
YOUR GUN. I'M GONNA NEED IT.
FFFT
GET YOUR OWN BLOODY GUN!
BLAM
FFFTTT
HANS!

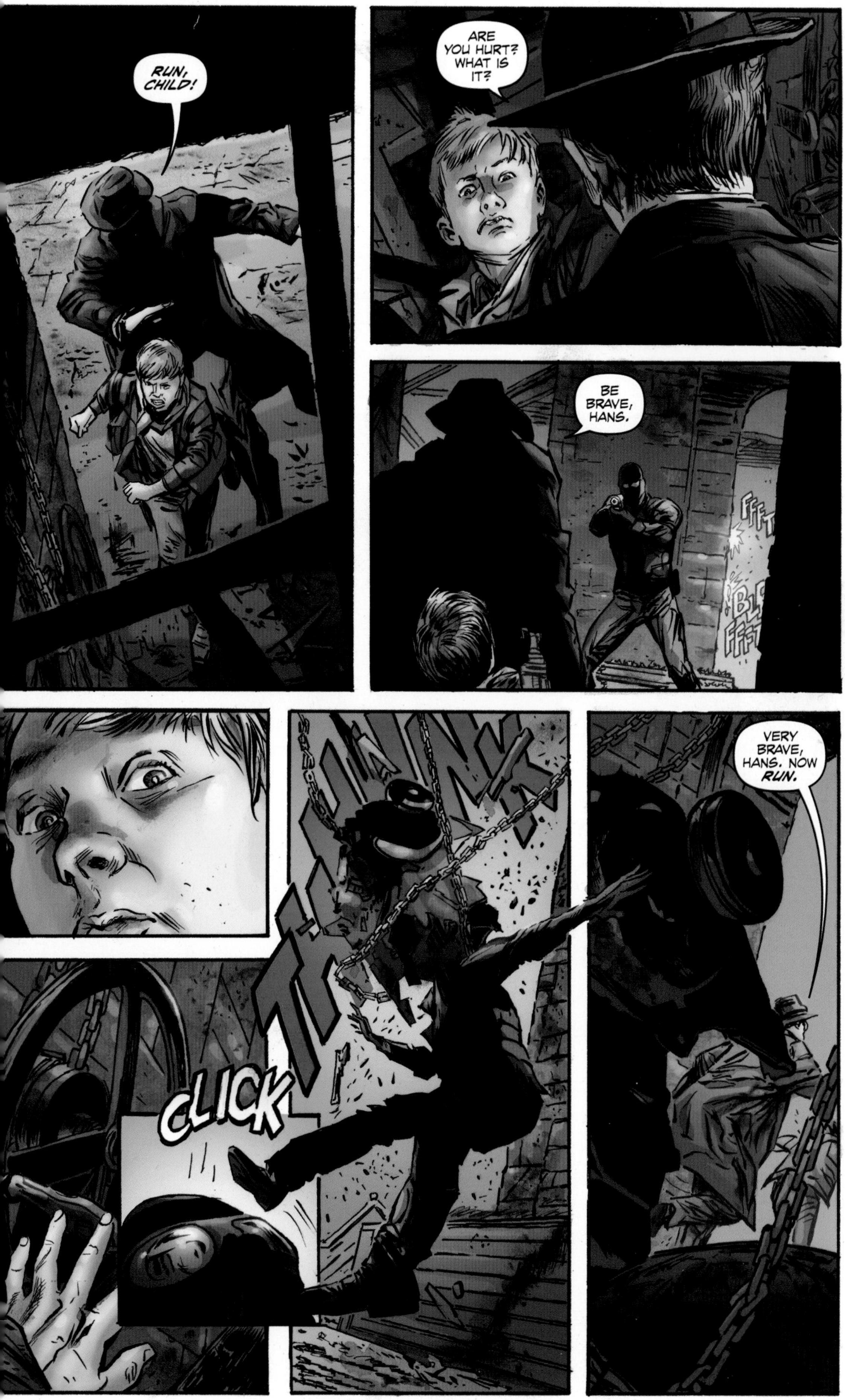
RUN, CHILD!
ARE YOU HURT? WHAT IS IT?
BE BRAVE, HANS.
VERY BRAVE, HANS. NOW RUN.
CLICK

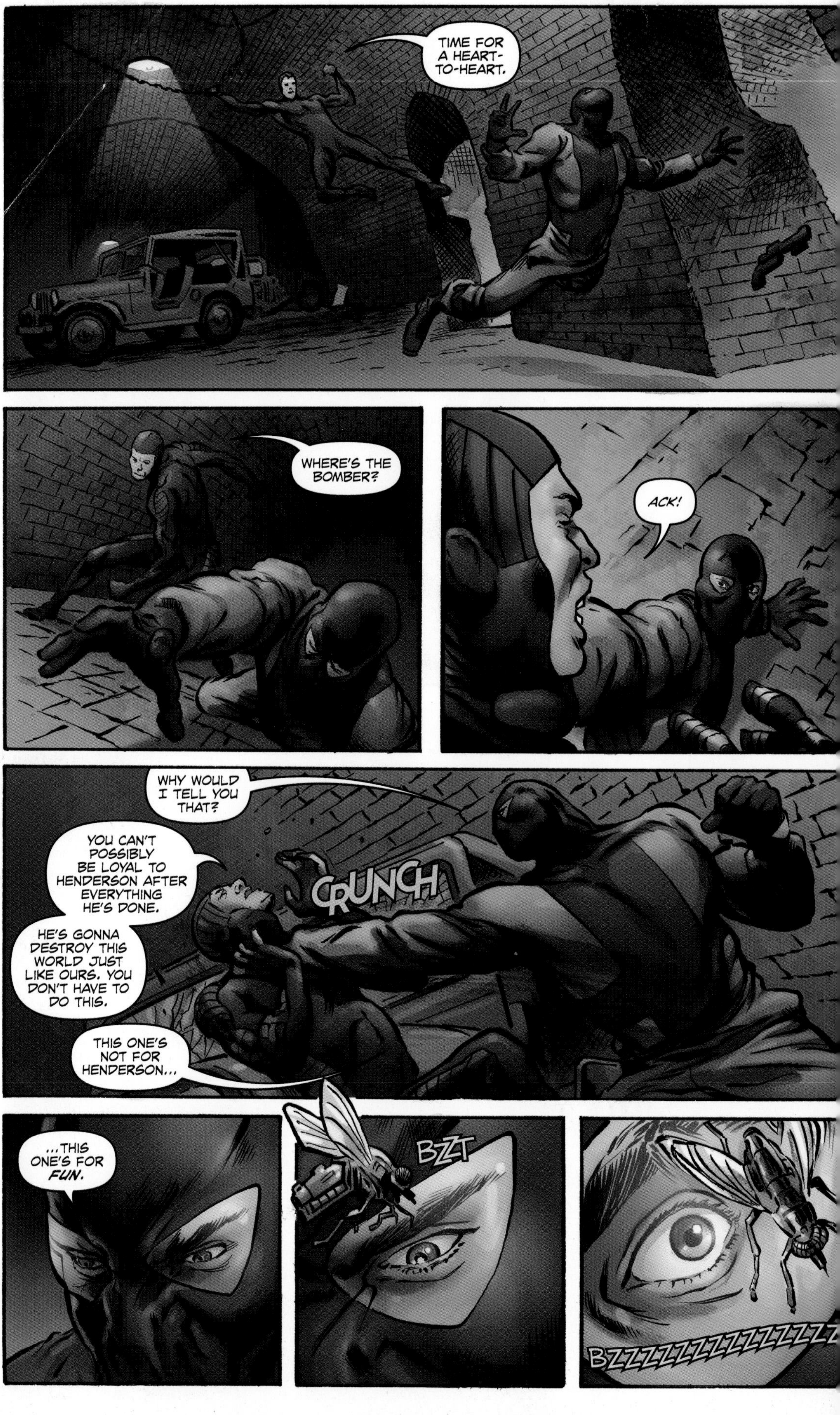
TIME FOR A HEART-TO-HEART.
WHERE'S THE BOMBER?
ACK!
WHY WOULD I TELL YOU THAT?
YOU CAN'T POSSIBLY BE LOYAL TO HENDERSON AFTER EVERYTHING HE'S DONE.
CRUNCH
HE'S GONNA DESTROY THIS WORLD JUST LIKE OURS. YOU DON'T HAVE TO DO THIS.
THIS ONE'S NOT FOR HENDERSON...
...THIS ONE'S FOR *FUN*.
BZZT
BZZZZZZZZZZZZZZZZZZZ

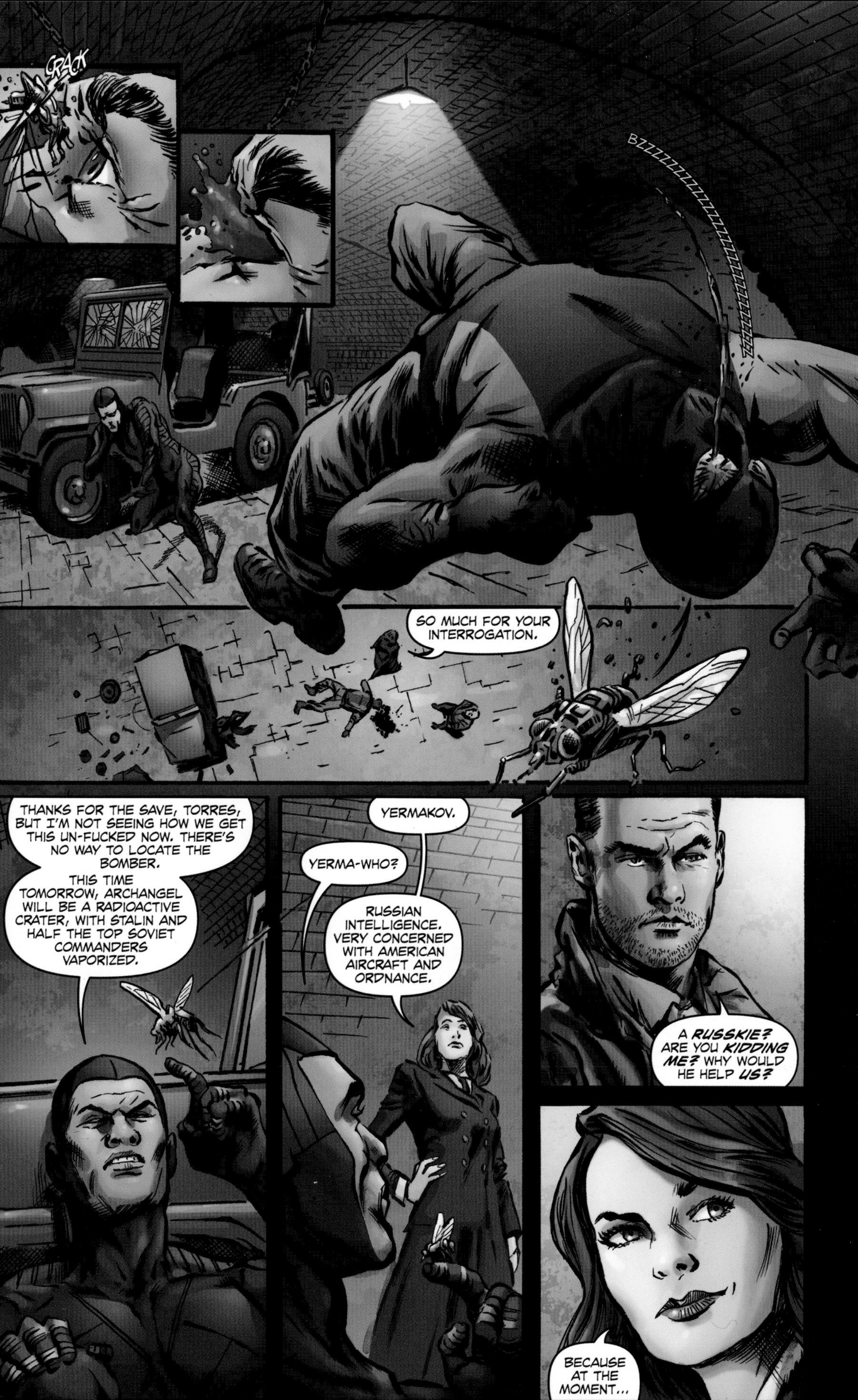
CRACK
BZZZZZZZZZZZZZZZZZZZZZZZZZ
SO MUCH FOR YOUR INTERROGATION.
THANKS FOR THE SAVE, TORRES, BUT I'M NOT SEEING HOW WE GET THIS UN-FUCKED NOW. THERE'S NO WAY TO LOCATE THE BOMBER.
THIS TIME TOMORROW, ARCHANGEL WILL BE A RADIOACTIVE CRATER, WITH STALIN AND HALF THE TOP SOVIET COMMANDERS VAPORIZED.
YERMAKOV.
YERMA-WHO?
RUSSIAN INTELLIGENCE. VERY CONCERNED WITH AMERICAN AIRCRAFT AND ORDNANCE.
A RUSSKIE? ARE YOU KIDDING ME? WHY WOULD HE HELP US?
BECAUSE AT THE MOMENT...

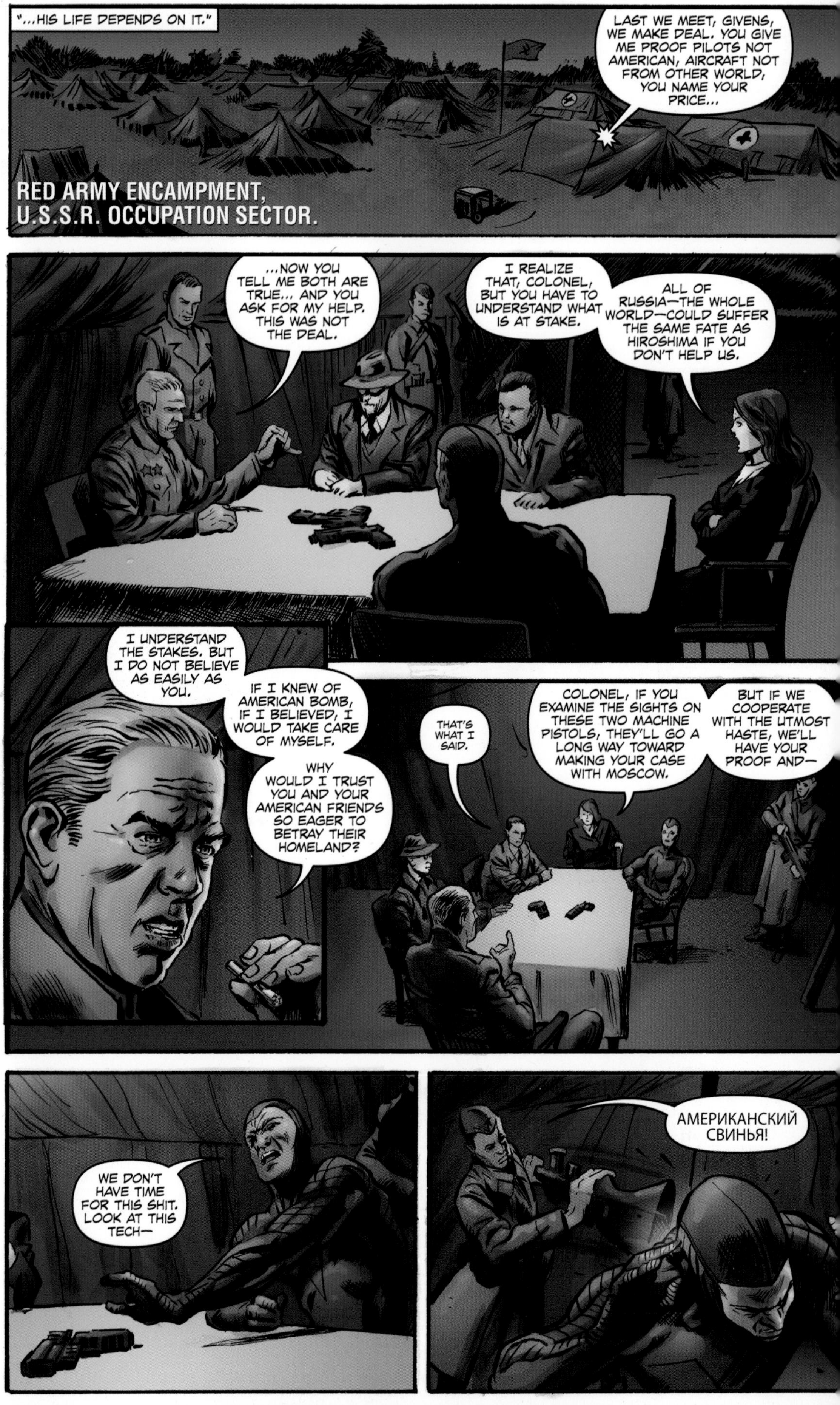
"...HIS LIFE DEPENDS ON IT."
LAST WE MEET, GIVENS, WE MAKE DEAL. YOU GIVE ME PROOF PILOTS NOT AMERICAN, AIRCRAFT NOT FROM OTHER WORLD, YOU NAME YOUR PRICE...
RED ARMY ENCAMPMENT, U.S.S.R. OCCUPATION SECTOR.
...NOW YOU TELL ME BOTH ARE TRUE... AND YOU ASK FOR MY HELP. THIS WAS NOT THE DEAL.
I REALIZE THAT, COLONEL, BUT YOU HAVE TO UNDERSTAND WHAT IS AT STAKE.
ALL OF RUSSIA—THE WHOLE WORLD—COULD SUFFER THE SAME FATE AS HIROSHIMA IF YOU DON'T HELP US.
I UNDERSTAND THE STAKES. BUT I DO NOT BELIEVE AS EASILY AS YOU.
IF I KNEW OF AMERICAN BOMB, IF I BELIEVED, I WOULD TAKE CARE OF MYSELF.
WHY WOULD I TRUST YOU AND YOUR AMERICAN FRIENDS SO EAGER TO BETRAY THEIR HOMELAND?
THAT'S WHAT I SAID.
COLONEL, IF YOU EXAMINE THE SIGHTS ON THESE TWO MACHINE PISTOLS, THEY'LL GO A LONG WAY TOWARD MAKING YOUR CASE WITH MOSCOW.
BUT IF WE COOPERATE WITH THE UTMOST HASTE, WE'LL HAVE YOUR PROOF AND—
WE DON'T HAVE TIME FOR THIS SHIT. LOOK AT THIS TECH—
АМЕРИКАНСКИЙ СВИНЬЯ!

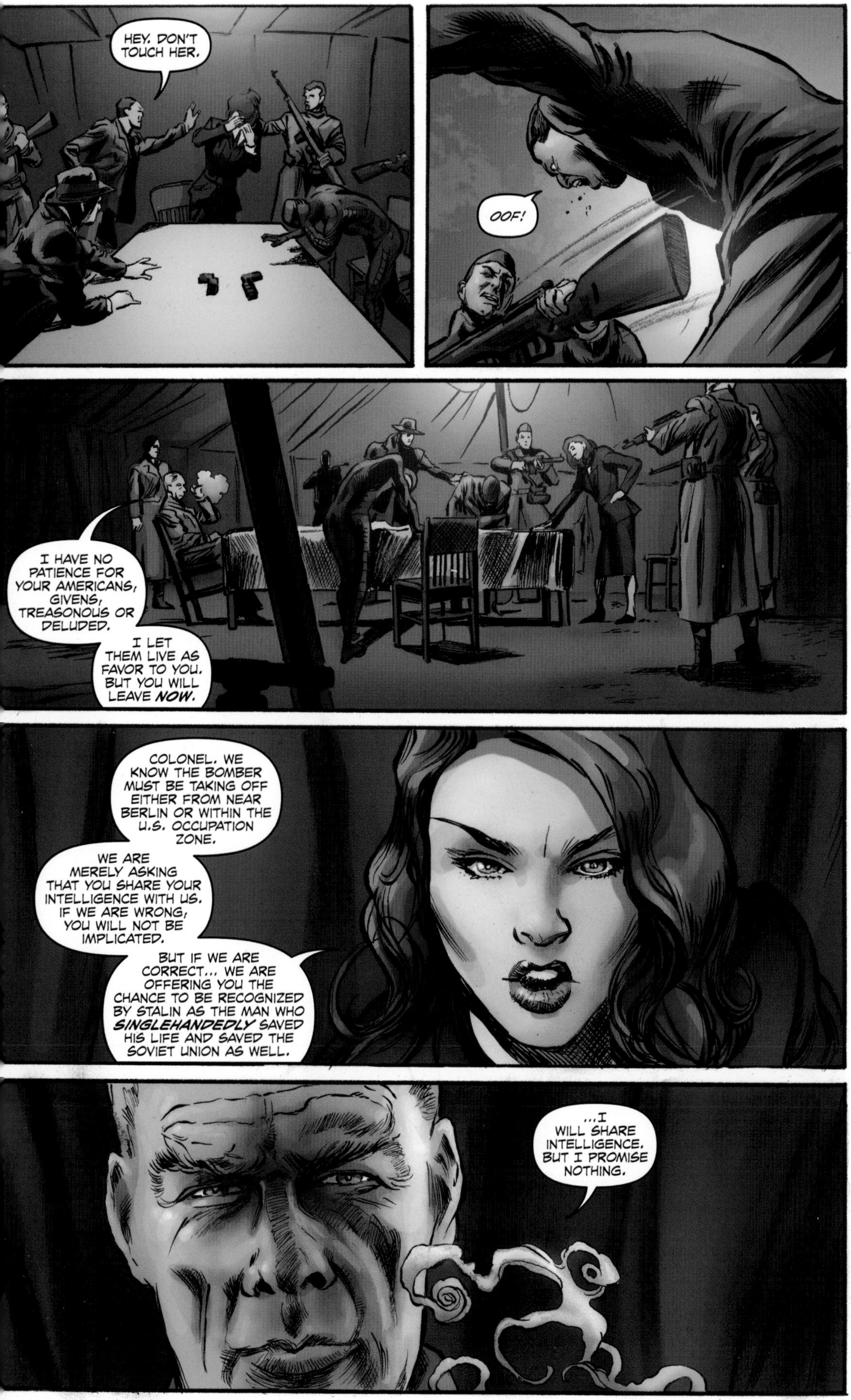

HEY. DON'T TOUCH HER.
OOF!
I HAVE NO PATIENCE FOR YOUR AMERICANS, GIVENS, TREASONOUS OR DELUDED.
I LET THEM LIVE AS FAVOR TO YOU. BUT YOU WILL LEAVE *NOW*.
COLONEL. WE KNOW THE BOMBER MUST BE TAKING OFF EITHER FROM NEAR BERLIN OR WITHIN THE U.S. OCCUPATION ZONE.
WE ARE MERELY ASKING THAT YOU SHARE YOUR INTELLIGENCE WITH US. IF WE ARE WRONG, YOU WILL NOT BE IMPLICATED.
BUT IF WE ARE CORRECT... WE ARE OFFERING YOU THE CHANCE TO BE RECOGNIZED BY STALIN AS THE MAN WHO *SINGLEHANDEDLY* SAVED HIS LIFE AND SAVED THE SOVIET UNION AS WELL.
...I WILL SHARE INTELLIGENCE. BUT I PROMISE NOTHING.

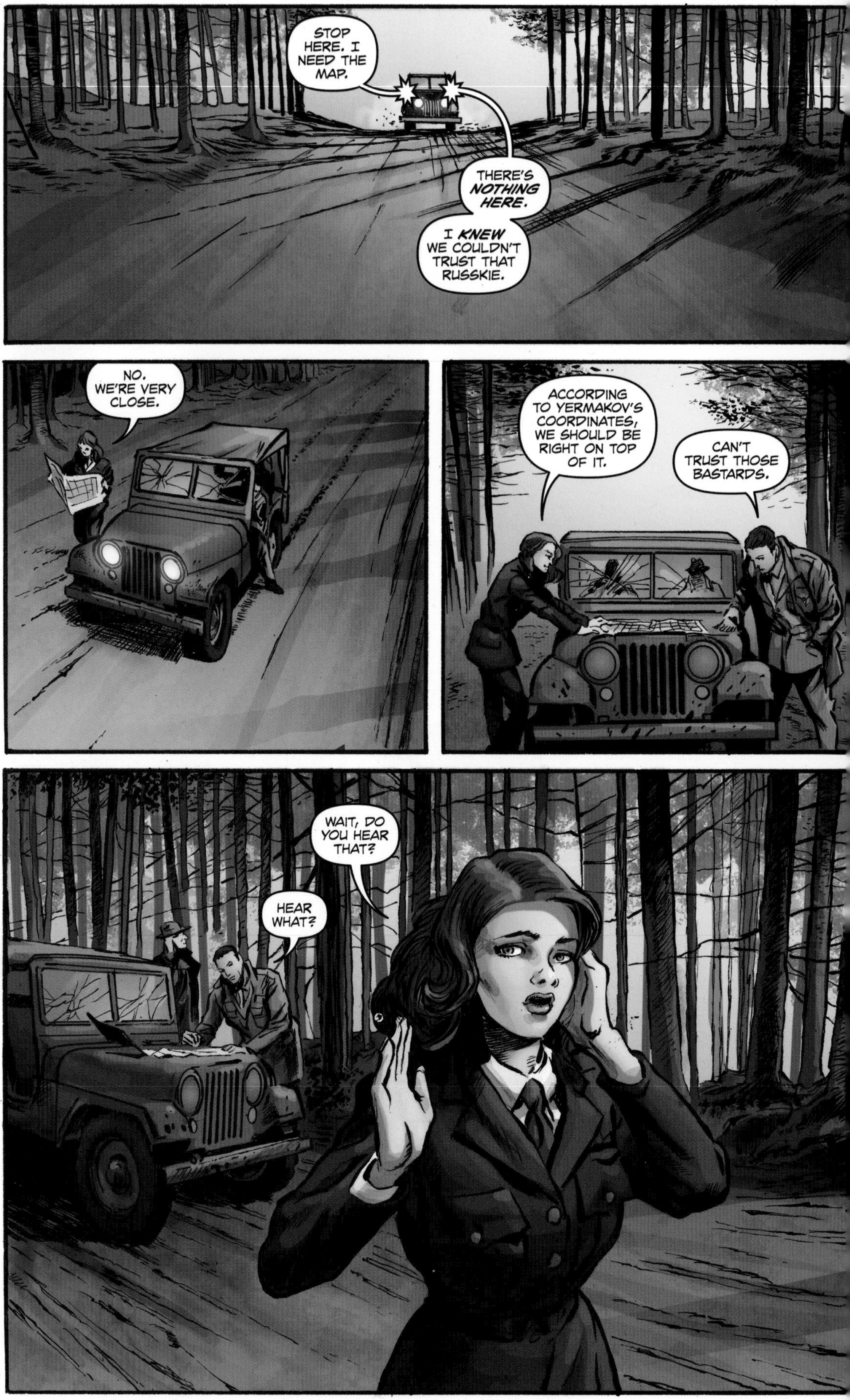
STOP HERE. I NEED THE MAP.
THERE'S *NOTHING HERE*.
I *KNEW* WE COULDN'T TRUST THAT RUSSKIE.
NO. WE'RE VERY CLOSE.
ACCORDING TO YERMAKOV'S COORDINATES, WE SHOULD BE RIGHT ON TOP OF IT.
CAN'T TRUST THOSE BASTARDS.
WAIT, DO YOU HEAR THAT?
HEAR WHAT?

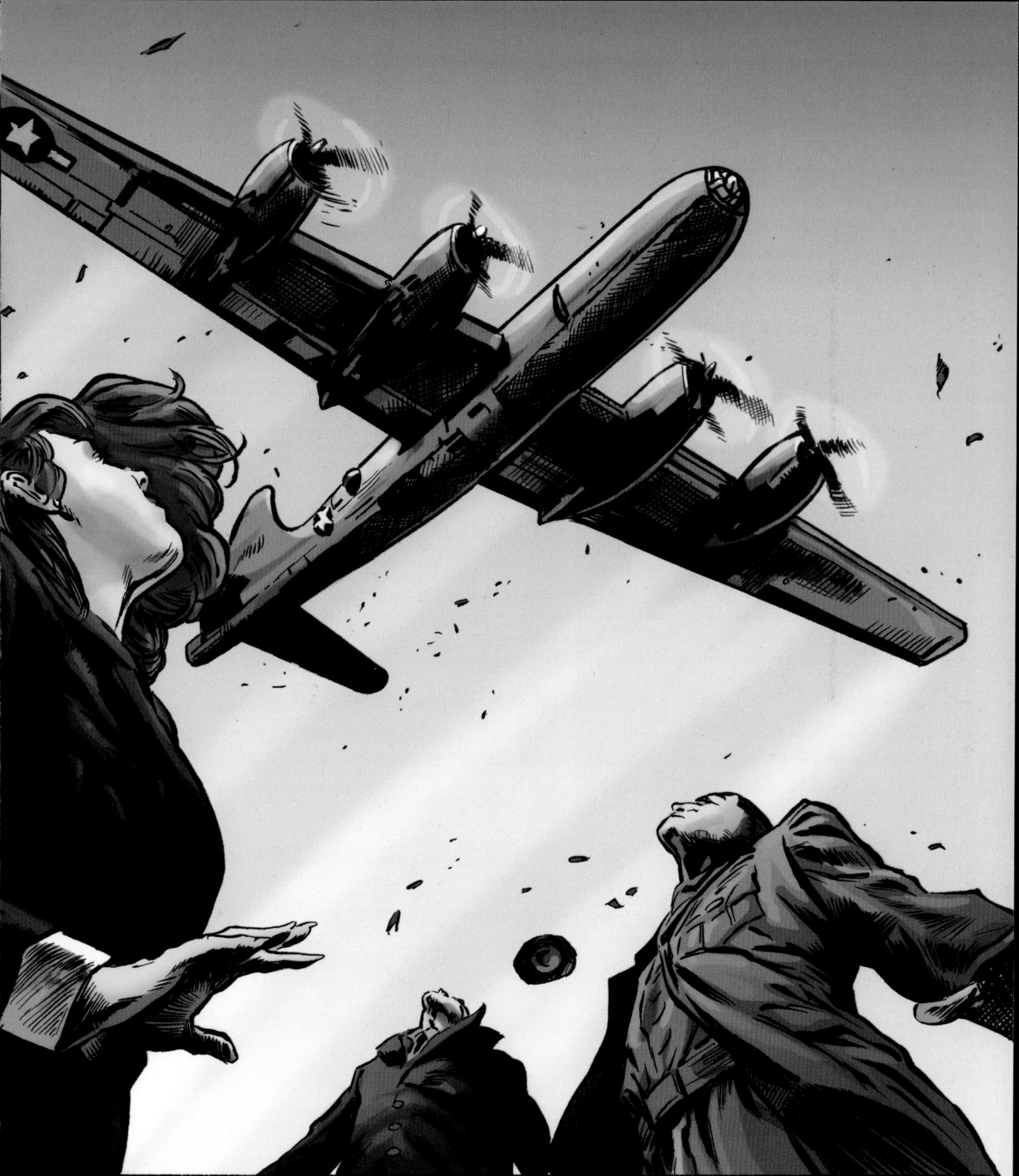

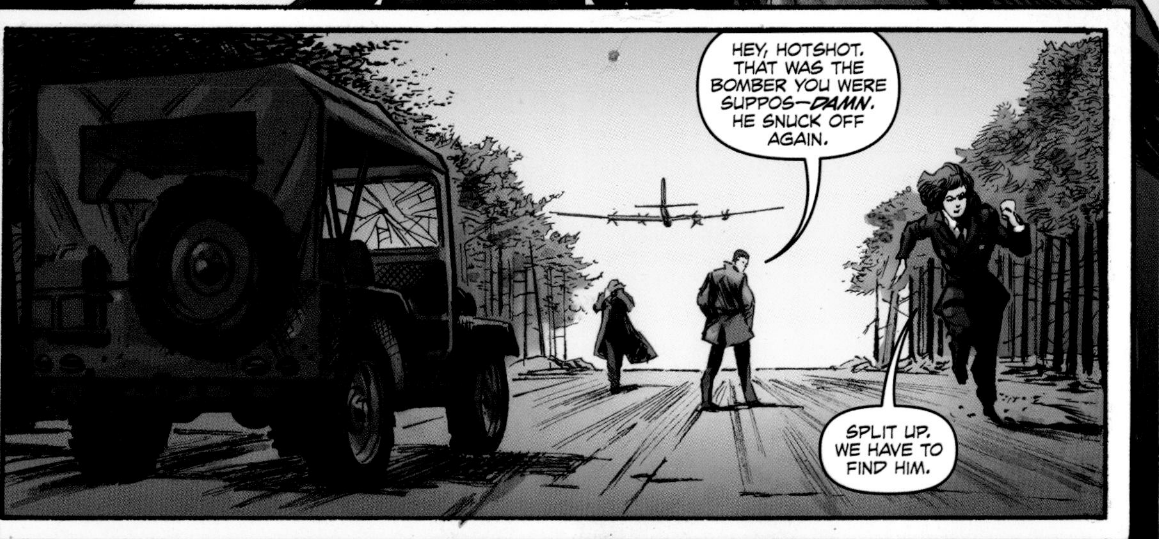

HEY, HOTSHOT. THAT WAS THE BOMBER YOU WERE SUPPOS—*DAMN*. HE SNUCK OFF AGAIN.
SPLIT UP. WE HAVE TO FIND HIM.

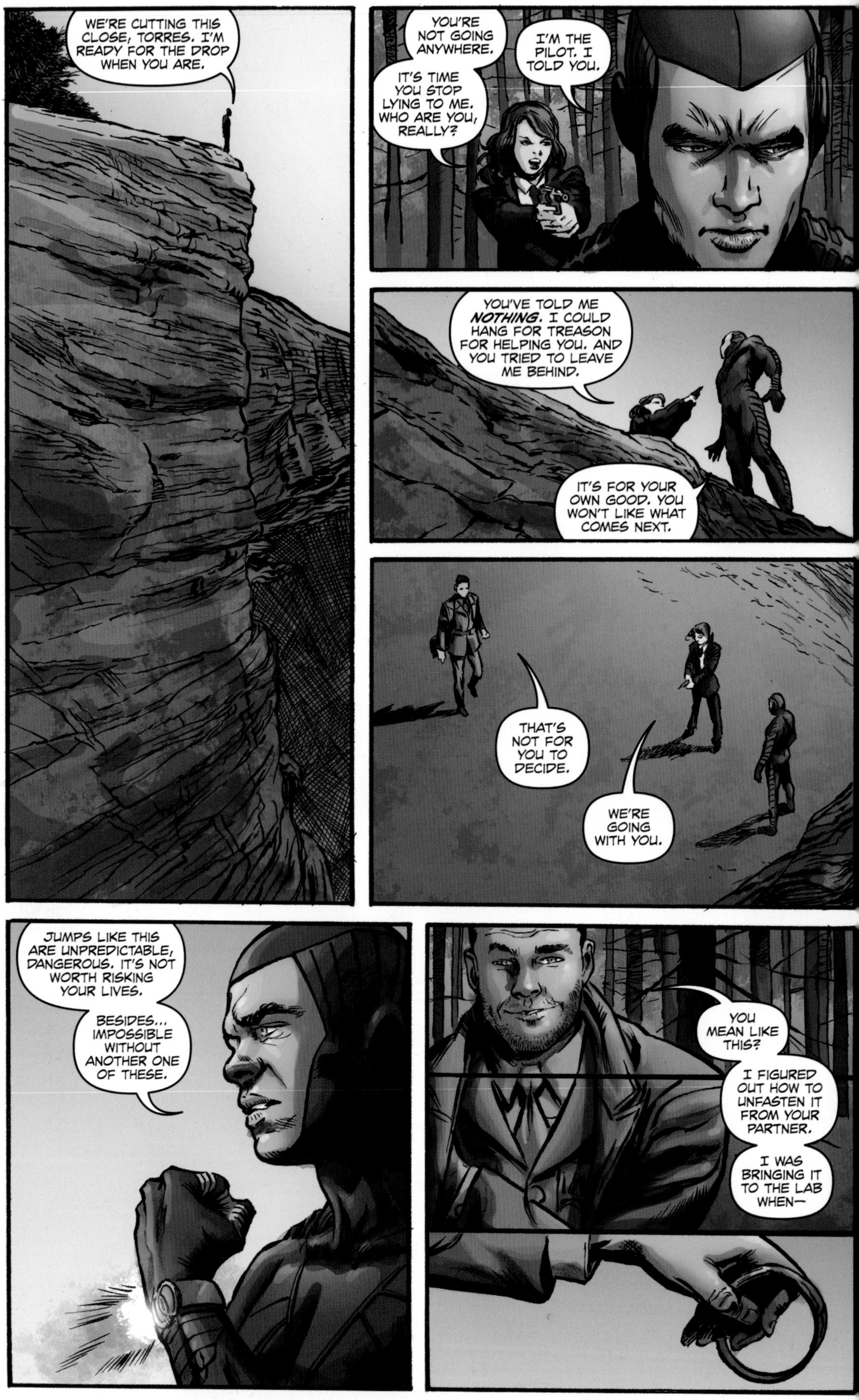
WE'RE CUTTING THIS CLOSE, TORRES. I'M READY FOR THE DROP WHEN YOU ARE.
YOU'RE NOT GOING ANYWHERE.
I'M THE PILOT. I TOLD YOU.
IT'S TIME YOU STOP LYING TO ME. WHO ARE YOU, REALLY?
YOU'VE TOLD ME *NOTHING*. I COULD HANG FOR TREASON FOR HELPING YOU. AND YOU TRIED TO LEAVE ME BEHIND.
IT'S FOR YOUR OWN GOOD. YOU WON'T LIKE WHAT COMES NEXT.
THAT'S NOT FOR YOU TO DECIDE.
WE'RE GOING WITH YOU.
JUMPS LIKE THIS ARE UNPREDICTABLE, DANGEROUS. IT'S NOT WORTH RISKING YOUR LIVES.
BESIDES... IMPOSSIBLE WITHOUT ANOTHER ONE OF THESE.
YOU MEAN LIKE THIS?
I FIGURED OUT HOW TO UNFASTEN IT FROM YOUR PARTNER.
I WAS BRINGING IT TO THE LAB WHEN—

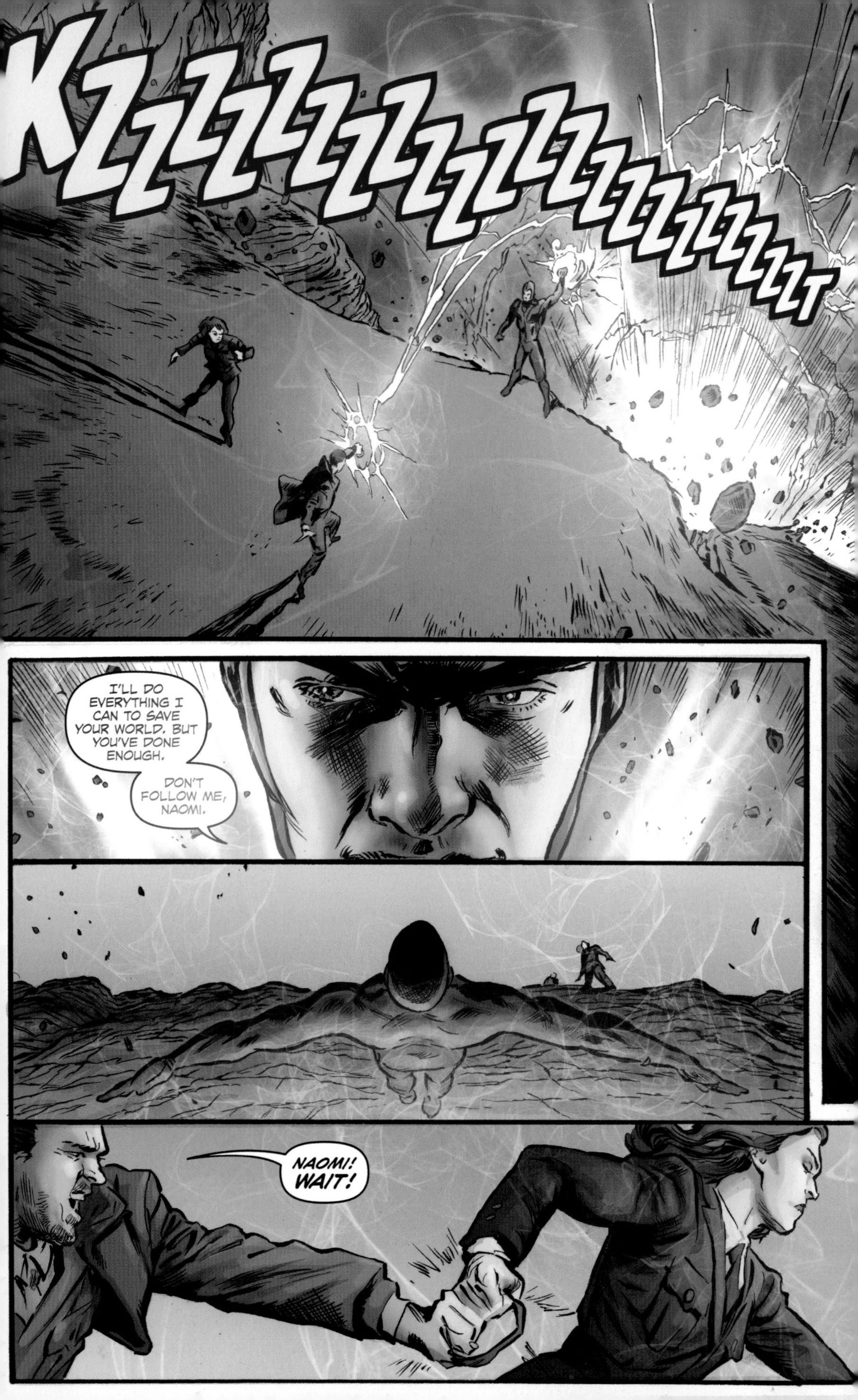
KZZZZZZZZZZZZZZZZZZZZT
I'LL DO EVERYTHING I CAN TO SAVE YOUR WORLD. BUT YOU'VE DONE ENOUGH.
DON'T FOLLOW ME, NAOMI.
NAOMI! WAIT!

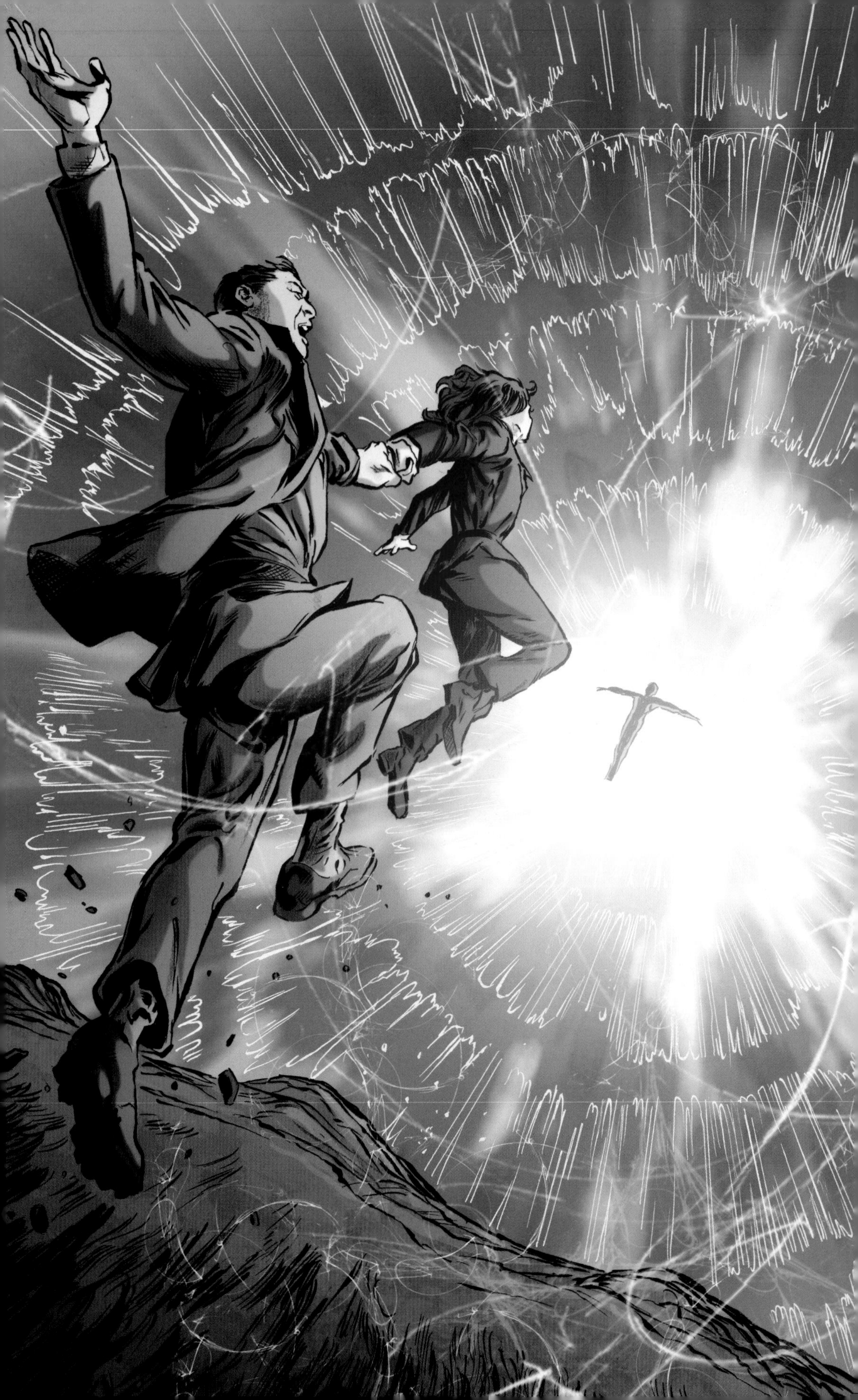

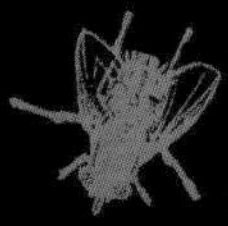

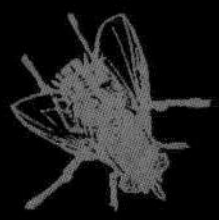

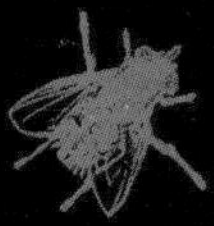

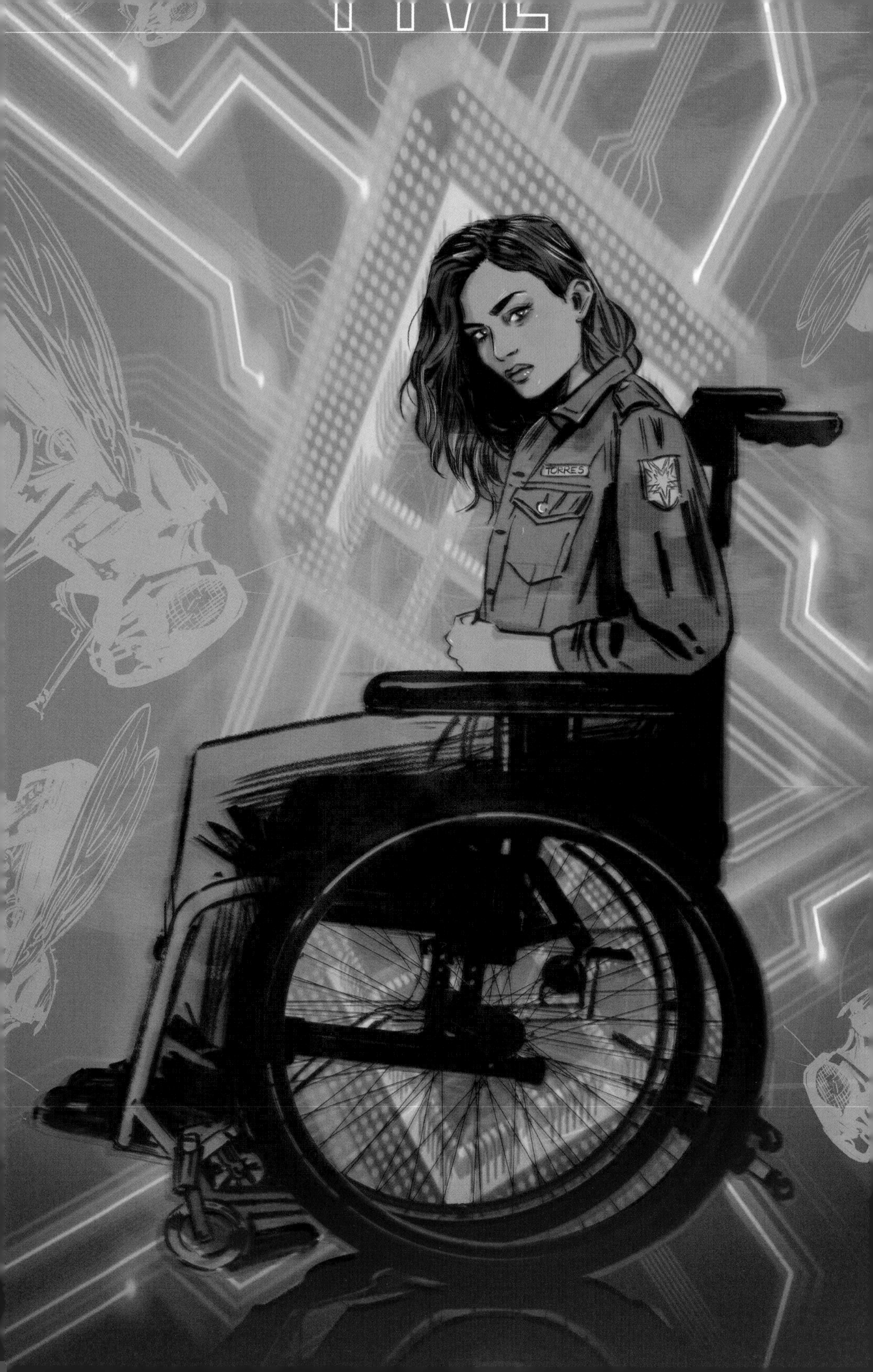
TORRES

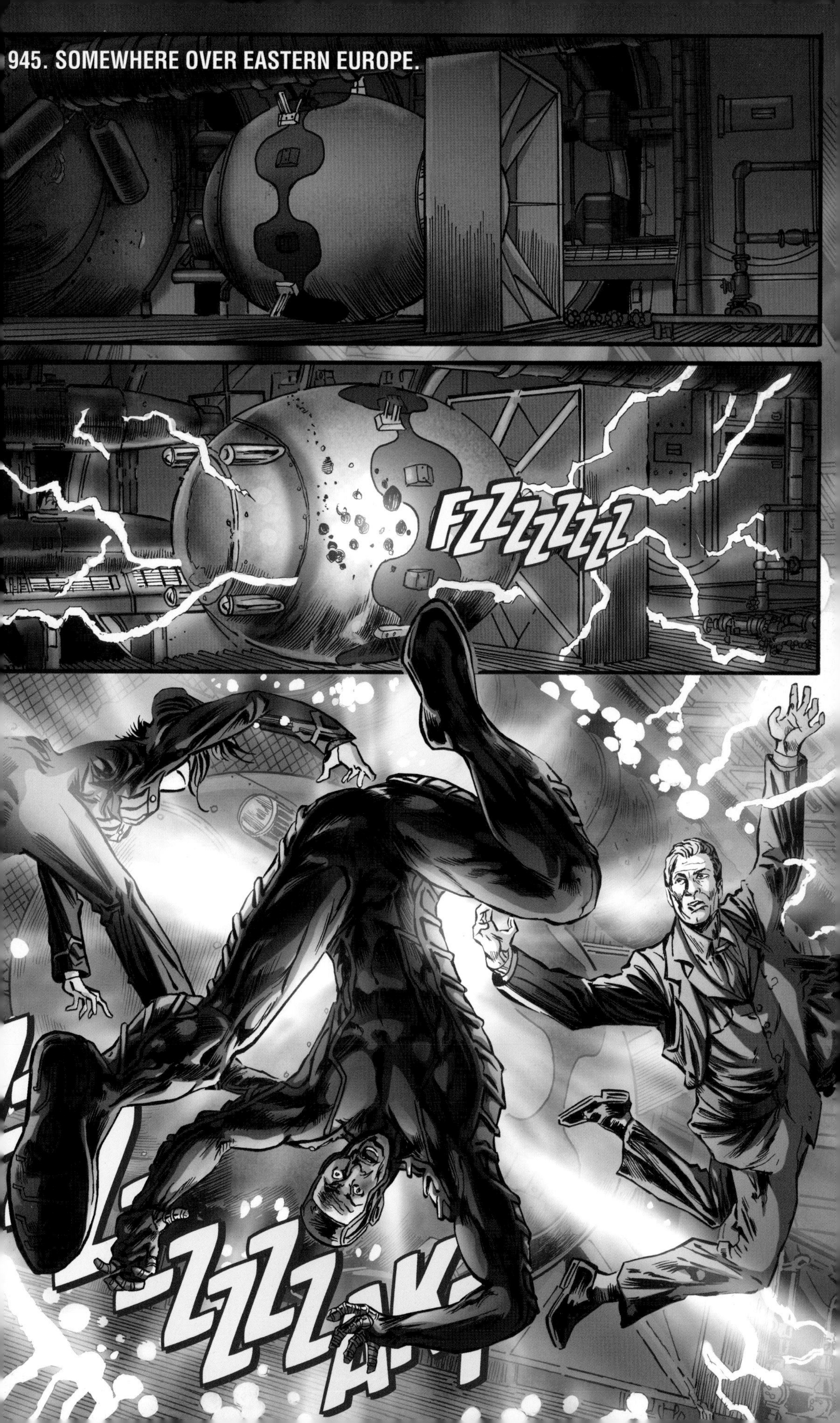
945. SOMEWHERE OVER EASTERN EUROPE.
FZZZZZZZZ

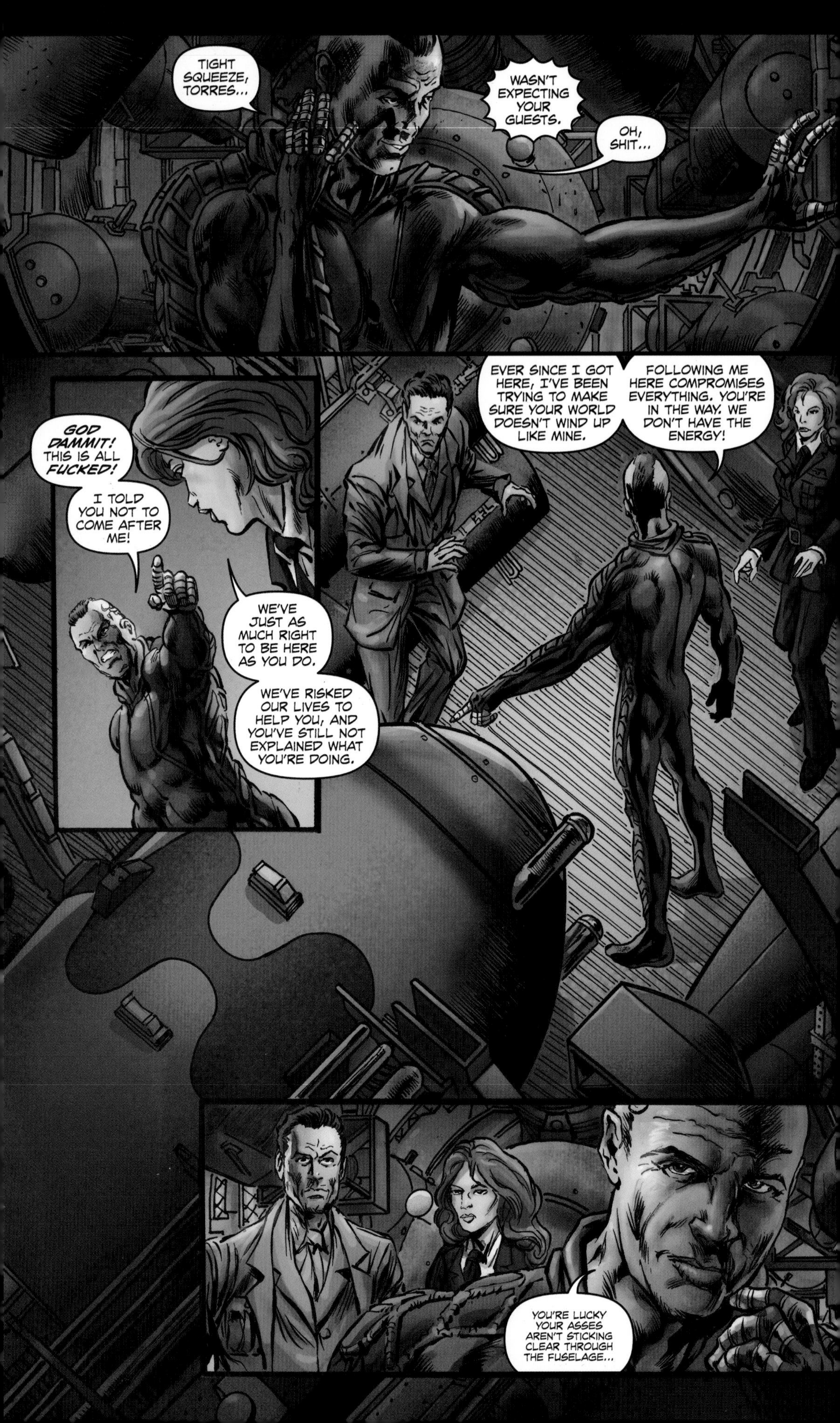
TIGHT SQUEEZE, TORRES...
WASN'T EXPECTING YOUR GUESTS.
OH, SHIT...
GOD DAMMIT! THIS IS ALL FUCKED!
I TOLD YOU NOT TO COME AFTER ME!
WE'VE JUST AS MUCH RIGHT TO BE HERE AS YOU DO.
WE'VE RISKED OUR LIVES TO HELP YOU, AND YOU'VE STILL NOT EXPLAINED WHAT YOU'RE DOING.
EVER SINCE I GOT HERE, I'VE BEEN TRYING TO MAKE SURE YOUR WORLD DOESN'T WIND UP LIKE MINE.
FOLLOWING ME HERE COMPROMISES EVERYTHING. YOU'RE IN THE WAY. WE DON'T HAVE THE ENERGY!
YOU'RE LUCKY YOUR ASSES AREN'T STICKING CLEAR THROUGH THE FUSELAGE...

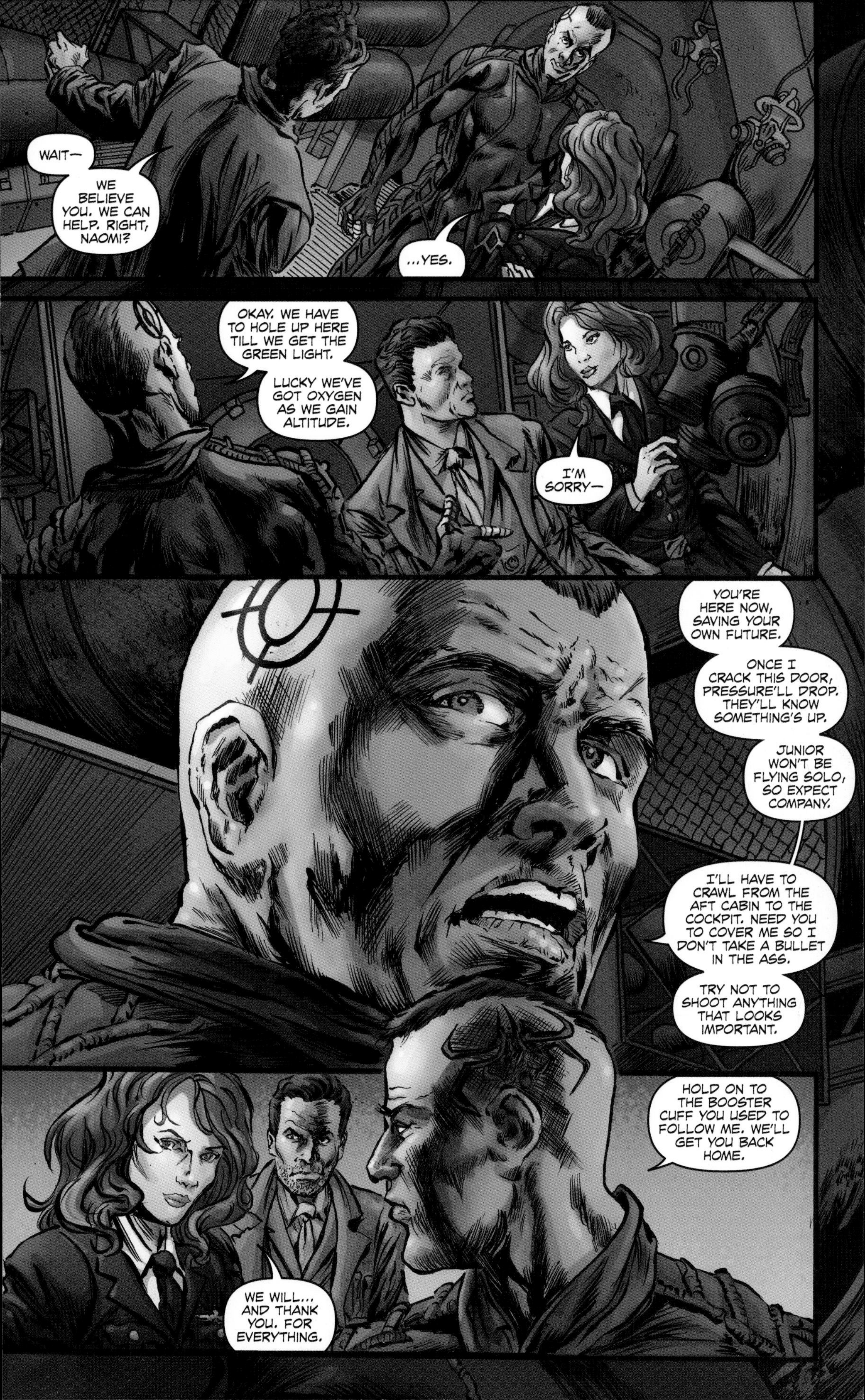
WAIT—
WE BELIEVE YOU. WE CAN HELP. RIGHT, NAOMI?
...YES.
OKAY. WE HAVE TO HOLE UP HERE TILL WE GET THE GREEN LIGHT.
LUCKY WE'VE GOT OXYGEN AS WE GAIN ALTITUDE.
I'M SORRY—
YOU'RE HERE NOW, SAVING YOUR OWN FUTURE.
ONCE I CRACK THIS DOOR, PRESSURE'LL DROP. THEY'LL KNOW SOMETHING'S UP.
JUNIOR WON'T BE FLYING SOLO, SO EXPECT COMPANY.
I'LL HAVE TO CRAWL FROM THE AFT CABIN TO THE COCKPIT. NEED YOU TO COVER ME SO I DON'T TAKE A BULLET IN THE ASS.
TRY NOT TO SHOOT ANYTHING THAT LOOKS IMPORTANT.
HOLD ON TO THE BOOSTER CUFF YOU USED TO FOLLOW ME. WE'LL GET YOU BACK HOME.
WE WILL... AND THANK YOU. FOR EVERYTHING.

2016. SNAKE MOUNTAIN, MONTANA. QUANTUM TRANSFER FACILITY.

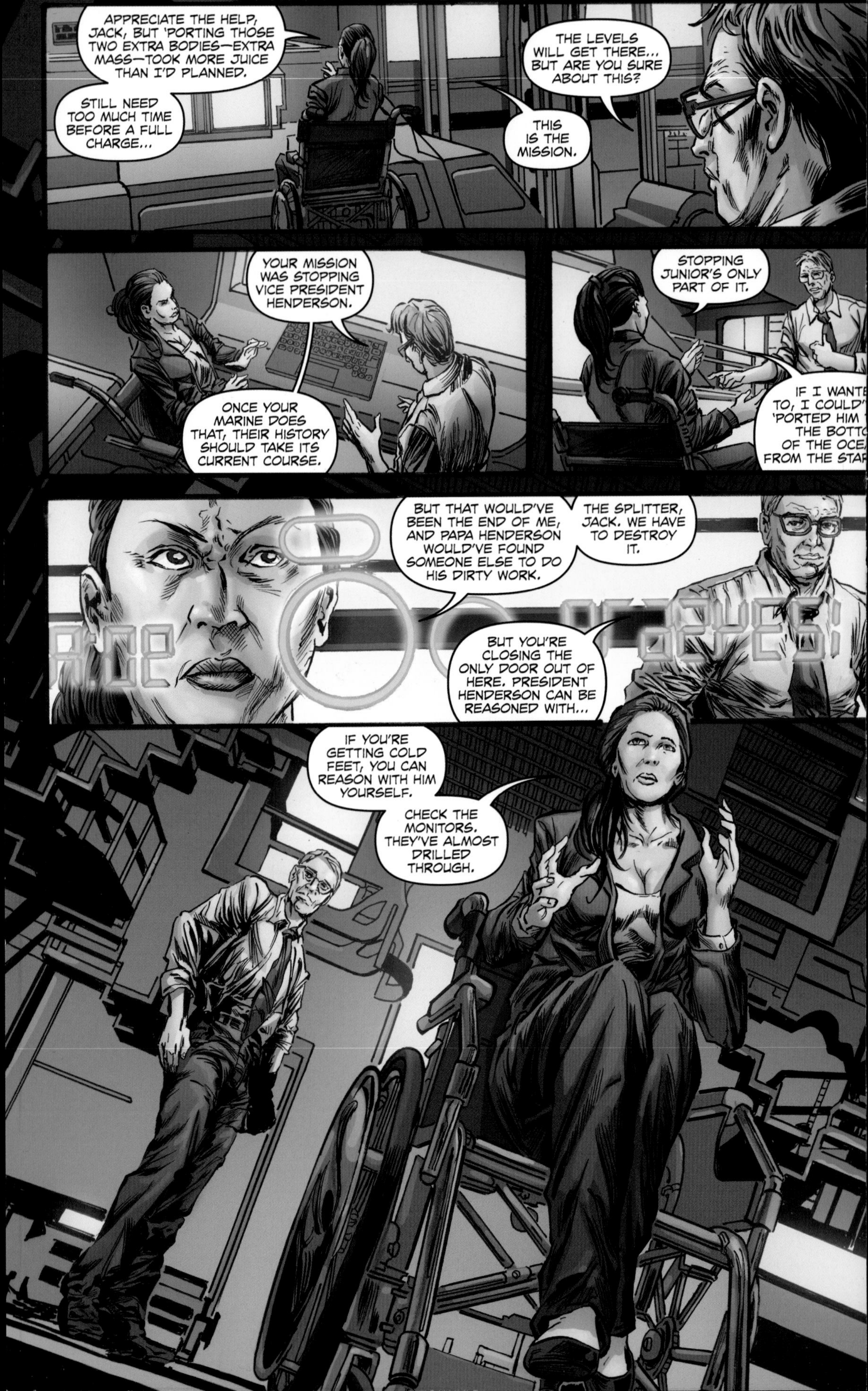
APPRECIATE THE HELP, JACK, BUT 'PORTING THOSE TWO EXTRA BODIES—EXTRA MASS—TOOK MORE JUICE THAN I'D PLANNED.
STILL NEED TOO MUCH TIME BEFORE A FULL CHARGE...
THE LEVELS WILL GET THERE... BUT ARE YOU SURE ABOUT THIS?
THIS IS THE MISSION.
YOUR MISSION WAS STOPPING VICE PRESIDENT HENDERSON.
ONCE YOUR MARINE DOES THAT, THEIR HISTORY SHOULD TAKE ITS CURRENT COURSE.
STOPPING JUNIOR'S ONLY PART OF IT.
IF I WANTE TO, I COULD' 'PORTED HIM THE BOTT OF THE OCE FROM THE STA
BUT THAT WOULD'VE BEEN THE END OF ME, AND PAPA HENDERSON WOULD'VE FOUND SOMEONE ELSE TO DO HIS DIRTY WORK.
THE SPLITTER, JACK. WE HAVE TO DESTROY IT.
BUT YOU'RE CLOSING THE ONLY DOOR OUT OF HERE. PRESIDENT HENDERSON CAN BE REASONED WITH...
IF YOU'RE GETTING COLD FEET, YOU CAN REASON WITH HIM YOURSELF.
CHECK THE MONITORS. THEY'VE ALMOST DRILLED THROUGH.

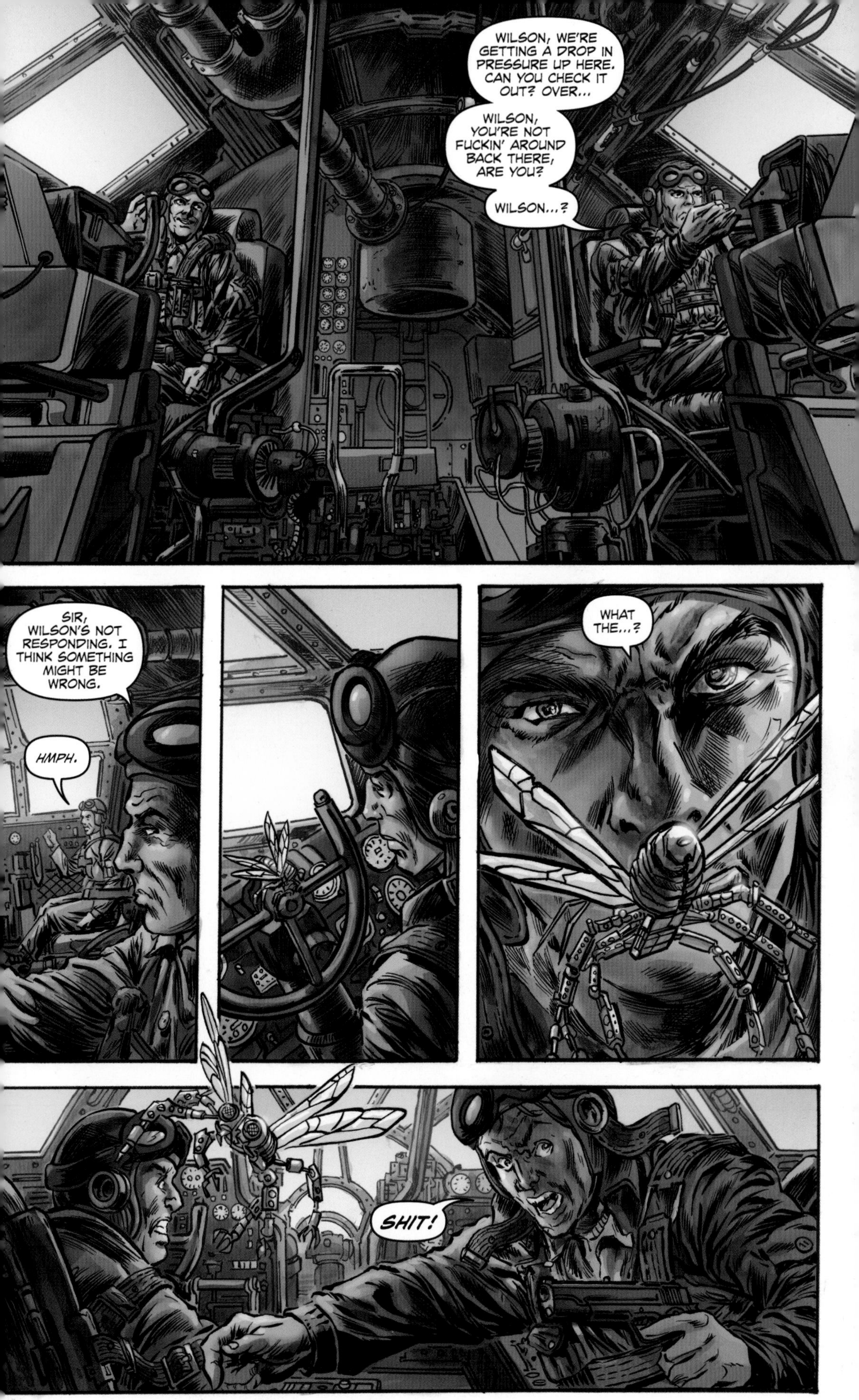
WILSON, WE'RE GETTING A DROP IN PRESSURE UP HERE. CAN YOU CHECK IT OUT? OVER...
WILSON, YOU'RE NOT FUCKIN' AROUND BACK THERE, ARE YOU?
WILSON...?
SIR, WILSON'S NOT RESPONDING. I THINK SOMETHING MIGHT BE WRONG.
HMPH.
WHAT THE...?
SHIT!

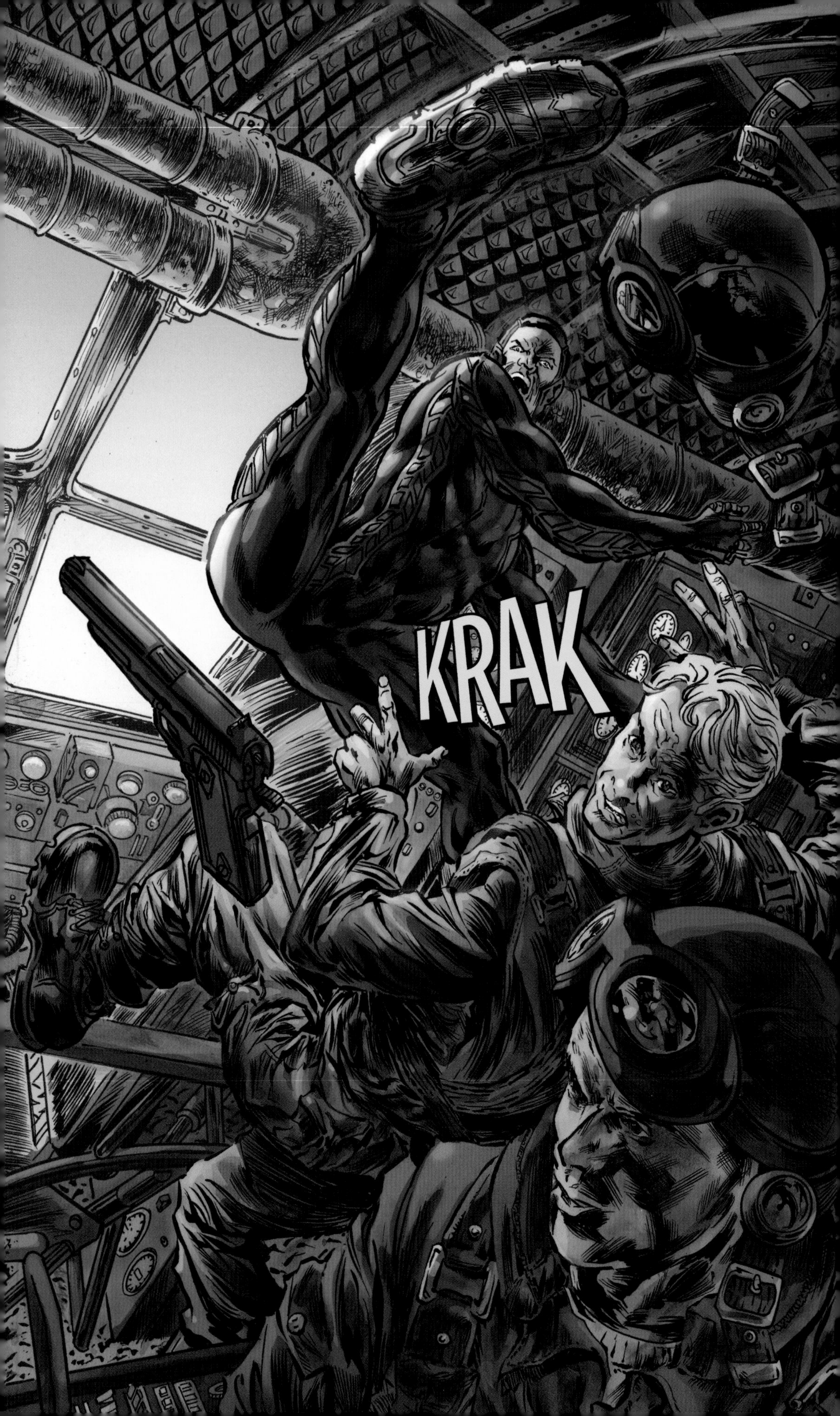
KRAK

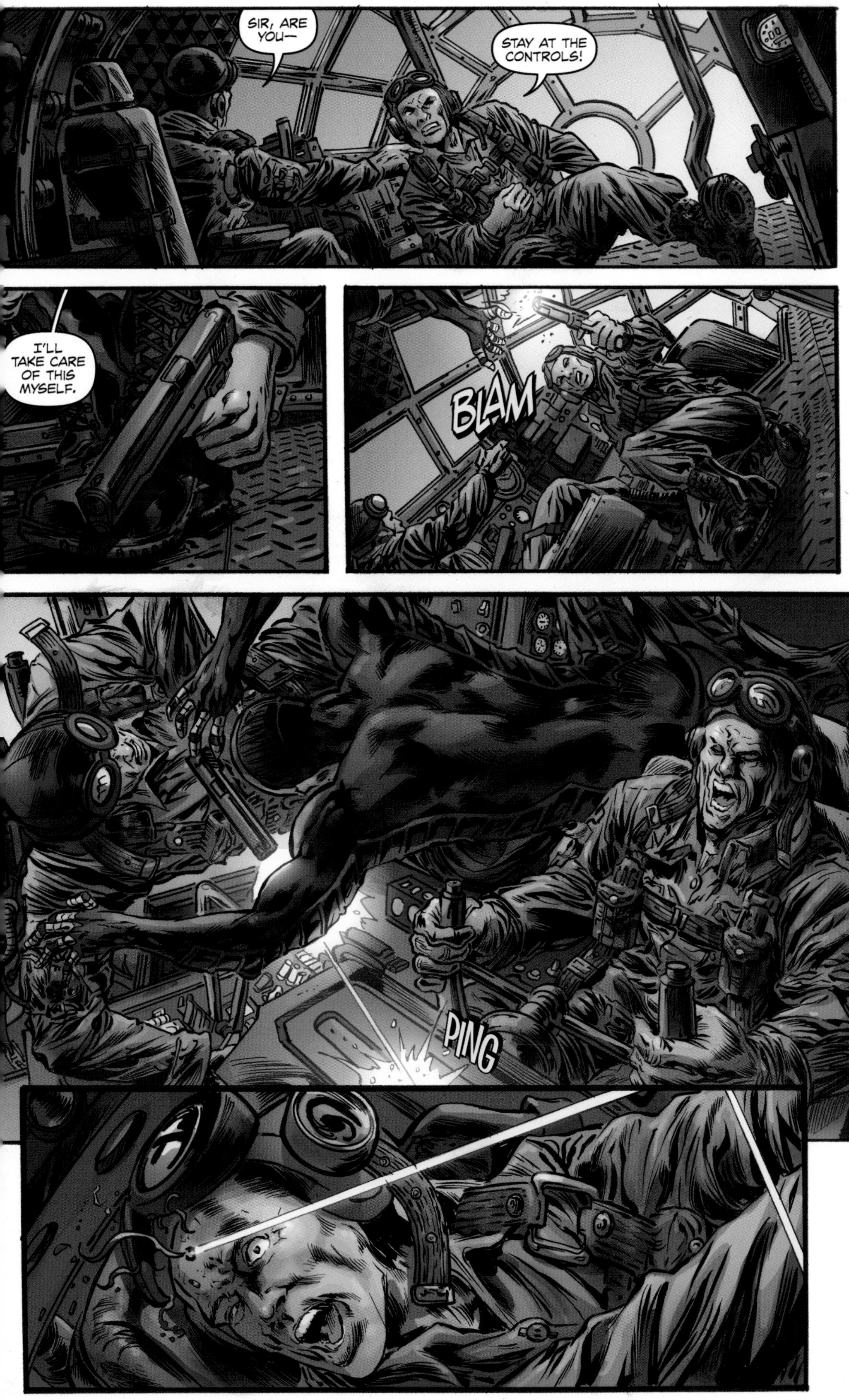
SIR, ARE YOU—
STAY AT THE CONTROLS!
I'LL TAKE CARE OF THIS MYSELF.
BLAM
PING

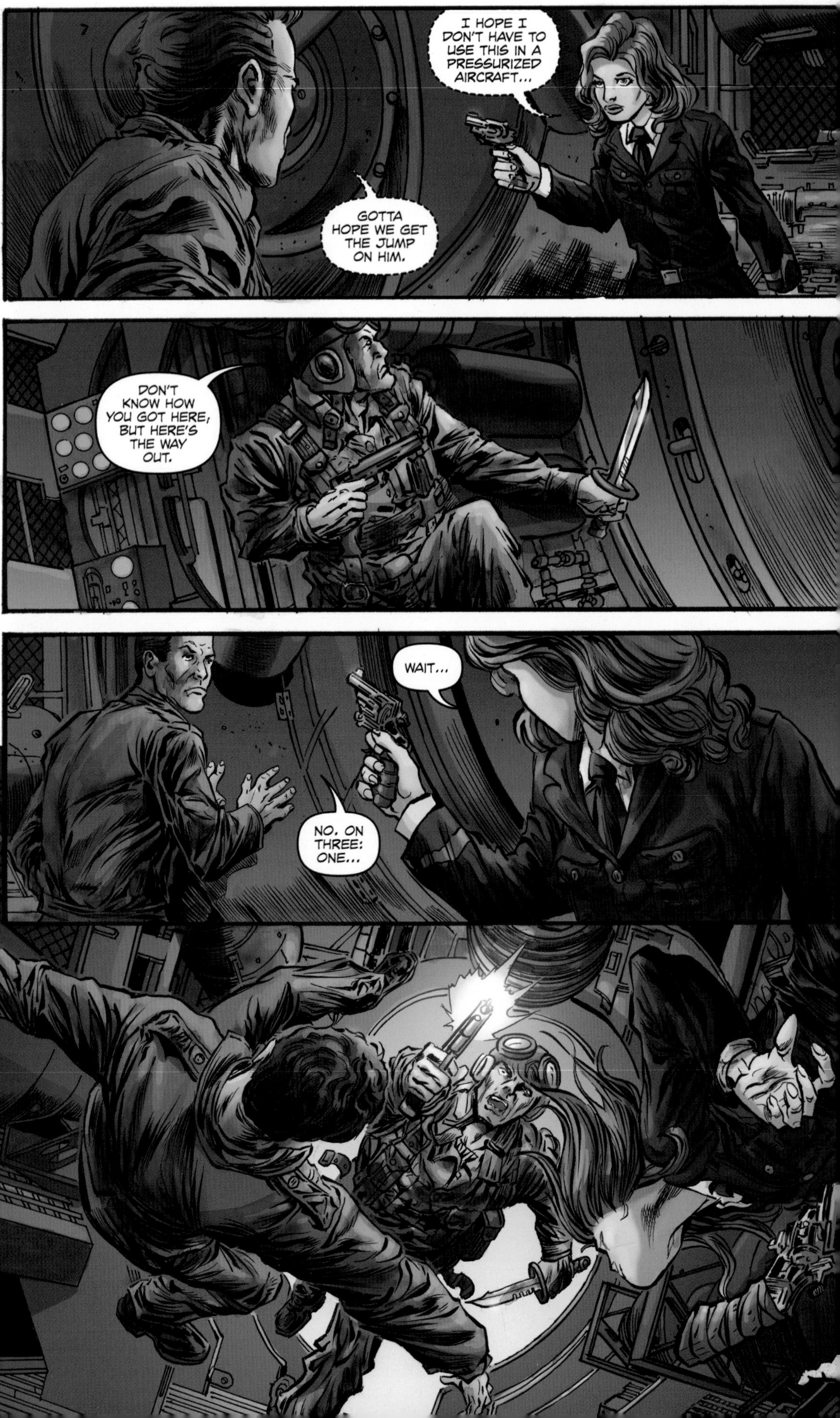
I HOPE I DON'T HAVE TO USE THIS IN A PRESSURIZED AIRCRAFT...
GOTTA HOPE WE GET THE JUMP ON HIM.
DON'T KNOW HOW YOU GOT HERE, BUT HERE'S THE WAY OUT.
WAIT...
NO. ON THREE: ONE...

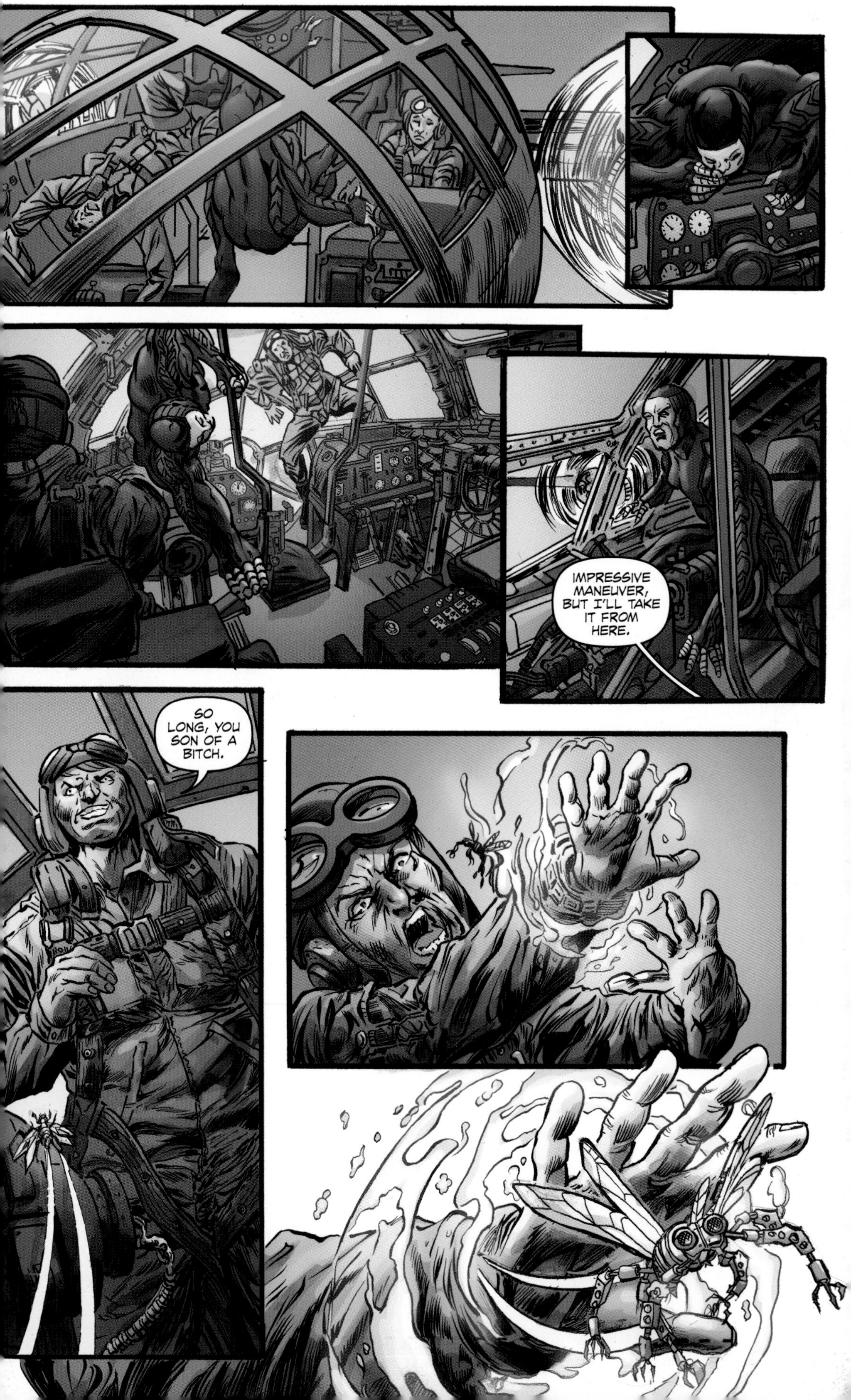
IMPRESSIVE MANEUVER, BUT I'LL TAKE IT FROM HERE.
SO LONG, YOU SON OF A BITCH.

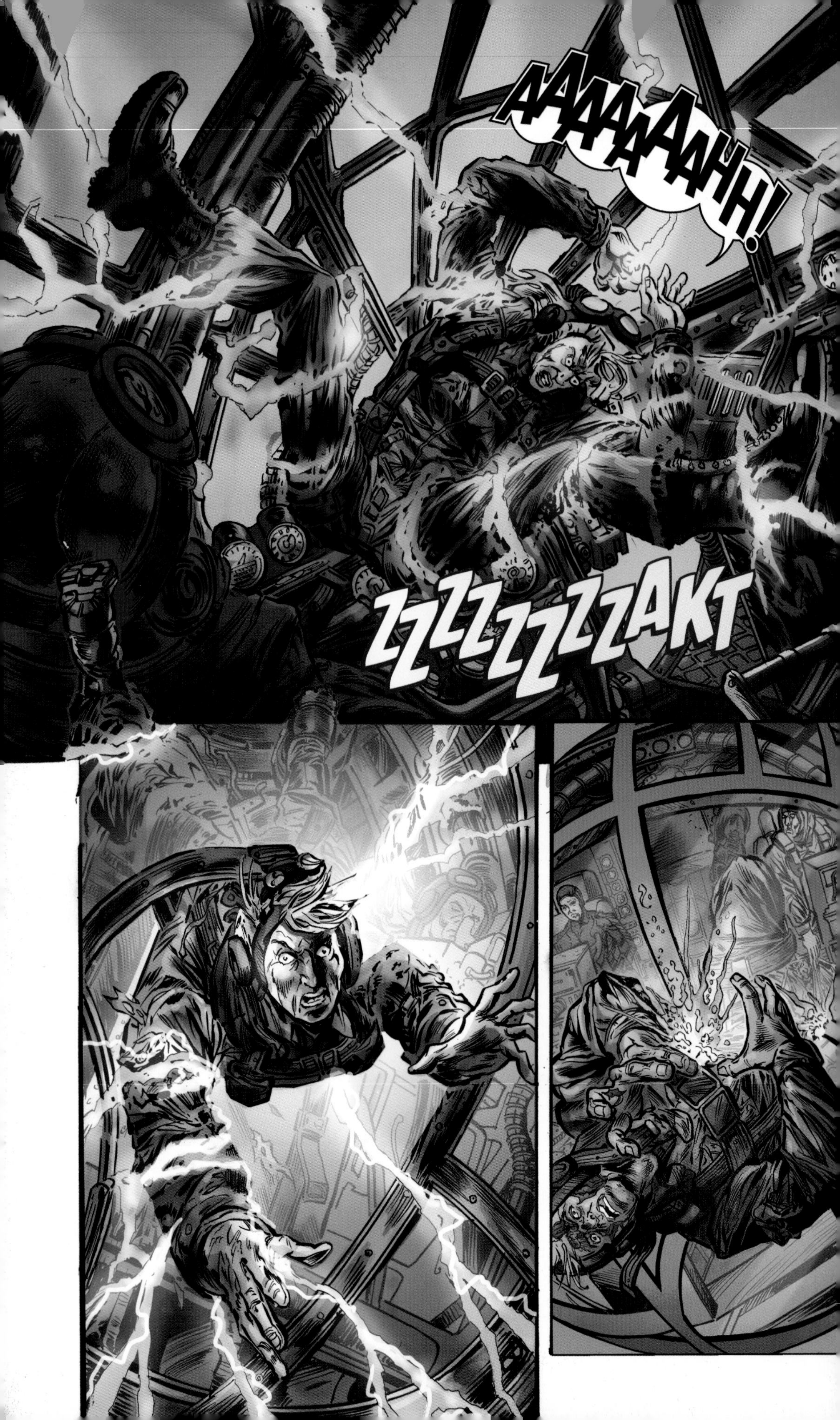
AAAAAAAHH!
ZZZZZZZZAKT

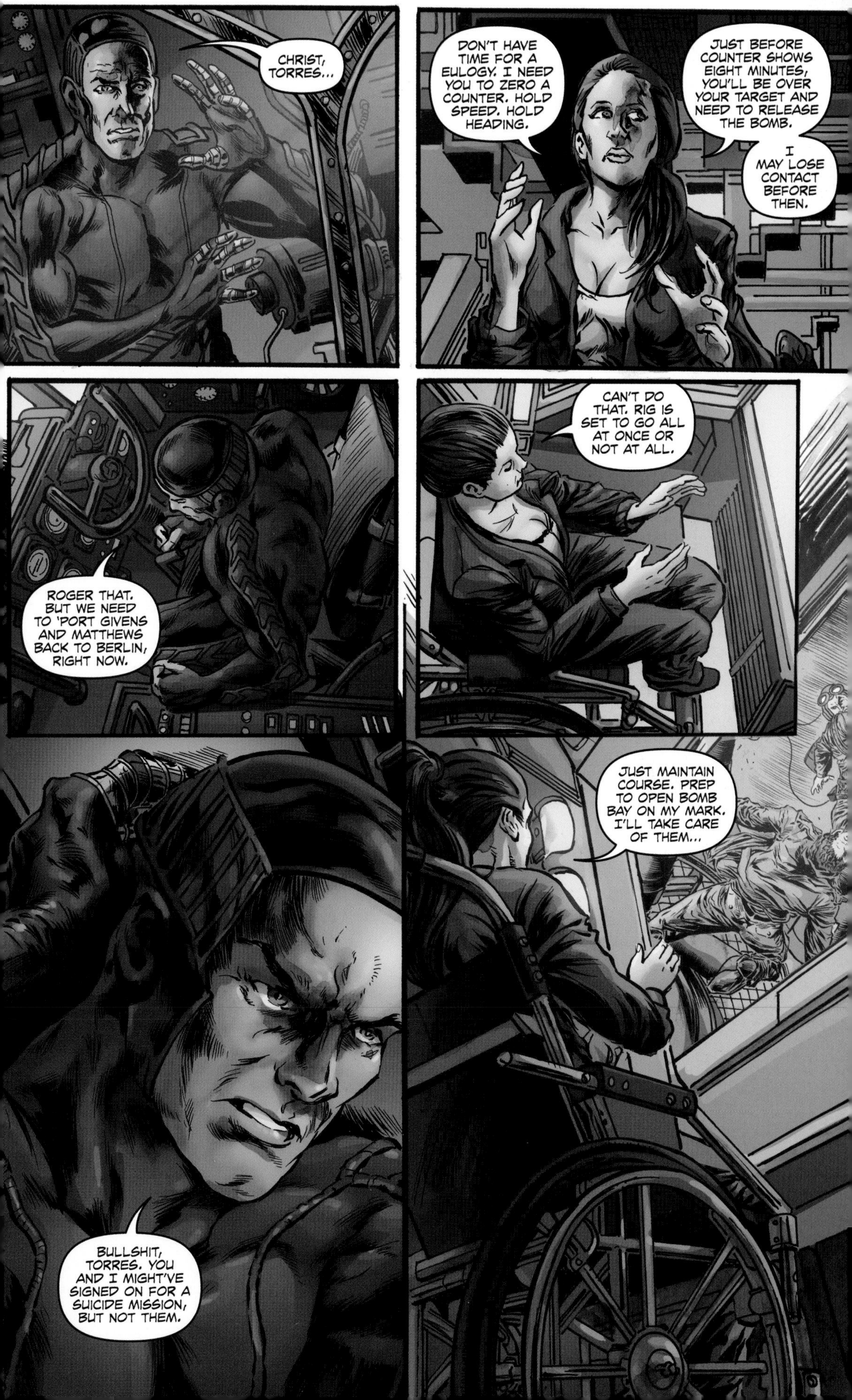
CHRIST, TORRES...
DON'T HAVE TIME FOR A EULOGY. I NEED YOU TO ZERO A COUNTER. HOLD SPEED. HOLD HEADING.
JUST BEFORE COUNTER SHOWS EIGHT MINUTES, YOU'LL BE OVER YOUR TARGET AND NEED TO RELEASE THE BOMB.
I MAY LOSE CONTACT BEFORE THEN.
ROGER THAT. BUT WE NEED TO 'PORT GIVENS AND MATTHEWS BACK TO BERLIN, RIGHT NOW.
CAN'T DO THAT. RIG IS SET TO GO ALL AT ONCE OR NOT AT ALL.
BULLSHIT, TORRES. YOU AND I MIGHT'VE SIGNED ON FOR A SUICIDE MISSION, BUT NOT THEM.
JUST MAINTAIN COURSE. PREP TO OPEN BOMB BAY ON MY MARK. I'LL TAKE CARE OF THEM...

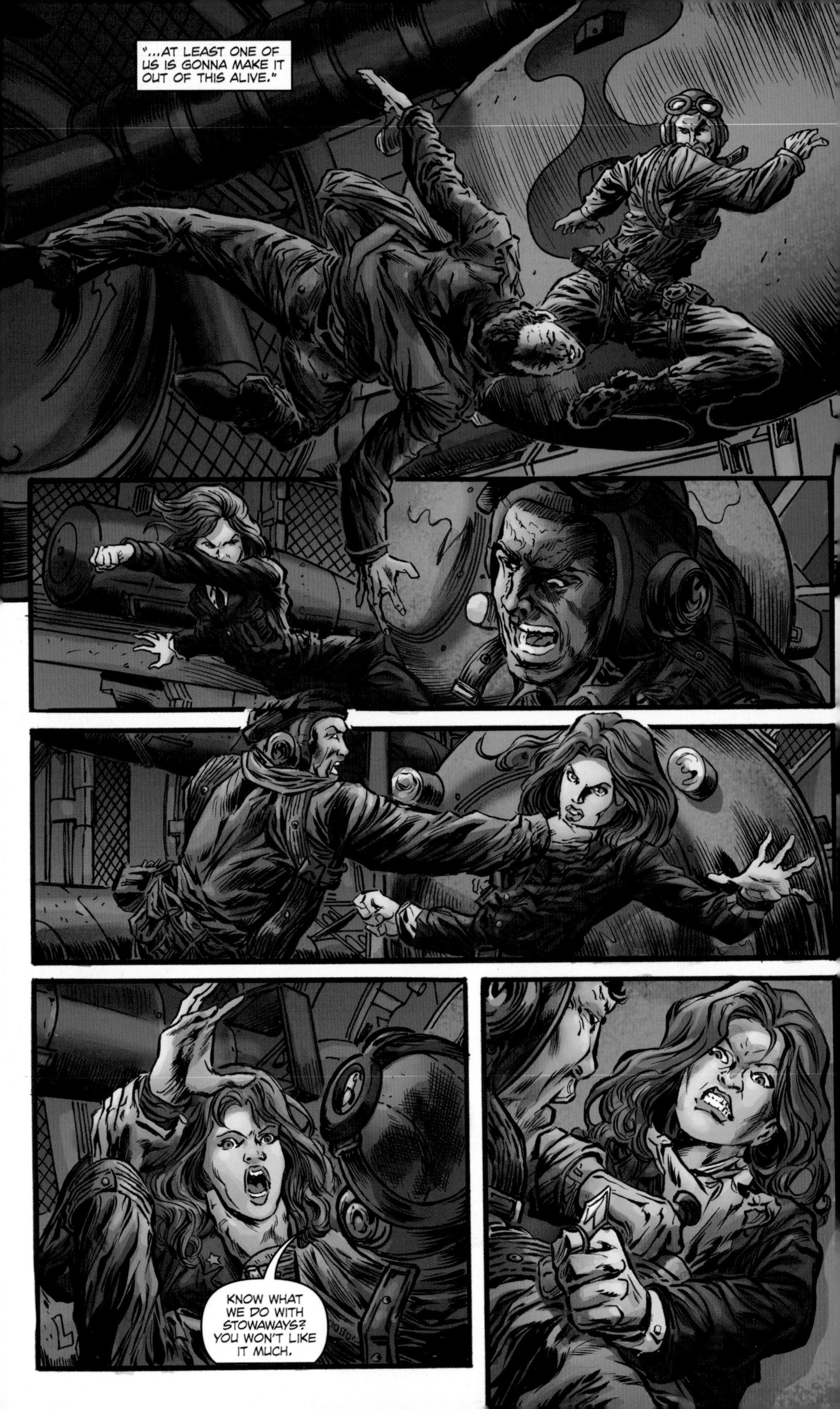
"...AT LEAST ONE OF US IS GONNA MAKE IT OUT OF THIS ALIVE."
KNOW WHAT WE DO WITH STOWAWAYS? YOU WON'T LIKE IT MUCH.

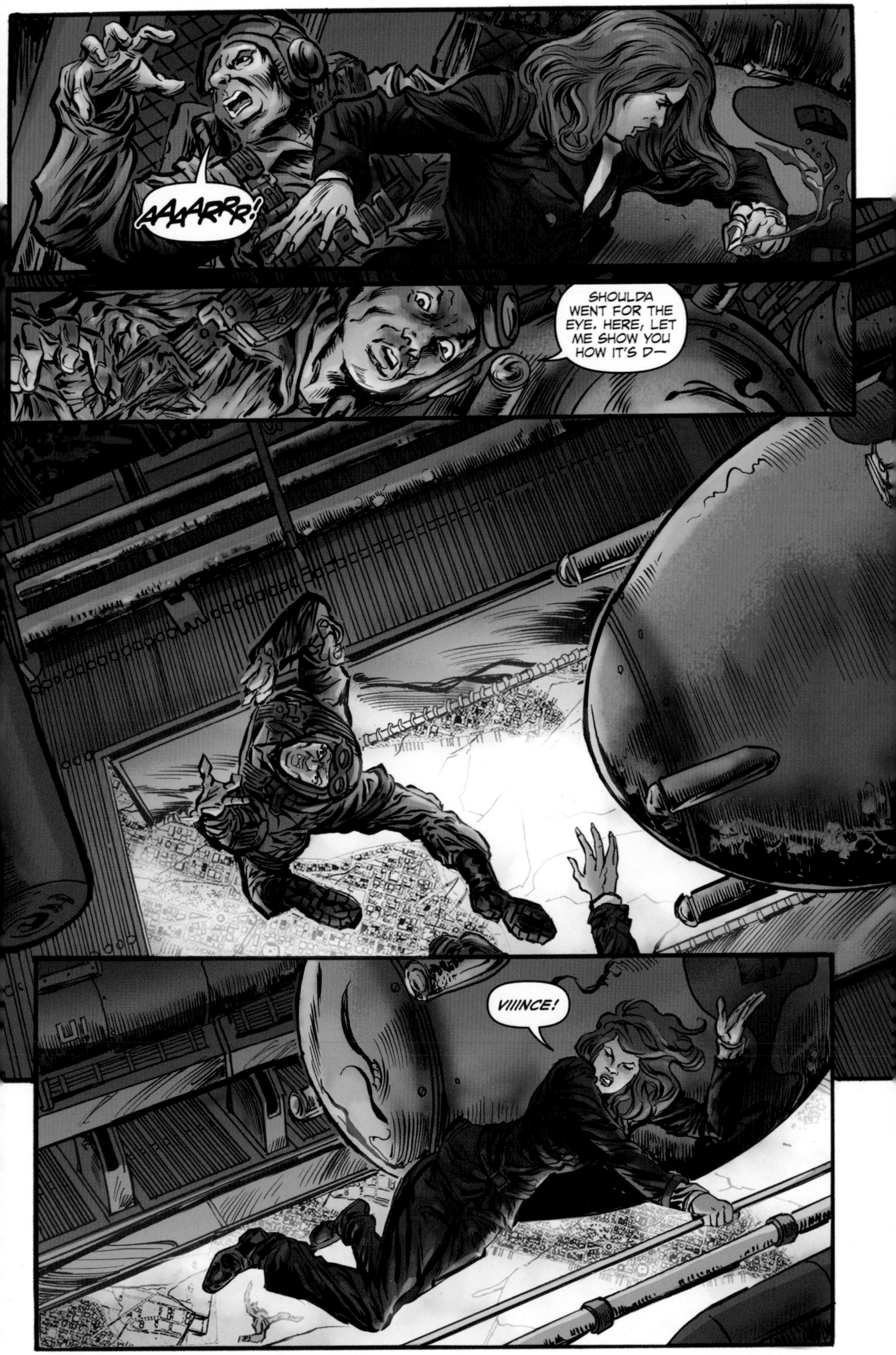
AAAARRR!
SHOULDA WENT FOR THE EYE. HERE, LET ME SHOW YOU HOW IT'S D—
VIIINCE!

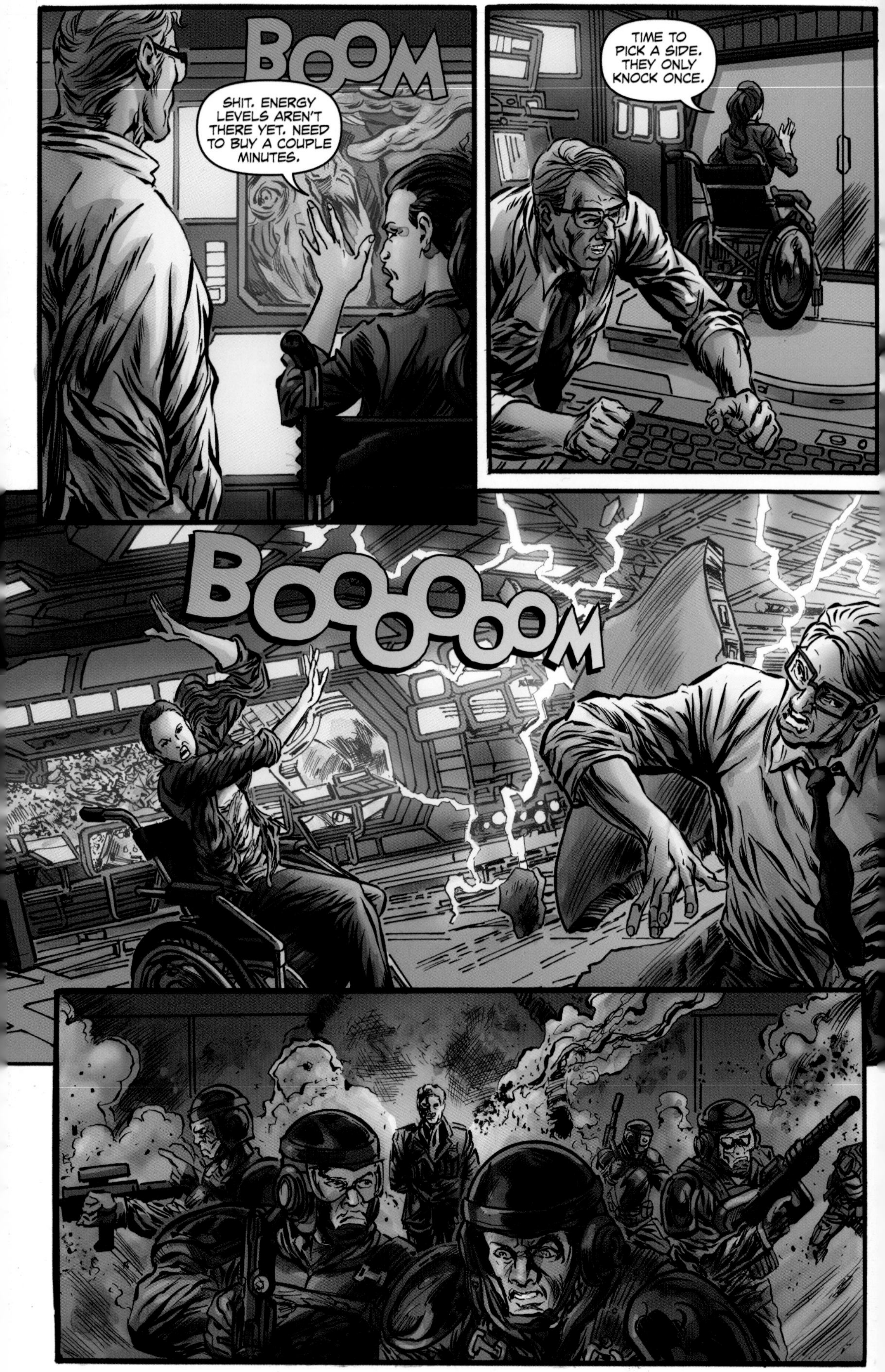
BOOM
SHIT. ENERGY LEVELS AREN'T THERE YET. NEED TO BUY A COUPLE MINUTES.
TIME TO PICK A SIDE. THEY ONLY KNOCK ONCE.
BOOOOOOOM

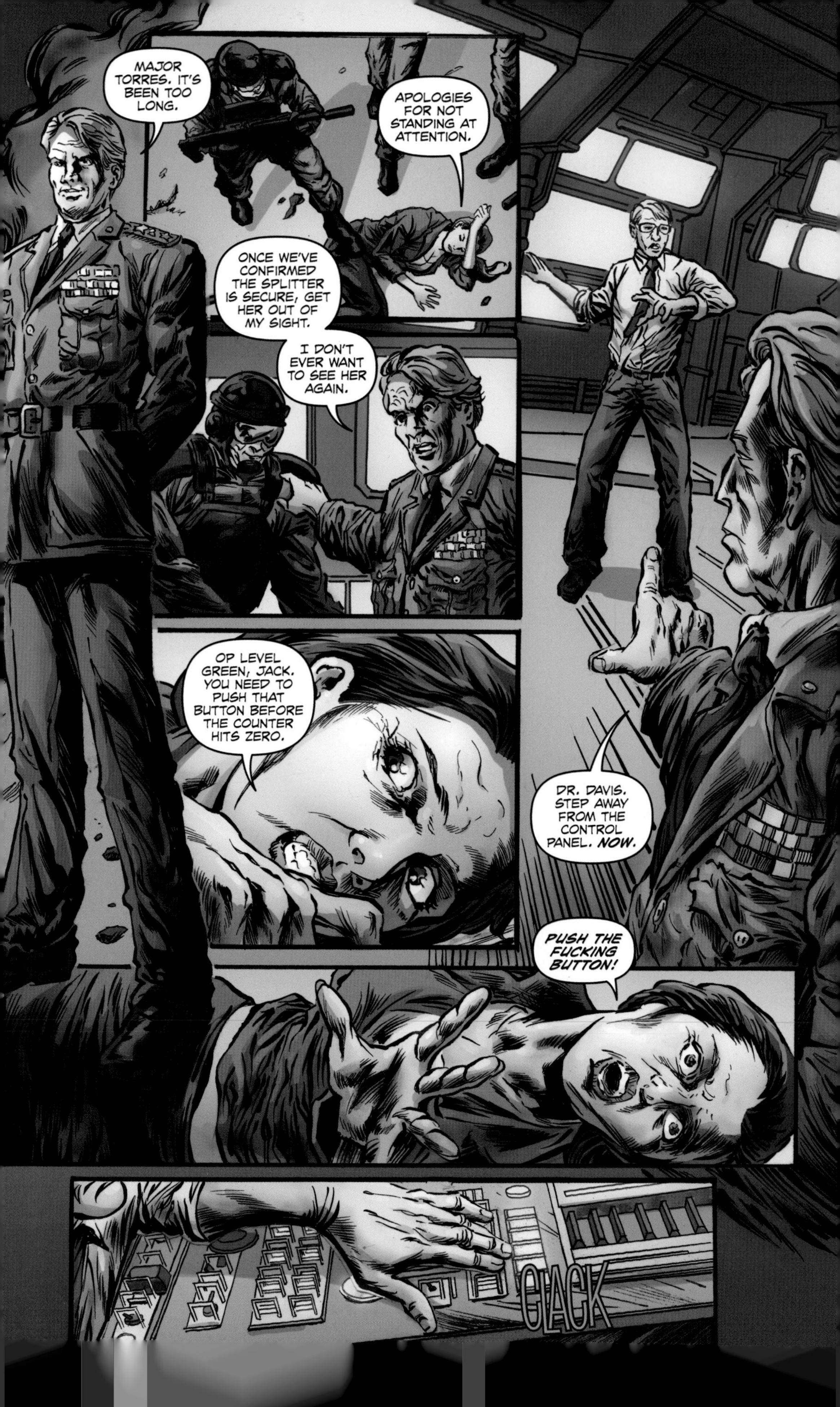
MAJOR TORRES. IT'S BEEN TOO LONG.
APOLOGIES FOR NOT STANDING AT ATTENTION.
ONCE WE'VE CONFIRMED THE SPLITTER IS SECURE, GET HER OUT OF MY SIGHT.
I DON'T EVER WANT TO SEE HER AGAIN.
OP LEVEL GREEN, JACK. YOU NEED TO PUSH THAT BUTTON BEFORE THE COUNTER HITS ZERO.
DR. DAVIS. STEP AWAY FROM THE CONTROL PANEL. NOW.
PUSH THE FUCKING BUTTON!
CLACK

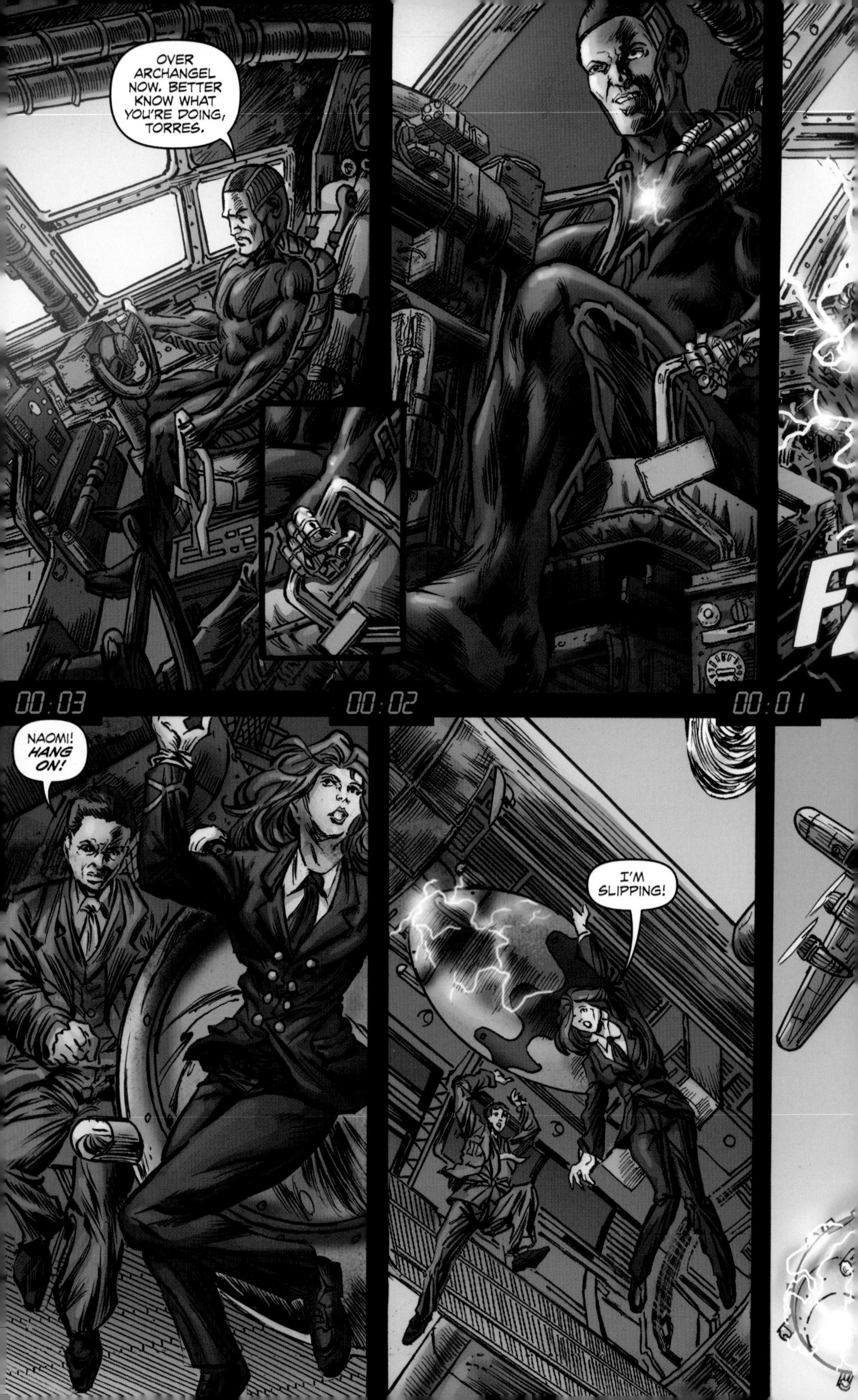
OVER ARCHANGEL NOW. BETTER KNOW WHAT YOU'RE DOING, TORRES.
00:03
00:02
00:01
NAOMI! HANG ON!
I'M SLIPPING!

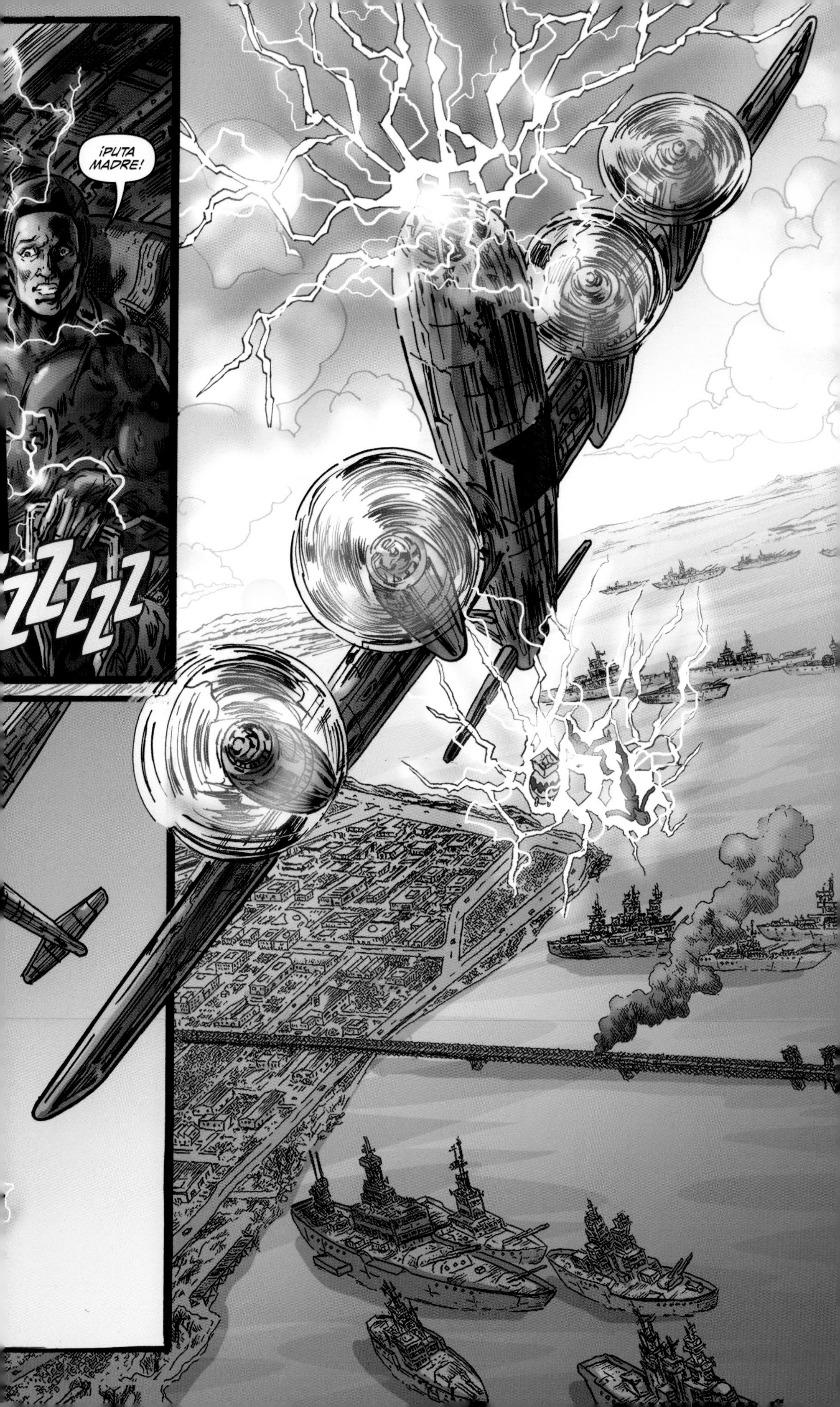
¡PUTA MADRE!
ZZZZZZ

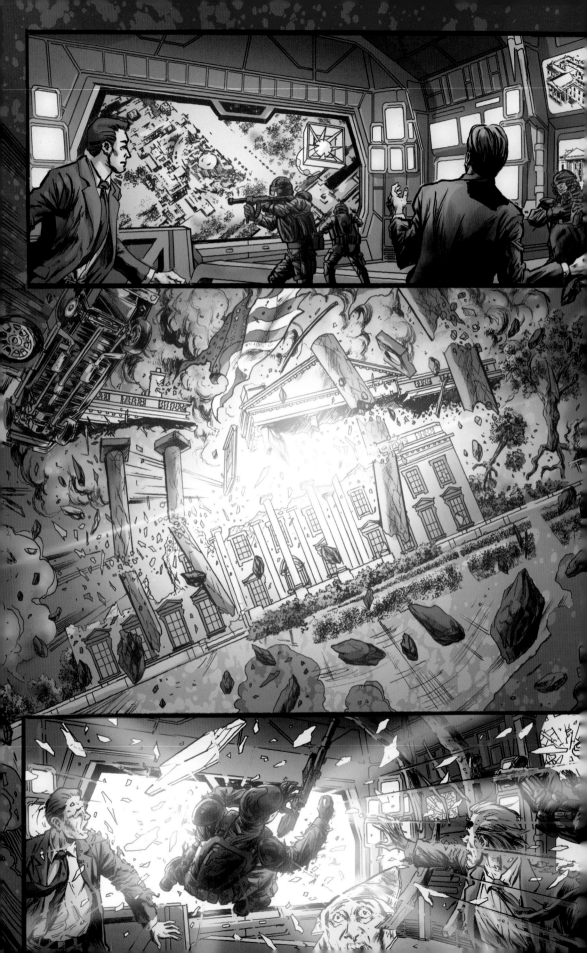

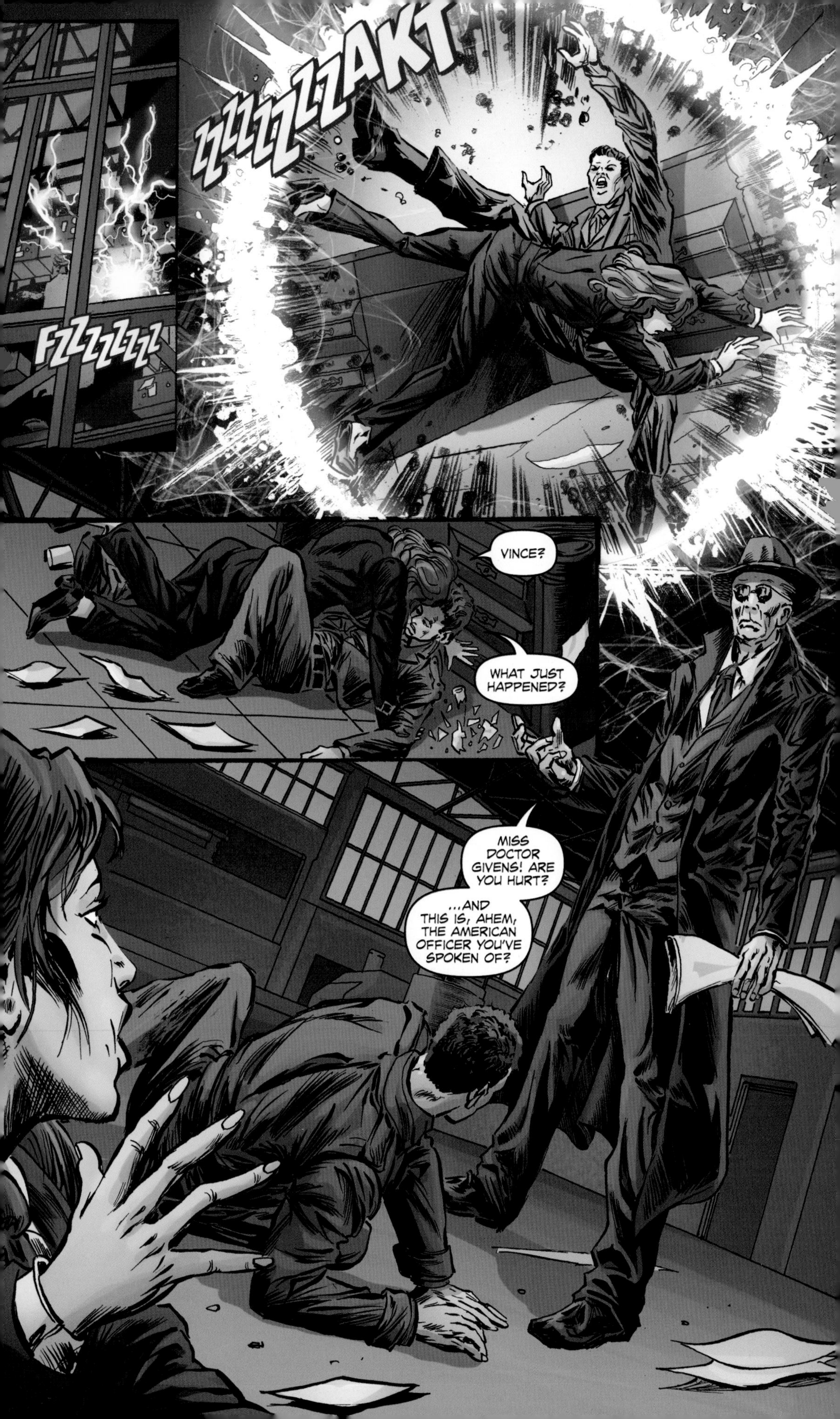
ZZZZZZZZAKT
FZZZZZZZ
VINCE?
WHAT JUST HAPPENED?
MISS DOCTOR GIVENS! ARE YOU HURT?
...AND THIS IS, AHEM, THE AMERICAN OFFICER YOU'VE SPOKEN OF?

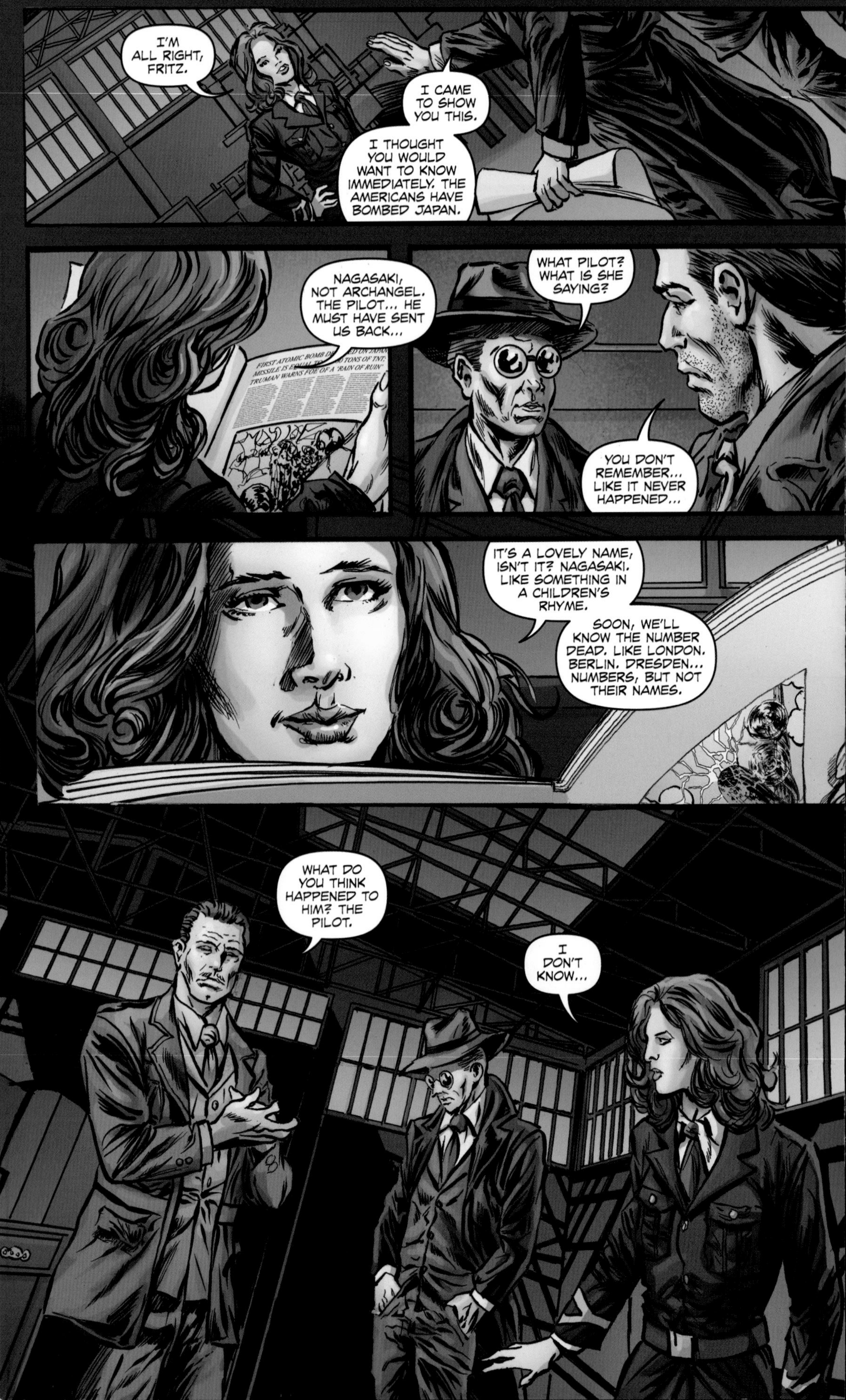
I'M ALL RIGHT, FRITZ.
I CAME TO SHOW YOU THIS.
I THOUGHT YOU WOULD WANT TO KNOW IMMEDIATELY. THE AMERICANS HAVE BOMBED JAPAN.
NAGASAKI, NOT ARCHANGEL. THE PILOT... HE MUST HAVE SENT US BACK...
TRUMAN WARNS FOE OF A 'RAIN OF RUIN'
WHAT PILOT? WHAT IS SHE SAYING?
YOU DON'T REMEMBER... LIKE IT NEVER HAPPENED...
IT'S A LOVELY NAME, ISN'T IT? NAGASAKI. LIKE SOMETHING IN A CHILDREN'S RHYME.
SOON, WE'LL KNOW THE NUMBER DEAD. LIKE LONDON. BERLIN. DRESDEN... NUMBERS, BUT NOT THEIR NAMES.
WHAT DO YOU THINK HAPPENED TO HIM? THE PILOT.
I DON'T KNOW...

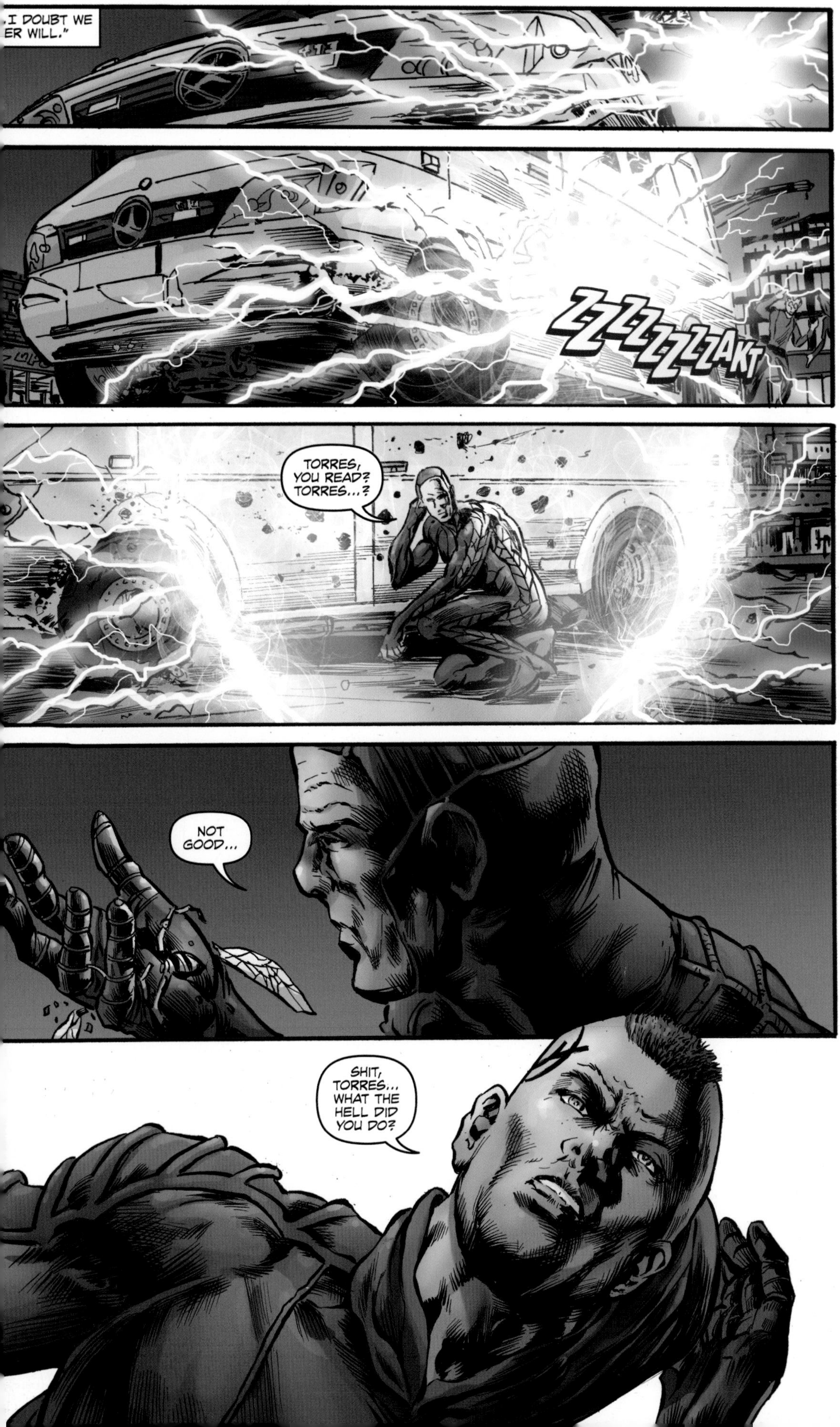
..I DOUBT WE ...ER WILL."
ZZZZZZZZZAKT
TORRES, YOU READ? TORRES...?
NOT GOOD...
SHIT, TORRES... WHAT THE HELL DID YOU DO?

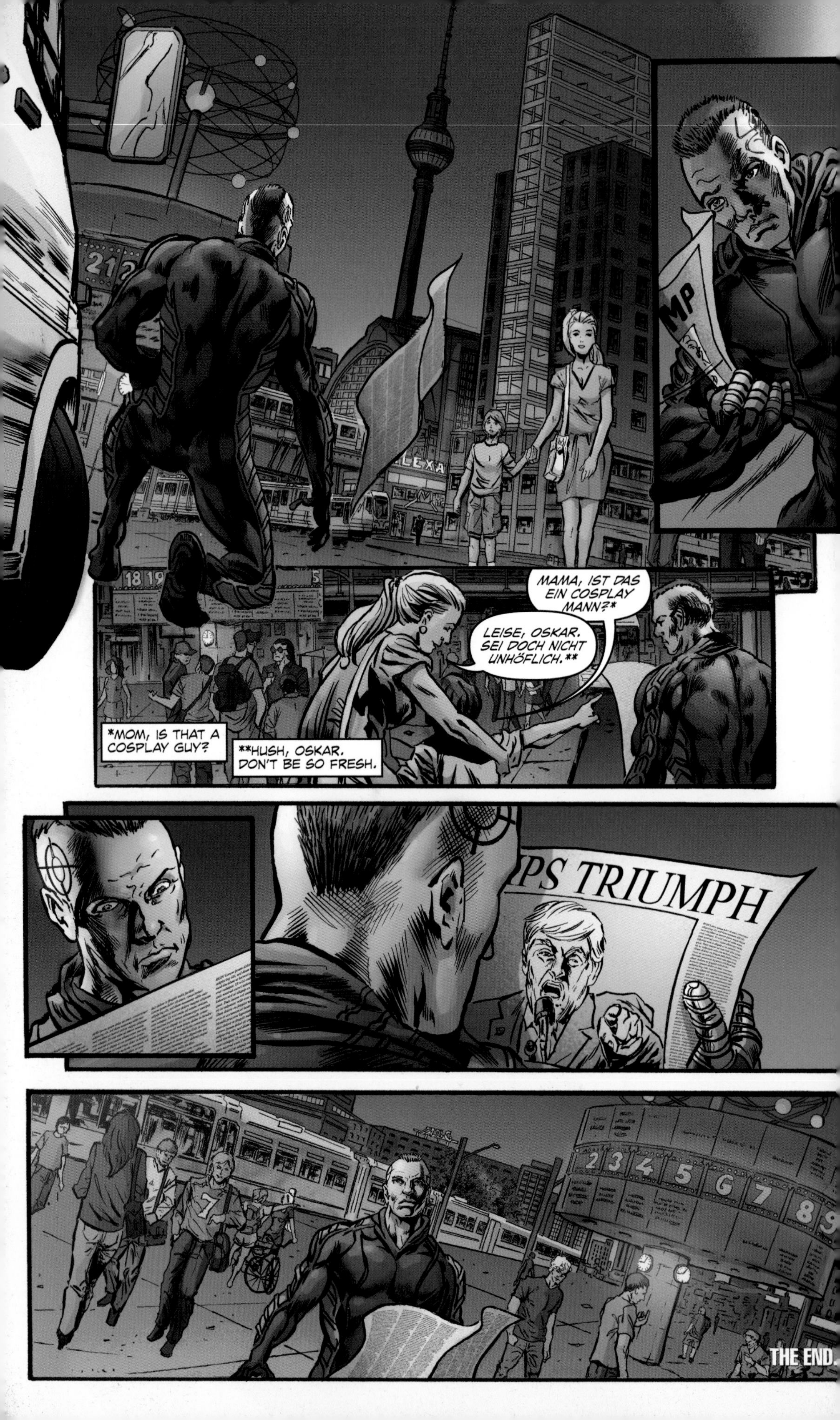
MAMA, IST DAS EIN COSPLAY MANN?*
LEISE, OSKAR. SEI DOCH NICHT UNHÖFLICH.**
*MOM, IS THAT A COSPLAY GUY?
**HUSH, OSKAR. DON'T BE SO FRESH.
PS TRIUMPH
THE END.

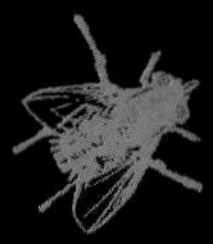

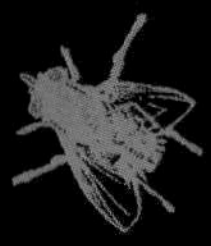

I discovered World War II when I was eight, in a mildewed trunk in the basement of a house under renovation. Workmen had left a kid-sized gap, through which I'd crawled to find World War II waiting, in the form of a small color print of dueling aircraft. Perhaps it had once been attached to a wartime calendar. Its back was blank, yellowed. It was the product of some unfamiliar process, perhaps a species of lithography. The colors were dull pastels. One of the two fighters, I would learn, was a RAF Spitfire, but at that point the roundels on its wings meant nothing to me. Neither did the Luftwaffe crosses on the other plane.

It caused me, somehow, this image, to experience a sort of conceptual vertigo, things in my head falling rapidly if only approximately together. How the grownups all referred to a time called The War, about which I had known, really, nothing, except for gathering somehow that during The War, which the grownups all remembered personally, things had been different. I found, looking at that print, the ability to conceptualize a previously unimaginable whole. I had seen black-and-white fragments of The War on television. I had seen The War in comics. There were plastic model kits of planes and vehicles from The War (but I was too young to build them yet). Yet I had never recognized these things as having The War in common.

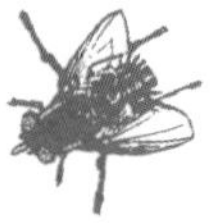

AFTERWORD

In those days there was no way for a curious child to instantly access everything about The War with a few keystrokes, but eventually I would learn quite a bit about The War. I found my way into my own favorite aspects of it, which might be thought of as The Weird War: the history of the OSS, of various resistance organizations, all the most secretive and/or deeply peculiar military operations, dubious narratives of Nazi occultism, wartime proto-UFOs...

So it was The Weird War that came back to me, several years ago, when my friend Michael St. John Smith first told me of a German producer he'd heard of, someone looking for material about Germany in World War II, for a German television mini-series. "Nazi flying saucers," I said, remembering the Third Reich's most wholly mythological secret weapon. I then told Mike whatever I remembered of foo-fighters and ghost rockets. Word of our discussion being eventually conveyed to the German television executive, he expressed, we were told, the frank disgust he felt for the utter goofy tastelessness of our suggestion. As sometimes happens, though, this rejection became our moment of collaborative triggering.

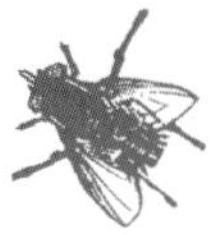

And that moment eventually became *Archangel,* though initially as several drafts of a feature screenplay, but culminating in a deal with IDW to turn it into a five-issue limited series.

While I've never doubted that comics are fully a medium in their own right, the experience of being part of creating one continually underlined that for me, and often in surprising ways. I realized that I'd never become as sophisticated a consumer of comics as I had of novels or films. I hadn't understood the number of creative decisions that have to be made, or the number of people required to make them.

Meanwhile, our story, having always involved an alternate time-track, found itself being revised in order to accommodate changes in the world (ours) in which it was being published. In the end (literally the very end of the book, and only amounting to the content of a few frames) it now concludes in a way that neither Mike nor I, as co-authors, nor anyone else involved, none of the other people crucial to its production, could possibly have imagined, when we began work on our first issue.

In Fritz Leiber's *The Big Time,* "change winds" blow, when one or the other side in the Change Wars succeeds in altering the course of history. And change winds have blown over *Archangel,* since we began to publish. The radioactive retro-future ruled over by President Henderson and Junior now seems quite differently possible, and will continue to, I imagine, one way or another.

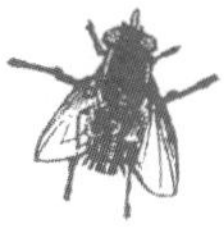

So our narrative, in order to belong more meaningfully to its day, must reflect that in the end. And does, I think, the message being delivered by a single windblown sheet of newsprint, and then by that final expression on the Pilot's face.

Knowing exactly how he feels, in June of 2017, we wish you all well, and most particularly everyone who helped make this series possible.

– William Gibson
8 June 2017

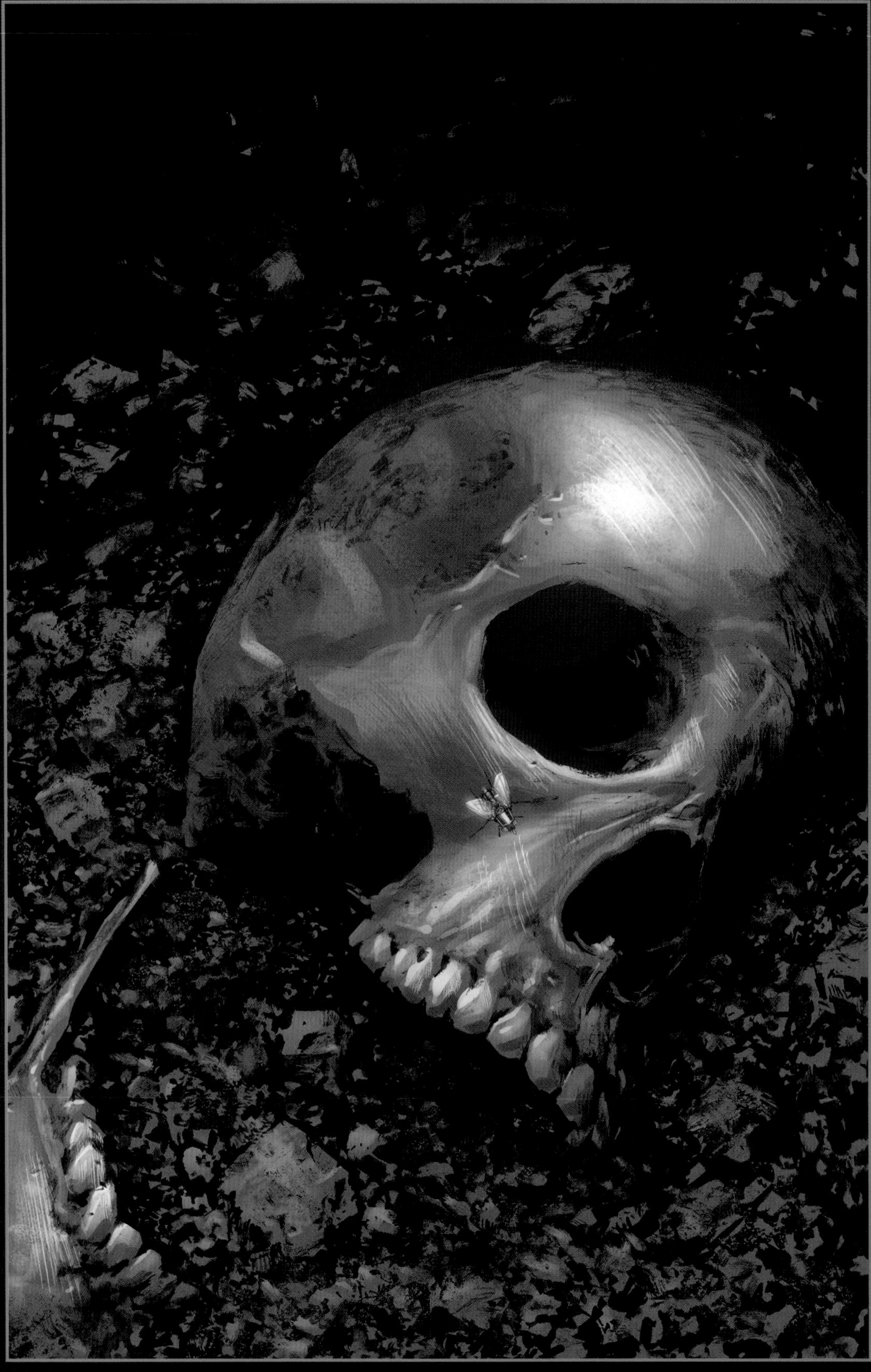

Art by BUTCH GUICE Colors by DIEGO RODRIGUEZ

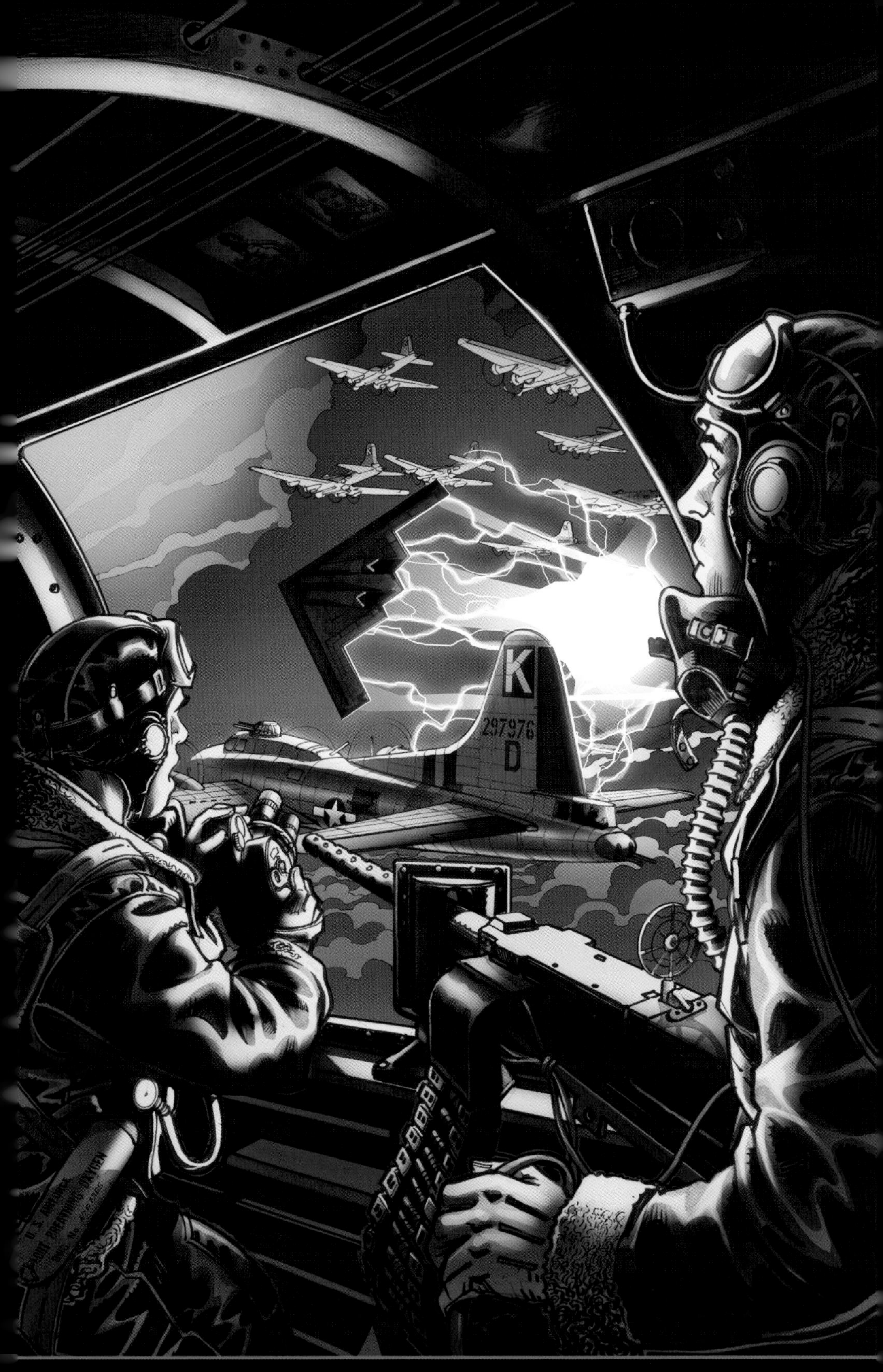
K
297976
D
U. S. ARMY AIR FORCE
PILOT BREATHING OXYGEN

DAVID FABBRI DIEGO RODRIGUEZ

WILLIAM GIBSON

ARCHANGEL

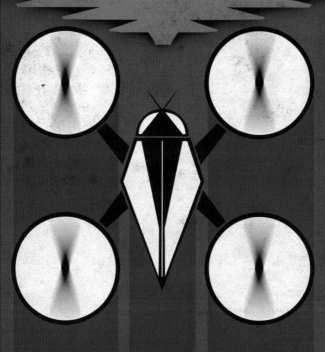

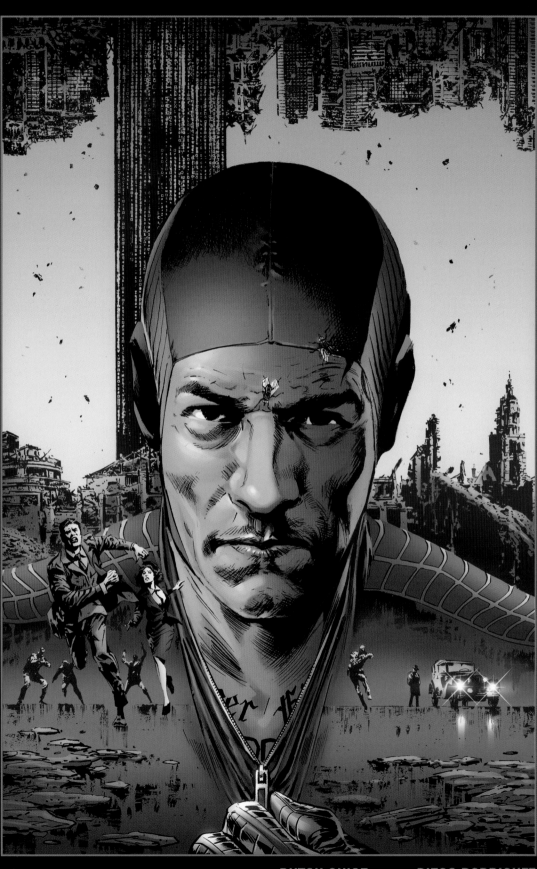

Art by BUTCH GUICE Colors by DIEGO RODRIGUEZ

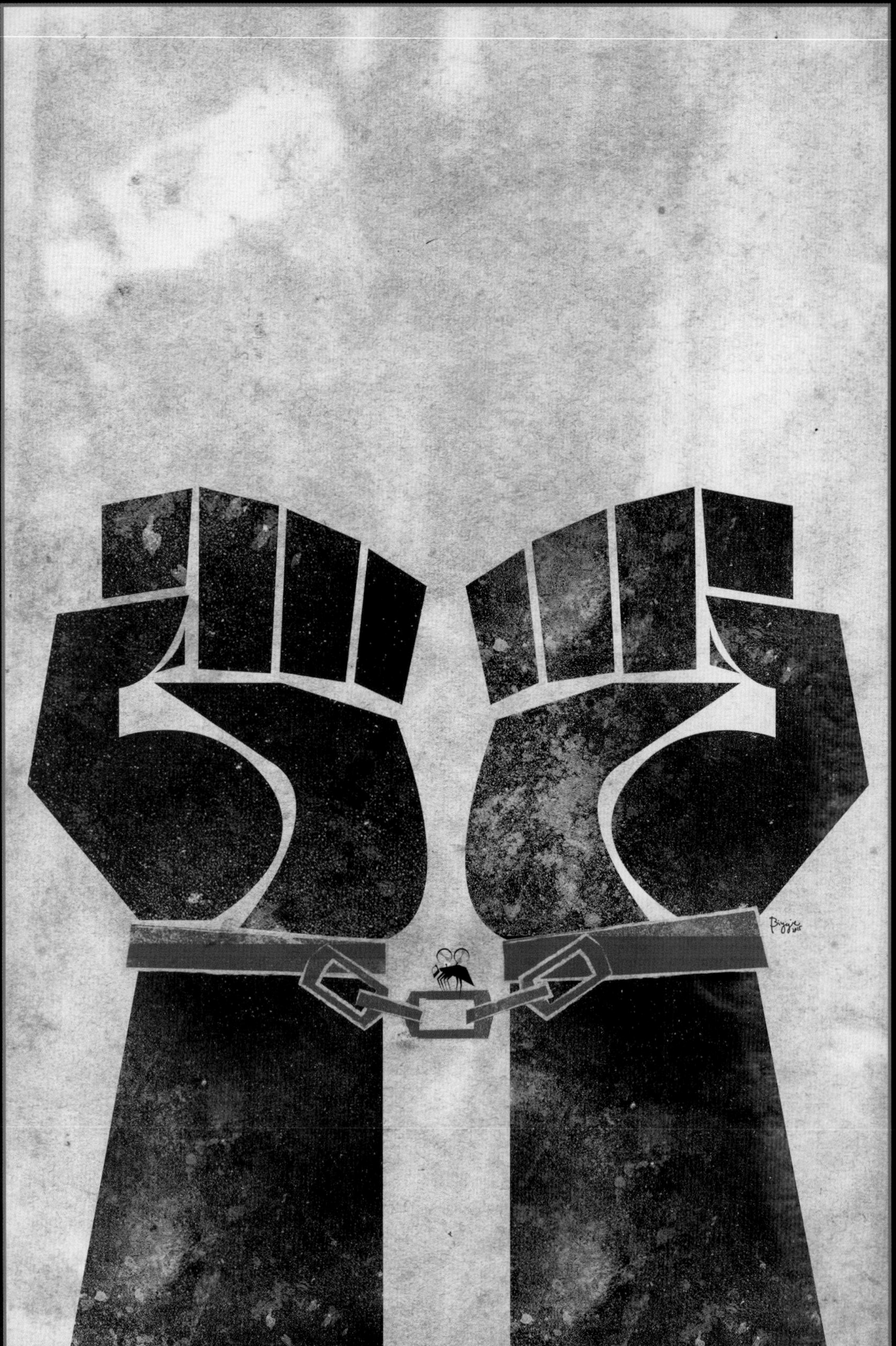

Art by **JAMES BIGGIE**

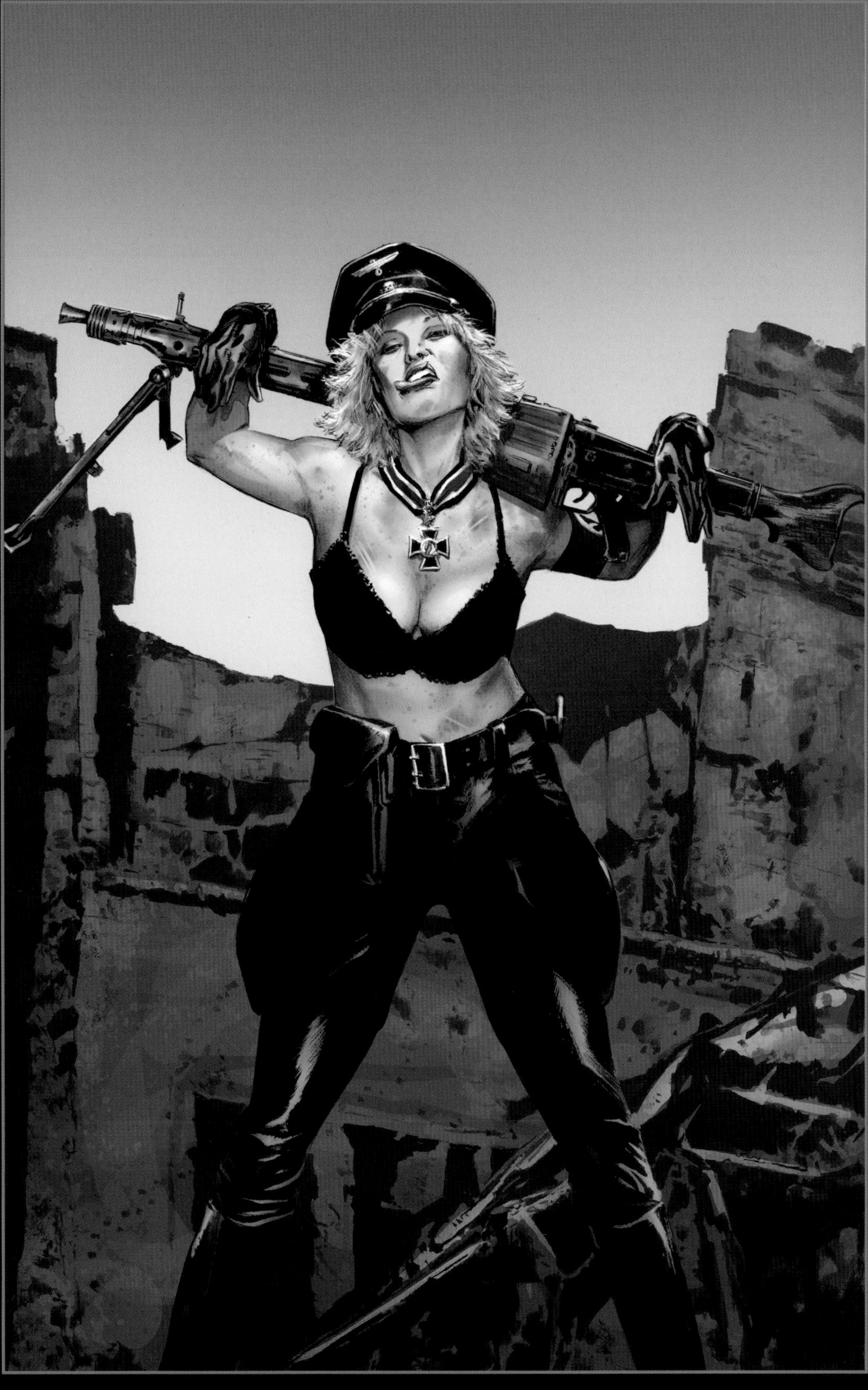

Art by BUTCH GUICE Colors by DIEGO RODRIGUEZ

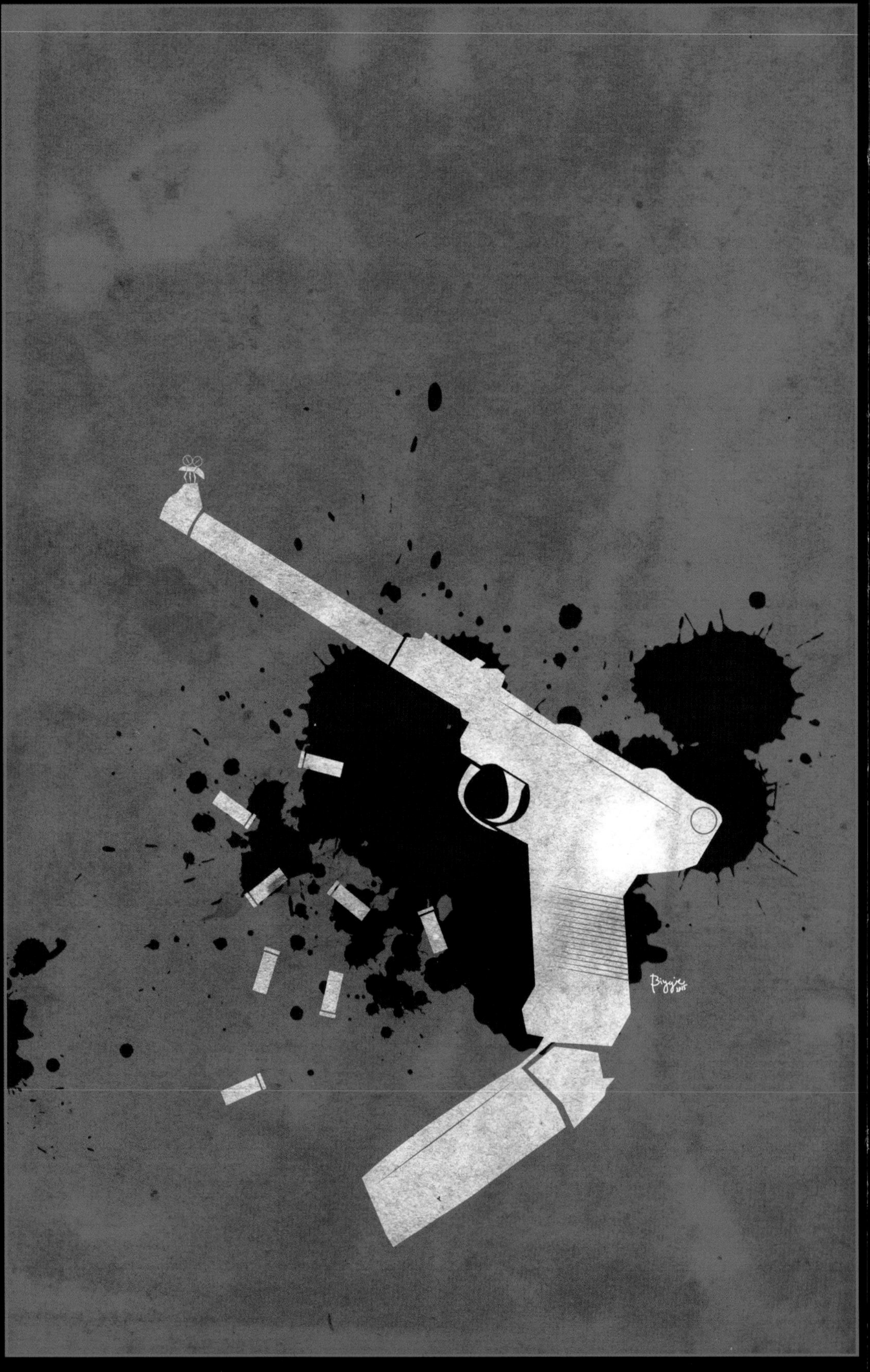

Art by JAMES BIGGIE

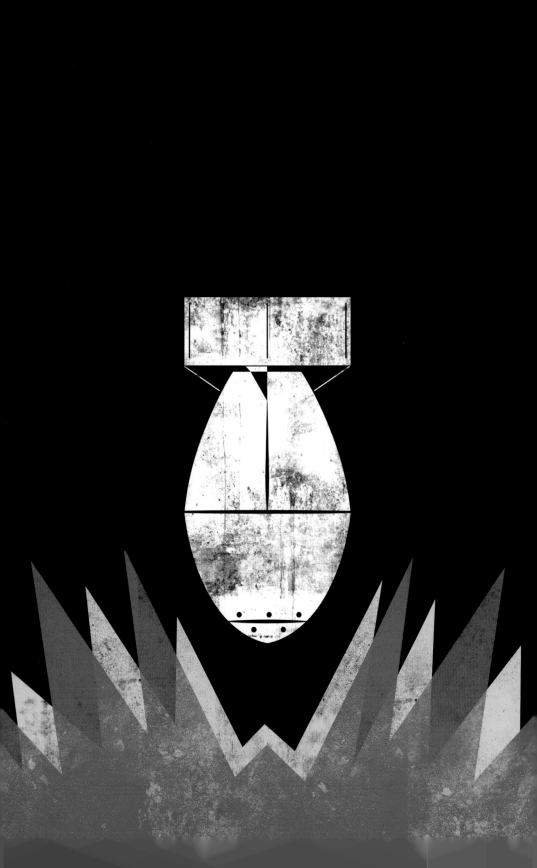

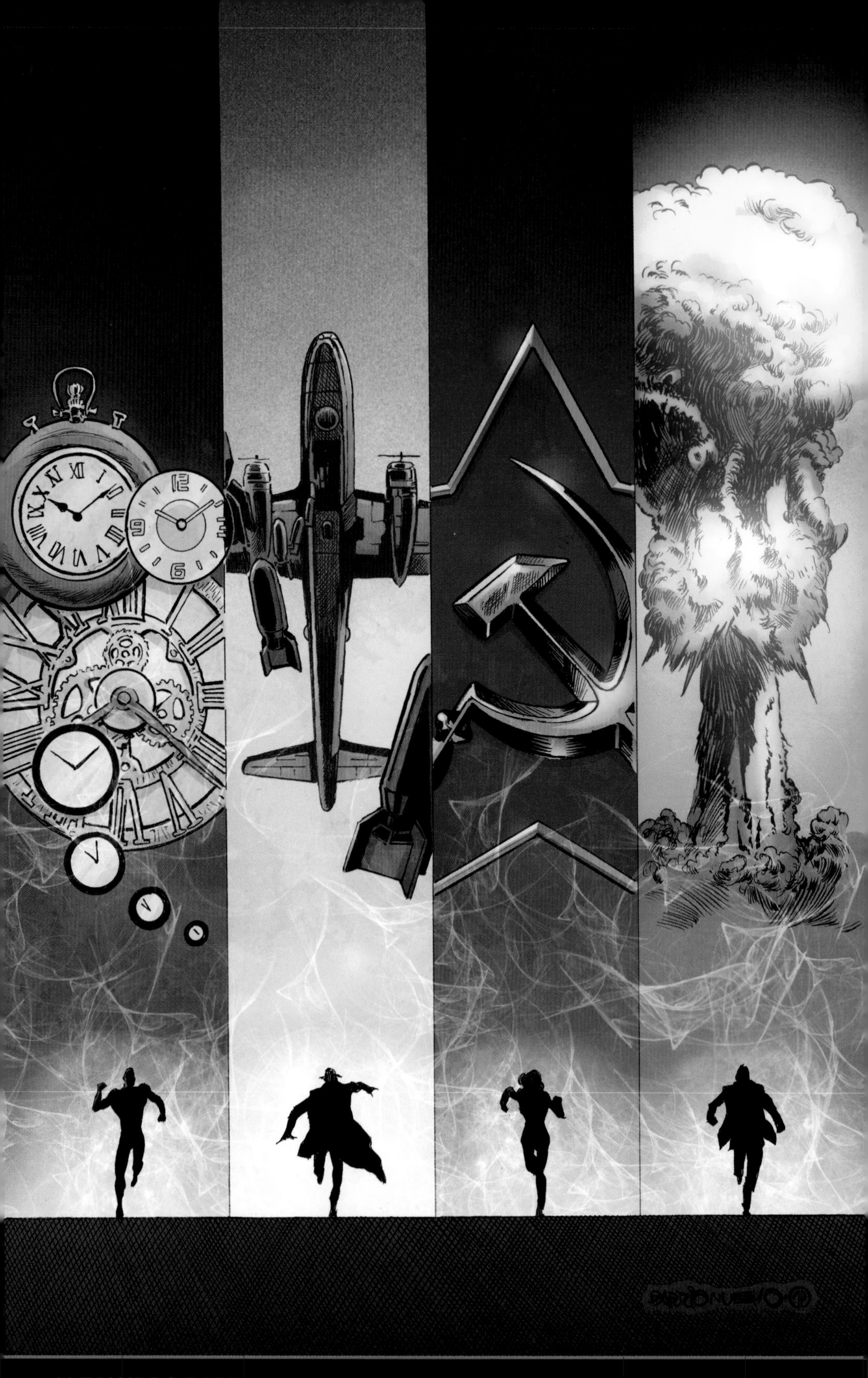

Art by ALEJANDRO BARR

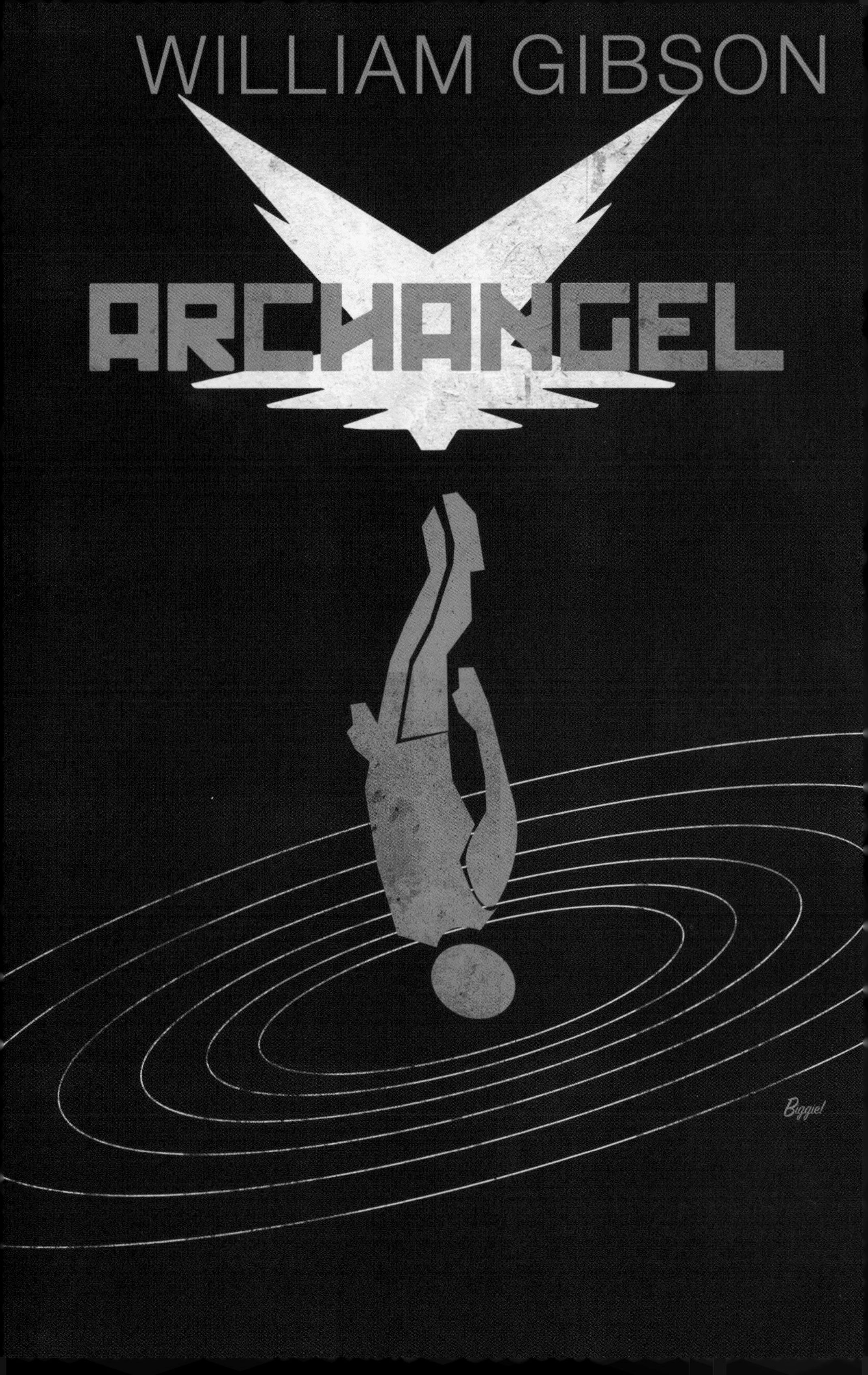
WILLIAM GIBSON
ARCHANGEL
Biggie!

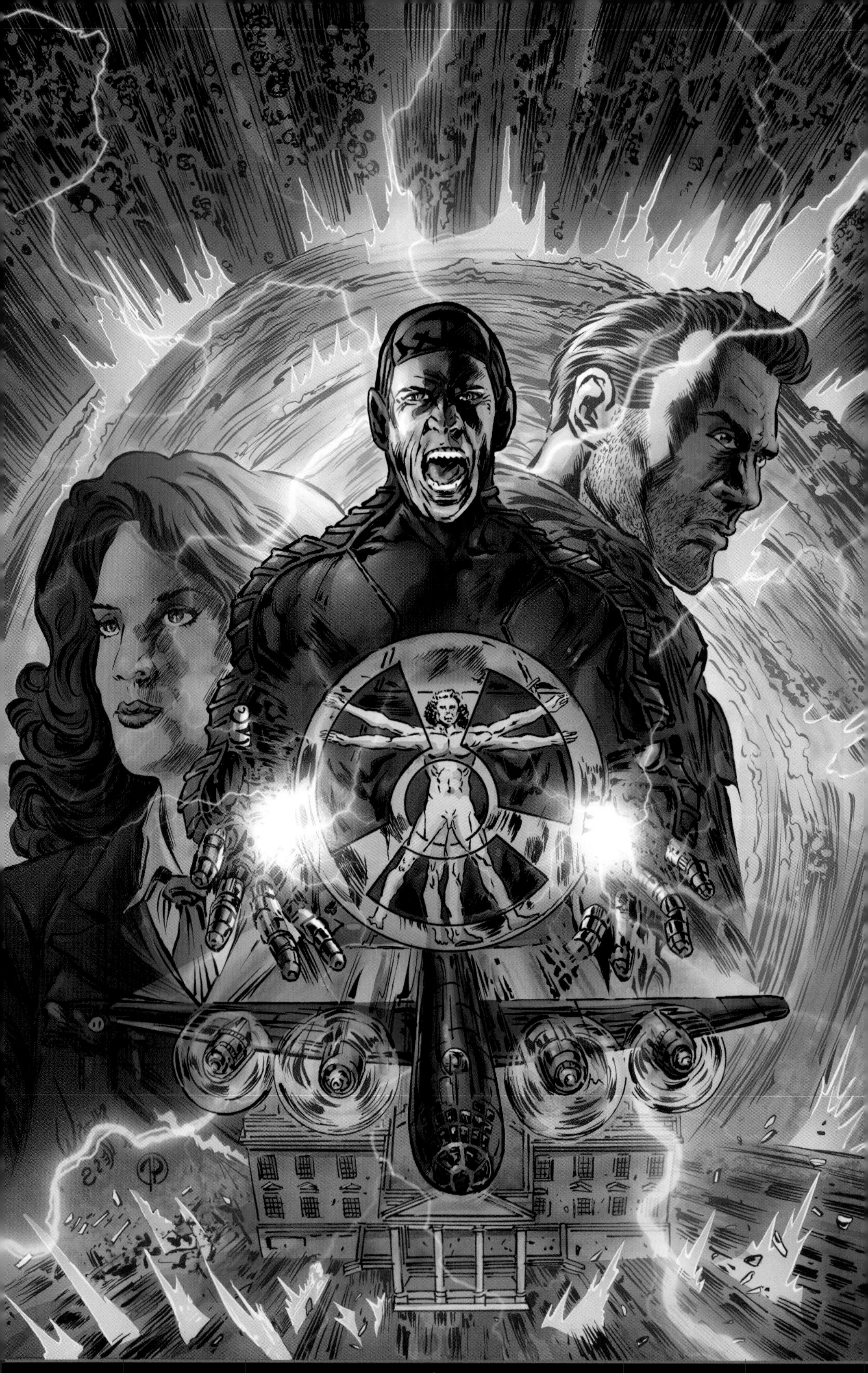

Art by **WAGNER REIS** Inks t

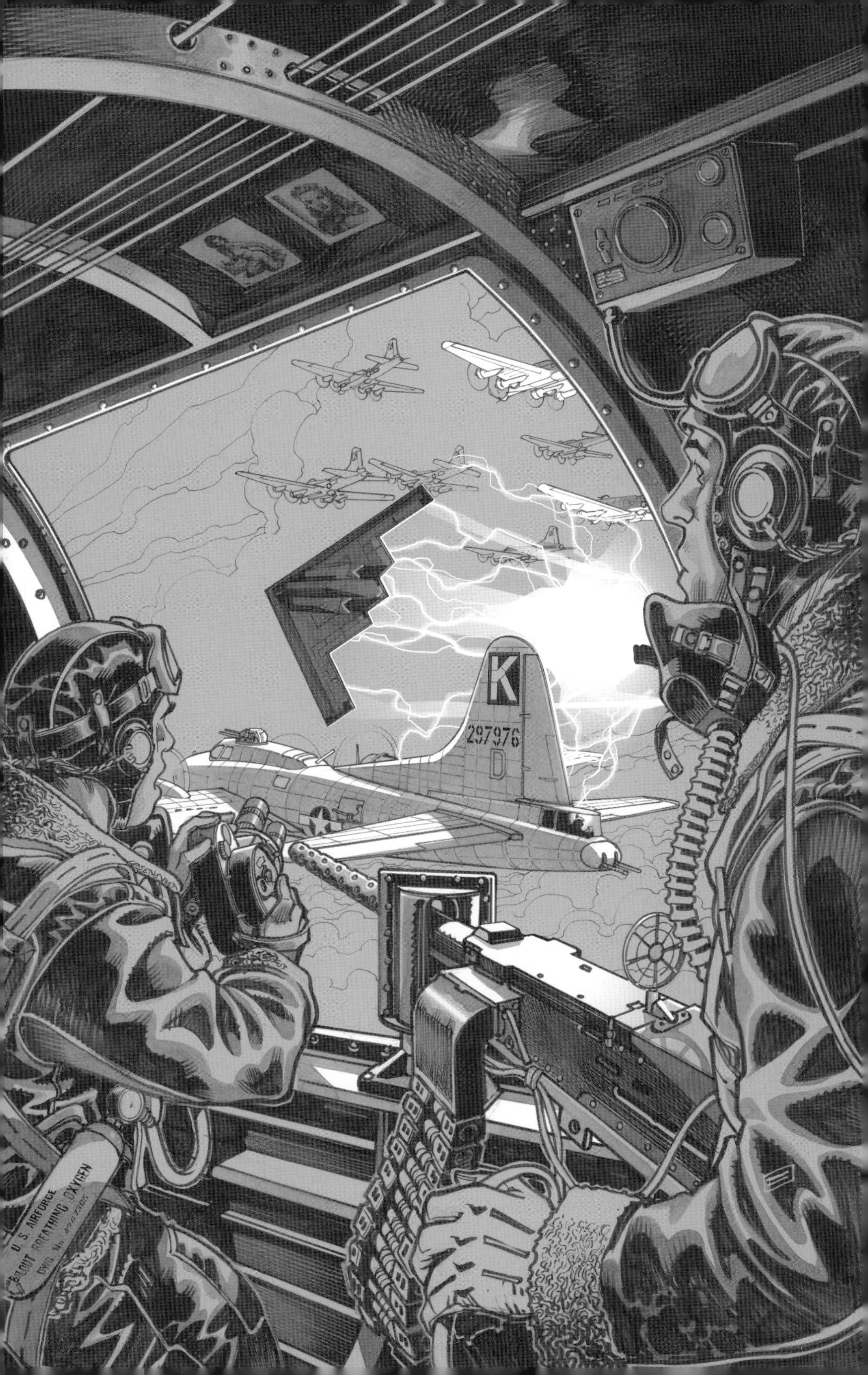
K
297976
D
U.S. AIRFORCE
BALOUT BREATHING OXYGEN
DWG. No

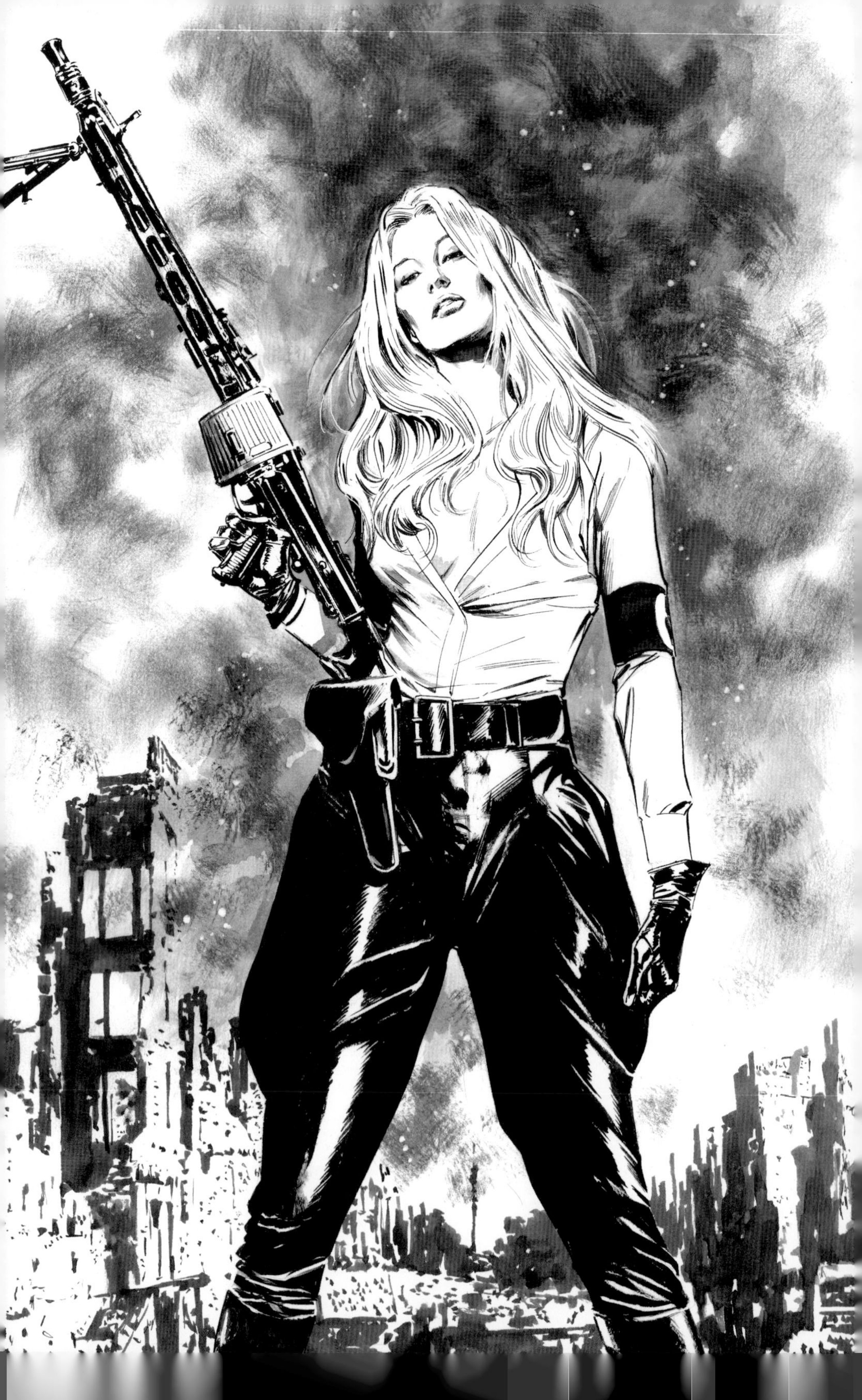

JUNIOR HENDERSON: U.S. Vice President of the dystopian alt-reality 2016. His father is the president. From page one, he takes the appearance of his Grandfather, Major Henderson (see below). He and his father are both horrible assholes. They never look like they aren't assholes. They are cruel, smug, narcissistic uber-thugs, wrapped sanctimoniously in what's left of the flag. Junior travels to our reality's 1945 to corrupt it for his own purposes.

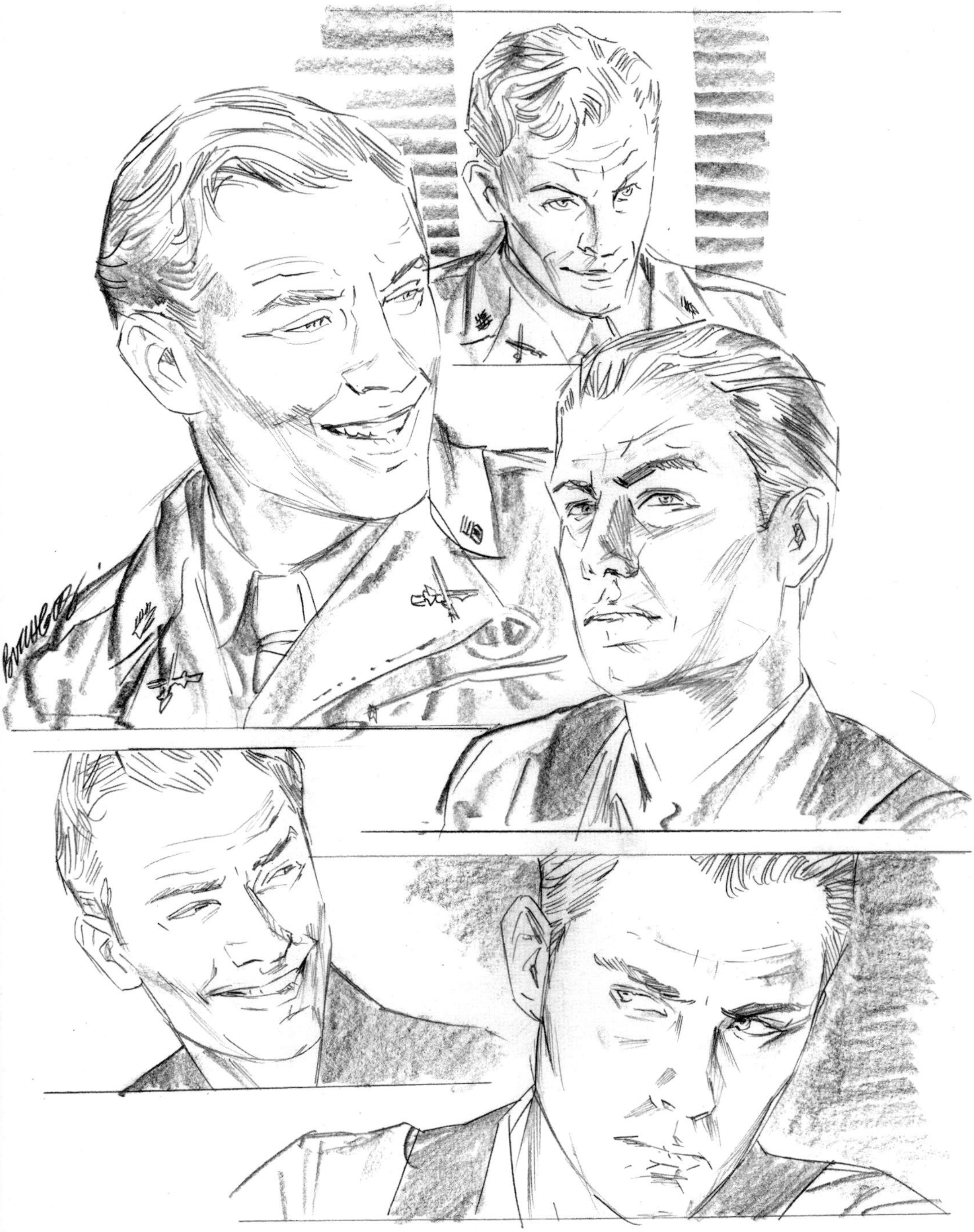

Tricky bit: Al, Junior's grandfather, wasn't an asshole, but by the time we meet Junior, his face has been altered to look exactly like Al's. But the asshole still has to show through.

MAJOR GUADALUPE TORRES: Face a study in determination, she pilots a noisy electric wheelchair and wears a brace on one leg. Her fatigues are faded and patched. Her uniform is a little shabby. Her world is ragged military, post-apocalyptic. They don't have a lot of stuff left, are running out of things, mending things, making do. All the spit-shine is reserved for Junior and his dad. She's hellbent on stopping Junior's plans in 1945.

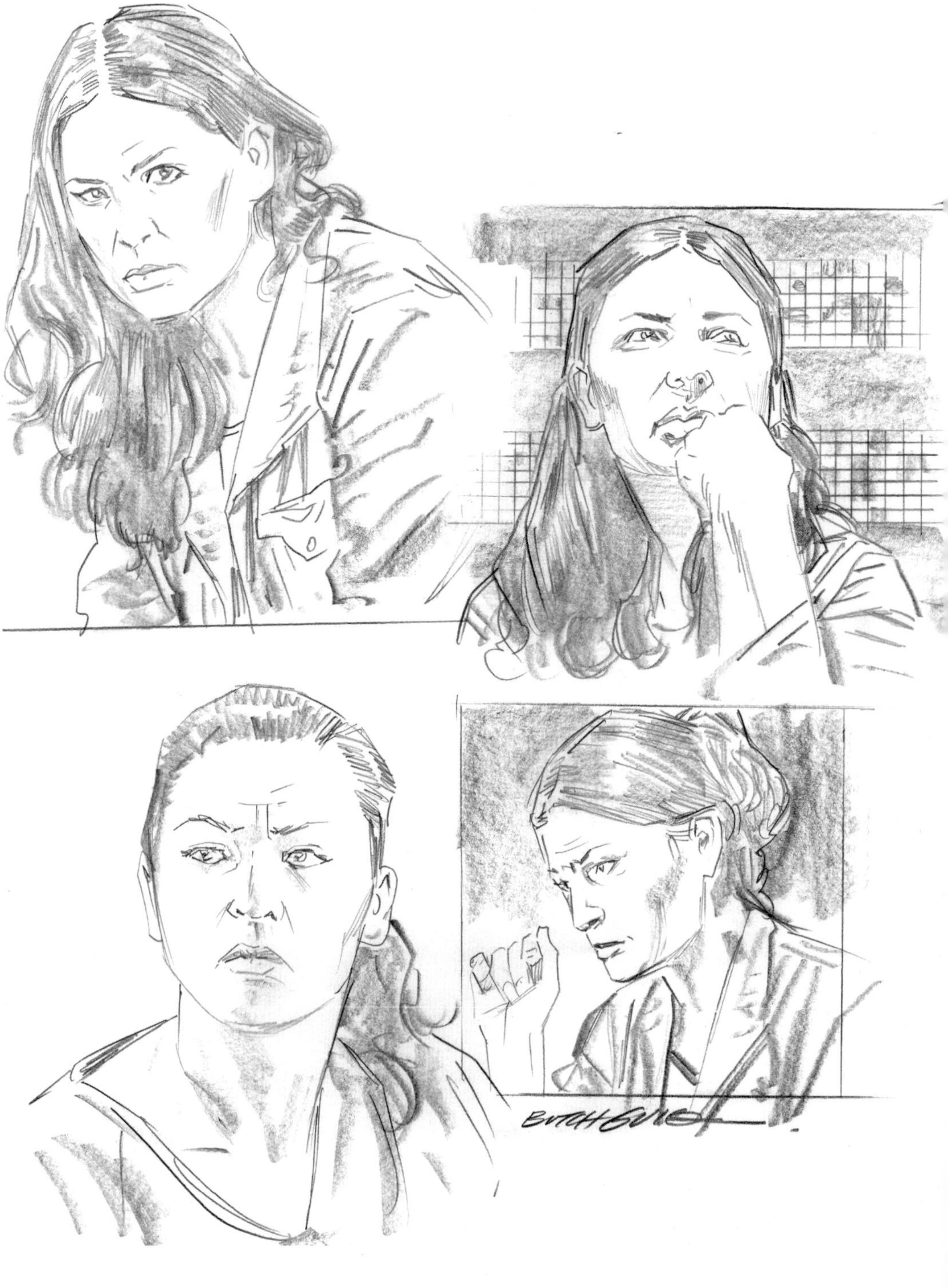
BUTCH GUICE

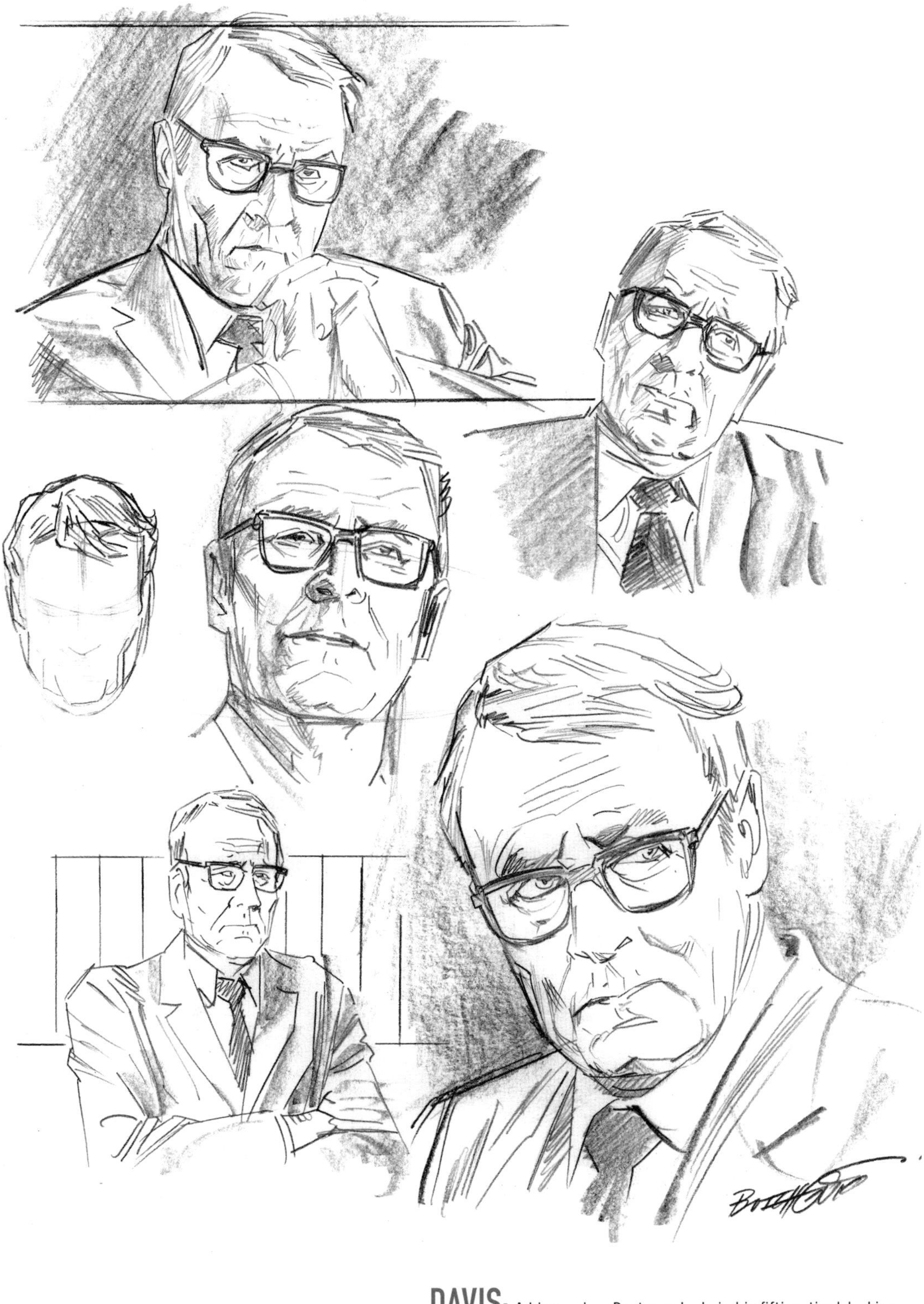

DAVIS: Addressed as Doctor or Jack, in his fifties, tired-looking but resolute in the face of his present task. He's the genius physicist behind the Splitter. He's loyal to the Hendersons more out of loyalty to what's left of the idea of America. He's a flawed character but not inherently evil. He accidentally winds up being the one who has to try to talk Torres out of wrecking their plans.

PILOT: Male, Marine, Hispanic. Dark tattoos from head to toe. Marine haircut, very short sides. Dressed in his camouflage/invisible creepsuit. The tattoos are black-work, like present day gang tattoos, extending up the neck and onto the sides of his skull. Tattoos look something like the style of MS 13 tattoos, La Mara Salvatrucha, but hybridized with USMC and apocalyptic symbols. Ornate "olde English" lettering styles. He's sent to 1945 to stop Junior.

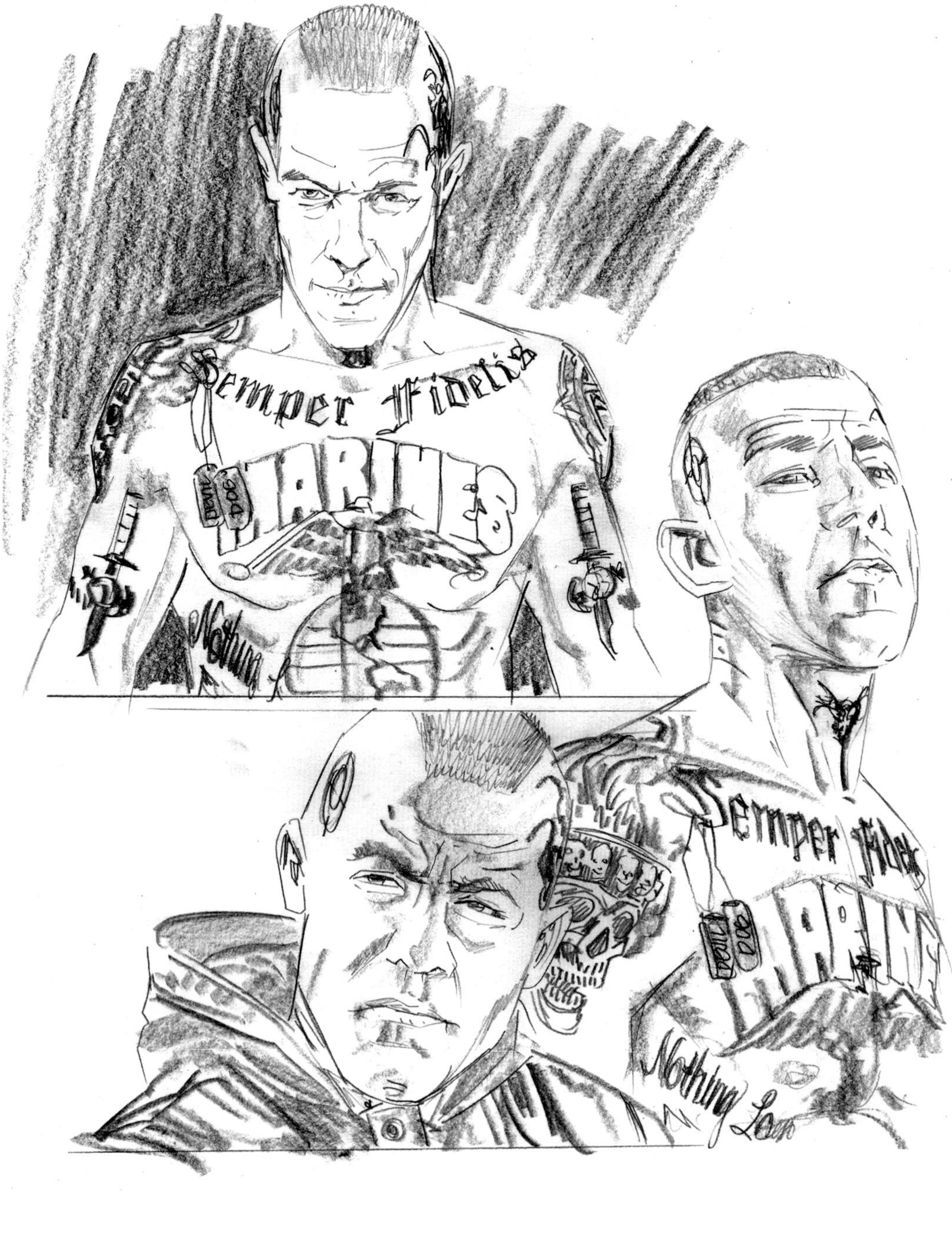
Semper Fidelis
Nothing

"MY MOOD BOARD:
ATMOSPHERIC. MELANCHOLY. OMINOUS. DIRTY."

ONE and **TWO, A** and **B:** Junior Henderson's personal bodyguards. Hulking, intimidating Blackwater contractor types. They are never named in the series and are the only characters that should have the hyper-muscular, "superhero" physique.

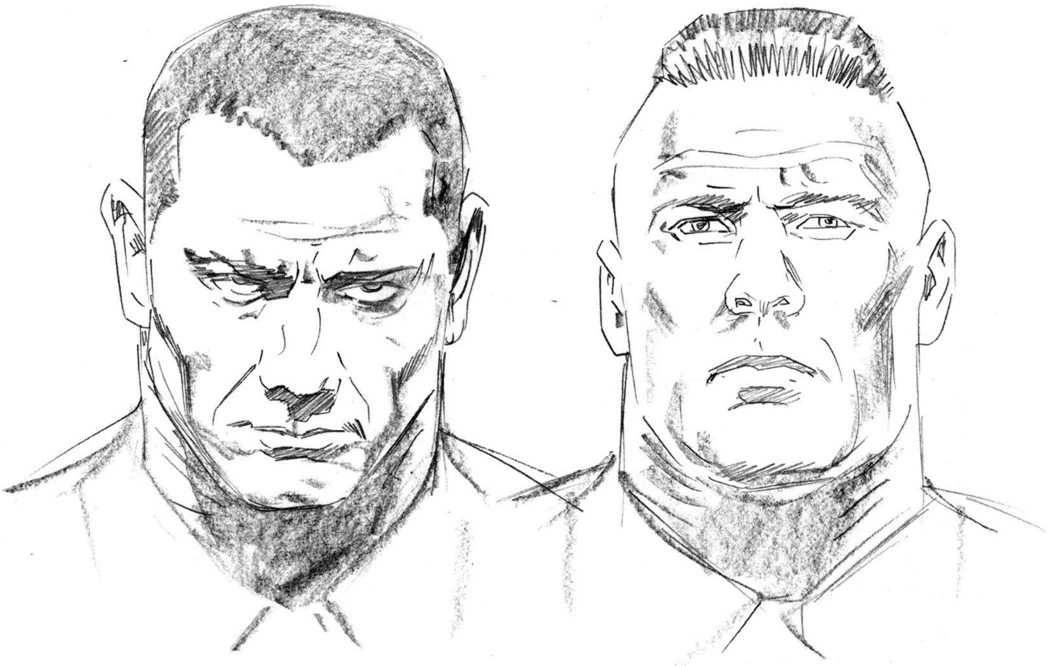

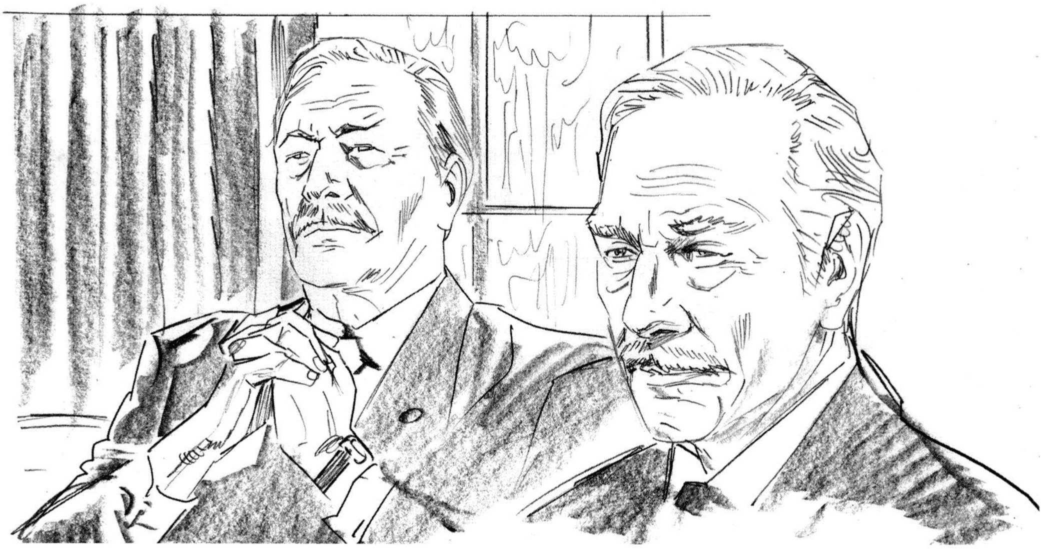

AIR COMMODORE GORDON TULLY:
British. Naomi's commanding officer. White-hair.

NAOMI GIVENS: British. Royal Air Force (RAF) uniform. A flight lieutenant, early 30s, attractive without seeming to try. She's our hero in 1945. Believes in the supernatural and unusual. Tully says of her, "Difficult enough being a woman in British Intelligence. Being a smart one is quite unforgivable." She is determined to succeed in male-dominated military.

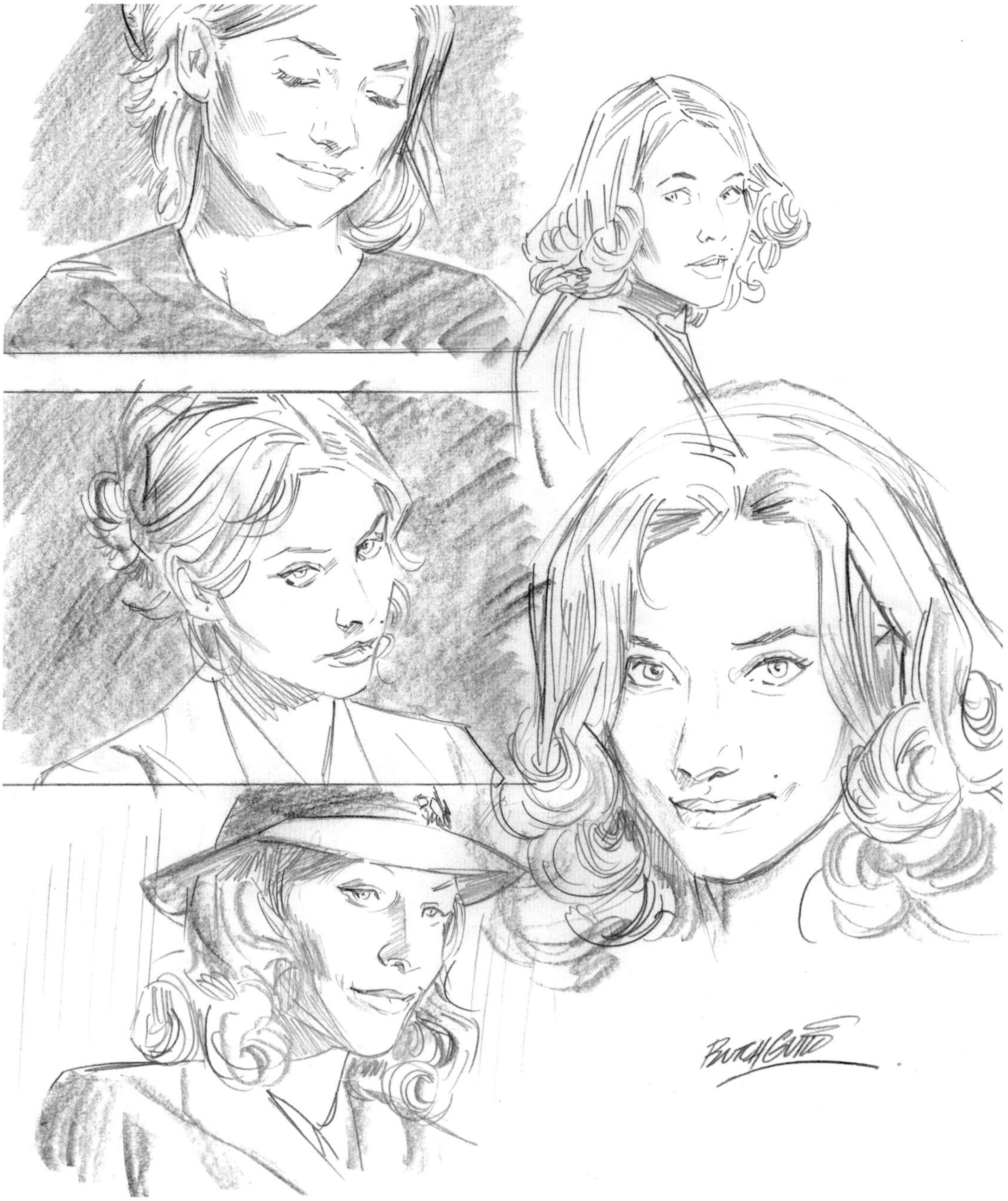

"I HAVE A CERTAIN KIND OF OVER-THE-TOP FEMALE CHARACTER WHO JUST NEVER GETS KILLED. THEY MAY NOT BE REALISTIC BUT I LOVE THEM, AND A LOT OF PEOPLE EVIDENTLY DO."

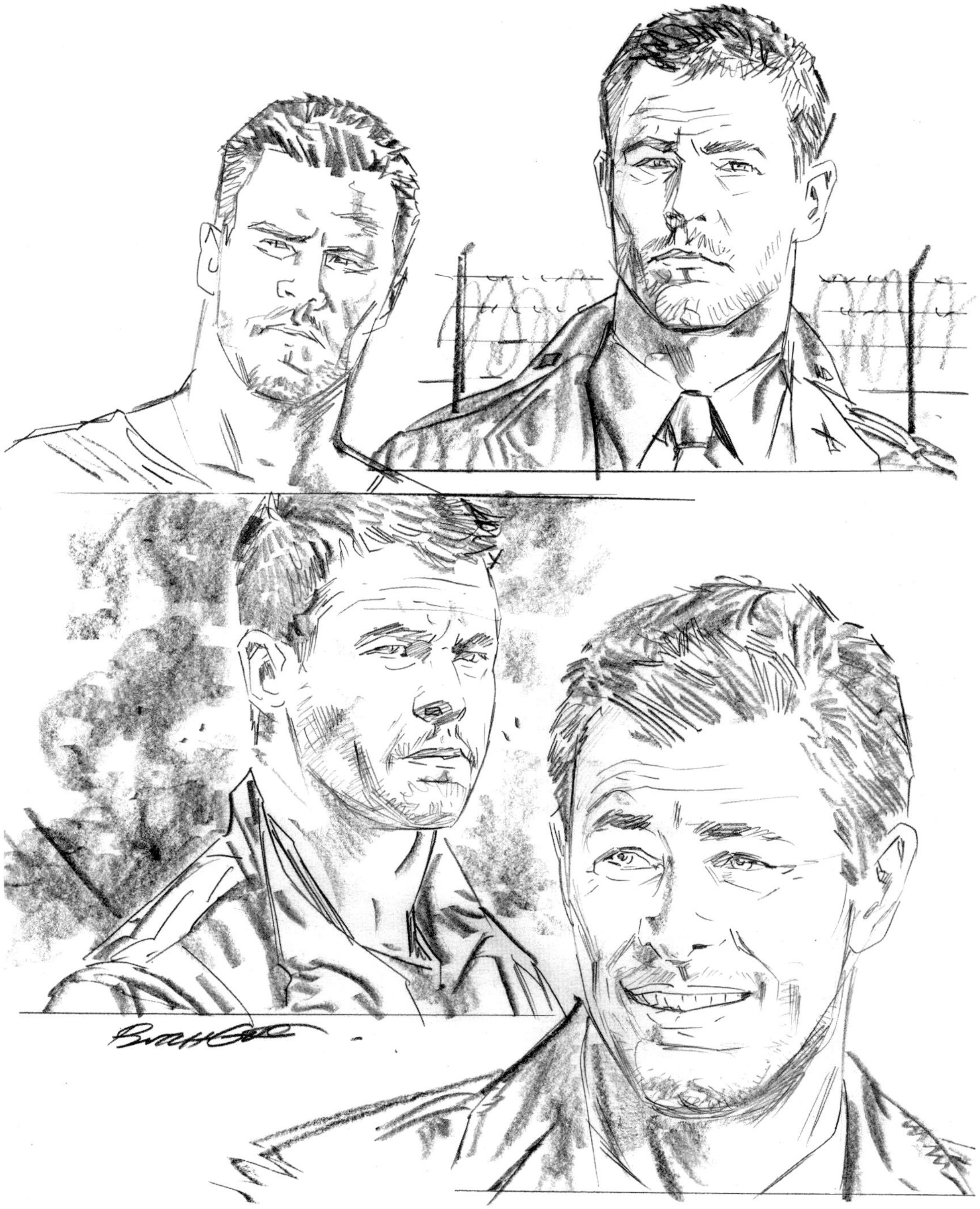

CAPTAIN VINCE MATTHEWS: American army uniform. Formerly romantically involved with Naomi. He's her male/U.S. counterpart throughout the story. Vince struggles between doing what is required as part of his position in the military and helping Naomi, whom he still loves. He's tough and doesn't believe the Pilot at first, but ultimately we like him and root for him.

FRITZ: Young, German. A decidedly unmilitary figure, his attempt at sharp civilian attire has been artfully assembled from available remnants. Has a sort of young Bowie élan. He's charming and clever. Acts as Naomi's street-smart driver and black market specialist.

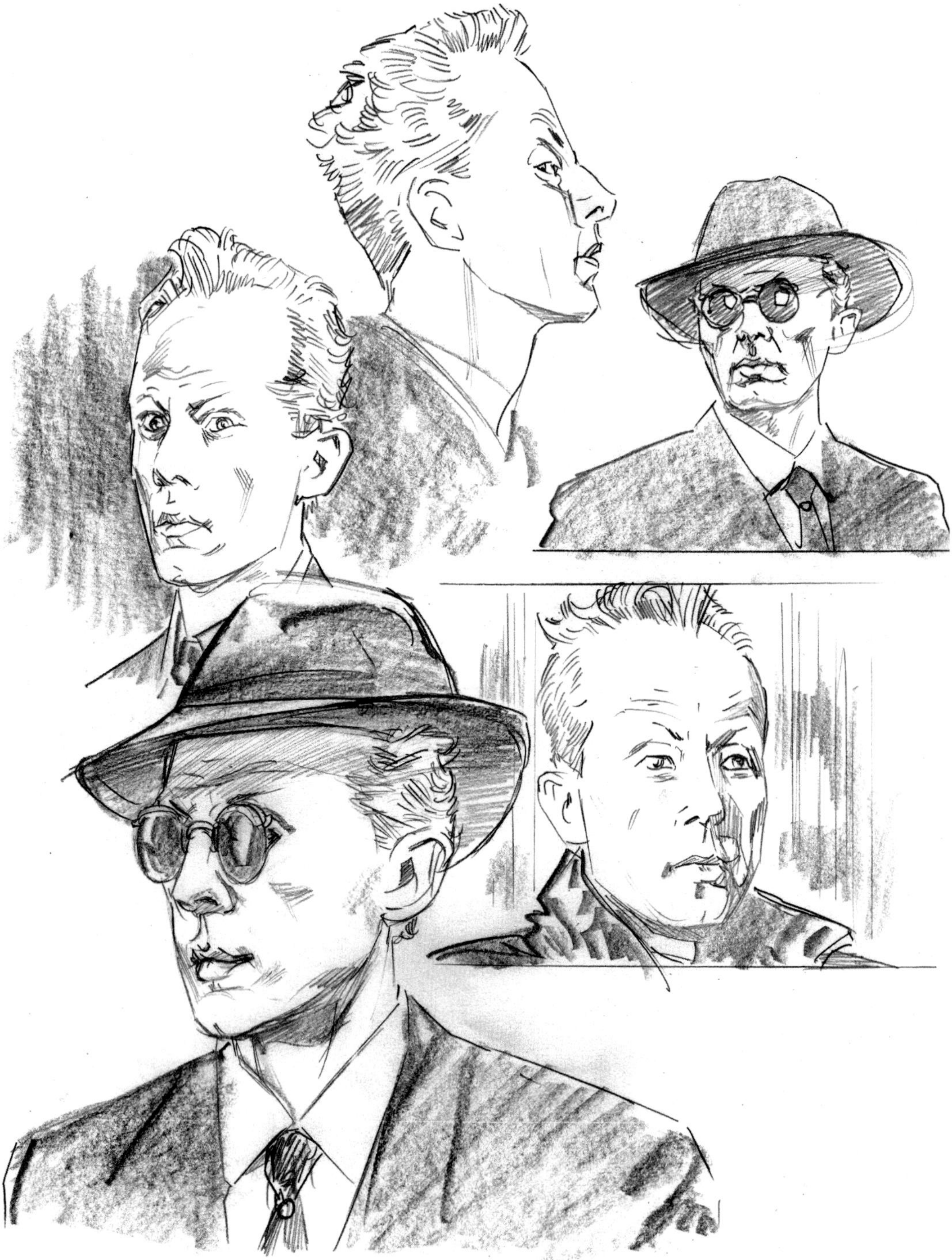

"EASILY THE MOST EXCITING ASPECT SO FAR HAS BEEN SEEING BUTCH BRING IT TO LIFE ON THE PAGE. TO ME, THAT'S ACTUALLY MORE AMAZING THAN SEEING SCREENPLAYS OF MINE FILMED, BECAUSE IT'S NOT THE RESULT OF HUNDREDS OF PEOPLE AND UMPTY MILLIONS OF DOLLARS, BUT OF THE TALENT OF ONE PERSON, SOMEONE WHO JUST SITS DOWN WITH A PEN AND *DOES IT BY HAND*. THAT CONTINUES TO BLOW ME AWAY."

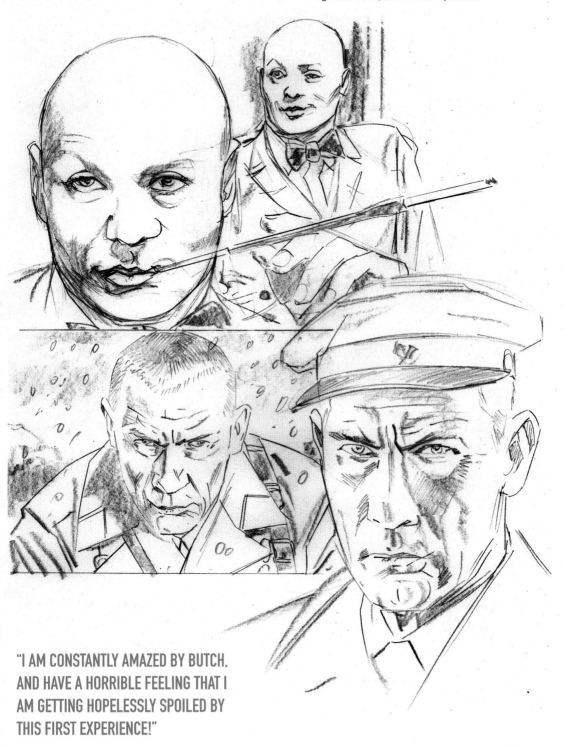

MR. BABY / HERR SÄUGLING: Who does indeed look very much like a newborn infant. Hairless, pink, rosebud mouth, no visible teeth. He's only five feet tall and dressed in an immaculate pale pre-war suit. German nightclub owner, black market specialist.

"I AM CONSTANTLY AMAZED BY BUTCH, AND HAVE A HORRIBLE FEELING THAT I AM GETTING HOPELESSLY SPOILED BY THIS FIRST EXPERIENCE!"

COLONEL YERMAKOV: Soviet. Intelligence officer. Tully's equivalent in the Red Army Air Force.